Gone Fishin' with the
Viking Fleet

The Forsberg Empire

75+ Years and Still Going Strong

By Captain Paul G. Forsberg

As Told to Manny Luftglass

Foreword By Fred Golofaro

Published by:
Gone Fishin' Enterprises

This is the Home Page of the Viking Website. It changes from time-to-time.

Gone Fishin' with The Viking Fleet

The Forsberg Empire

75+ Years and Still Going Strong

By Captain Paul G. Forsberg

As Told to Manny Luftglass

© 2013 Paul G. Forsberg

Published by:
Gone Fishin' Enterprises, PO Box 556, Annandale, NJ 08801

EAN: 978-0-9860434-0-6   ISBN: 0-9860434-0-0
UPC: 7 93380 12836-2

Photo Credits: Viking Fleet Website, Fred Golofaro, Captain Paul G. Forsberg, Manny Luftglass, Steve Gatto/Museum of New Jersey Marine History, Evelyn Bartram Dudas, Bart Malone, Miss Barnegat Light, Captain Fred E. Bird, Montauk Public Library Archives, Barbara Luftglass/Morea, John Badkin, Harrry Klauber, Chris Mahlstadt, *New York Daily News, New York Times, Providence Evening Bulletin.*

Book Design & Typography: TeleSet, Inc., Hillsborough, NJ
Transcribed by: Medxscribe, Inc.
PRINTED IN THE UNITED STATES OF AMERICA

To my father
who inspired me and taught me all I know;
to my mother
whose unwavering faith in my endeavors
kept me on course;
and also to my family
whose love and dedication to the Viking Fleet
has enabled us to grow and prosper.

Table of Contents

Chapter Three: 1940s

Chapter Four: 1950s

Chapter Five: 2013

Chapter Six: 4 Generations

Chapter Thirteen: 1970s

Chapter Fourteen: 1970s-80s

Chapter Fifteen: 1980s

Chapter Sixteen: 1990s

Chapter Seventeen: 2000s

Introduction

By Captain Paul G. Forsberg

This is a book about a family and a fleet.

In fact, it's about *my family* and *our fleet.*

Forsberg was the name when the operation began in 1936 and Forsberg remains the name that owns and controls the fleet.

While some of the boats that were owned by our family had other names, those that made headlines across the east coast all wore the name "Viking," with a number or word following it. So, whether it was *Viking I, Viking VII, Viking Star, Viking Freedom,* or any others, all of our boats had the word "Viking" printed on their hulls.

The man who helped me with this book, Manny Luftglass, thinks of our operation as "The Forsberg Empire."

The Viking/Forsberg combination is usually recognizable to anglers and writers of fishing lore.

Here's a photo of our charter boat the *Viking IV*, in Freeport.

Foreword

By Fred Golofaro
Senior Editor of The Fisherman Magazine

aptain Paul's career path was established early on as the son of Capt. Carl Forsberg, who pioneered fishing at Cox's Ledge, and captained the first open boat to fish that area. Paul soon made his own mark in the industry and was most instrumental in growing the *Viking Fleet* from his dad's first boat, the 65-foot Price-built *Viking Star,* to the current fleet of seven vessels, including the 140-foot *Viking Starship,* the largest open boat on the Atlantic Coast. The *Viking Fleet* celebrated its 75th anniversary in 2011.

Paul is widely recognized as being among the most innovative of party boat skippers. He invented the first heated handrail, and he is solely and partly responsible for discovering wrecks like the *Andrea Doria, Grecian, Suffolk,* the American sub *Bass,* and the German sub U-853. He also pioneered new fishing grounds such as the Pinnacle, the Apple Tree, Lumber Yard, Old 40L, and Old Faithful.

Fred Golofaro, Senior Editor of *The Fisherman Magazine* with the Montauk Lighthouse in the background

Paul was always looking to push the envelope when it came to seeking out new fishing areas, especially those which required lengthy or multi day trips. He brought species like swordfish, tuna and tilefish within reach of party boat anglers, men and women who otherwise had no access to these offshore fisheries. He also coined phrases such as "Valley of the Giants" and "Gorillagator Blues" as he marketed new and exciting fisheries.

As much as he is known for being a pioneer and innovator, Captain Paul has probably had an even greater impact on fishery management and its affect on the party boat industry. He is an advisor to the Scup Management Board, and regularly attends state and federal fisheries management meetings for a multitude of species up and down the coast at his own expense. Often, his is the only voice speaking out on behalf of the party boat industry. His testimony has been directly responsible for avoiding the needless closures of several species; actions which would have crippled the open boat fleet had Paul not been there to speak on their behalf.

Few individuals have impacted the open boat industry to the degree that Captain Paul Forsberg has, and no one from the industry has been more involved in the regulatory process. He remains a dynamic force, even as he spends much of the winter prowling Florida's Gulf Coast aboard his *Viking Freedom,* a steel-hulled fishing sail boat he built himself in Montauk.

The Author

Captain Paul G. Forsberg

In my Viking Fleet cap and shirt.

Some might say that Paul Forsberg was born with a fishing rod in his hands. It is often said that, "All fishermen are liars except you and me, and I'm not so doggone sure about you." But instead of saying that he was born with a rod in his hands, let's just say that shortly after he was able to walk, he was able to hold a fishing pole. Even though he was born left-handed, his dad Carl quickly taught him how to turn the reel handle with that other hand, the one that most of you use; the right one.

The idea for this book had been in Captain Forsberg's head for quite a while but with the countless activities he has been involved in, there was simply no chance to even begin to put it into print. But one day he got a call and that was when his idea began to spring forth. The call was from writer Manny Luftglass, on behalf of the well-known *Fisherman Magazine,* asking Paul if he would like to see a feature article appear in "The Fisherman" about the

"Forsberg Empire." Forsberg moved forward quickly and instead of simply telling Manny yes, he asked him if he had written any books about fishing. Since Manny already had fourteen books in print that started with the words "Gone Fishin'," it became Paul's wish to get his family's story into a book. The article was published, of course, but more importantly to Captain Forsberg was the fact that his book would be produced by their joint efforts.

Much of the material found in this book came directly from Paul himself who sat in his car, at his home, and on board one Viking vessel or another, telling his story into a tape recorder. A "transcriber" listened to the words, many tens of thousands of them, and typed them into a somewhat orderly form. After rewrites and helpful pre-editing by Paul's significant other, Patricia, Manny Luftglass and Paul produced what makes up this book.

The Publisher

Manny Luftglass /
Gone Fishn' Enterprises

Manny Luftglass is the writer of more than 3,000 fishing columns, feature articles and reports that all started with his by-line, "Gone Fishin'" and, including this one, he has written and/or published 22 books to date, most of which starting with the words "Gone Fishin'." A former business insurance agency owner, twice-elected Mayor (Somerville, N.J.), environmental and peace activist, he prefers to be viewed simply now as an angler who likes to write about fishing, and he does plenty of both.

He has fished in at least a dozen countries and an equal number of states. But of the many ports he has fished out of, Montauk Point is perhaps his favorite saltwater one of all, and for that matter, fishing on board one of the Viking vessels brings back his fondest memories. He caught his biggest codfish ever on a Viking vessel, a 42 pounder!

Chapter One

1930s

How *The Viking Fleet* Began

According to *Webster's New World Dictionary of the American Language,* a "Viking" was "any of the Scandinavian pirates of the 8th to 10th centuries." It also defines a "pirate" as "one who practices piracy." Carry that further and they define "piracy" in part, as "robbery of ships on the high seas."

Well, while none of our Captains truly ever meant to "rob" others, you can say that many a competitor has had their "feathers ruffled," watching *Viking* vessels tie up at the dock with passengers unloading and carrying an abundance of fish to their cars even when fishing was not quite as good for others. Without doubt, no Forsberg ever intended to "steal" from anyone else but, hey, producing better catches was and is always our goal and more often than not, we achieve that goal!

Truth be known, the name *"Viking"* was given to the first boat in the fleet by my father, Captain Carl, purely as a way to settle a bit of a dispute with my

New York Daily News, May 4, 1956. Sport Highlights by Curt Brall.

mom! You see, he had first named the boat "Doris," the name of his sister. But my mom, Adele, was not too happy with that, thinking that he should have named it "Adele" instead. This created quite a problem and the wind-up was to use a name signifying his Scandinavian roots, "*Viking*," and that satisfied my mother completely.

So, a pirate ship? No, just a settlement of a minor family squabble.

Early Family Memories

My father's dad was born in Sweden and dad was born in America. My mom Adele was born in France. She and her parents moved to America via Ellis Island when she was about six years of age. It was tough for her since she knew no English and her family only spoke French at home. However, she managed to learn English in their local school in Mountain View, New Jersey. Dad and my mother were both raised in that suburb of Passaic County.

Mom's father couldn't find a job locally but finally got some work on the Alaskan Railroad. He was a chef and went to Alaska cooking for the workers who were laying the tracks for the railroad. While there he tried panning for gold and went broke. He and a friend jumped on freight trains and hitchhiked all the way from Alaska to New Jersey. They actually made the newspapers doing it. They just worked their way back, walking, hitching rides, etc., wherever they could until they got to N. J.

Mom's dad began selling coffee and French croissants on the street in front of the local railroad station in Mountain View. He eventually built a little shed so that he would have some protection from the cold and nasty weather. He wound up buying the piece of property he was situated on and the shed kept growing and growing until it became a French restaurant. It sat 35 people and became well known and popular. My grandfather stayed in the kitchen and cooked while my grandmother was out front. Mom was a waitress and did the ordering for the restaurant up until she married my father.

My mom learned how to cook from her dad who became known as a great

Here's mom and I.

chef. She could always make a meal from scratch and make it taste good no matter what it consisted of. That was really a blessing for us children as we grew up. After they married, mom worked side by side with dad, they clearly were workaholics, and of course, she raised four kids along the way. Brother Carl was #1, four years later; I was born and three years after, my sister Audrey was born, and lastly came Jon.

Mom ran the business side of the *Viking* fleet. I don't think that dad ever wrote a single check, mom did it all. He ran the boats and kept them operating smoothly and was fishing hard all the time.

How The *Viking* Business Began

But before there was to be a fishing business, let's discuss how it all began. My father's dad was a naval architect who worked for the City of New York building bridges, tunnels and piers.

Grandpa was on a New York team of architects and on the side he designed sailboats, having established quite a reputation for designing sailing vessels of that era. All the boats then, were, of course, built out of wood. He also designed yachts, oyster boats, and commercial fishing boats and later on, wound up designing my father's first newly built fishing boat.

My father got a job through his father as a "groundhog." If you don't know what that means, just imagine an animal digging holes in the ground to reach the safety of his family hideaway. Well, a groundhog then and now was a person who dug holes too, but these were more often than not holes in the ground, building tunnels for the New York City subway system.

One day my father was using a cart that was on the subway tracks to remove dirt that he and his co-workers had piled up. The cart must have hit something and as it was moving, it jumped off the tracks. Dad and a few co-workers got some "jimmy" bars. As they were attempting to "jimmy" the cart back onto the track, he slipped and fell and wheels of the heavy metal cart ran over his right hand!

The wheel cut off his pinky and mangled the rest of his right-hand fingers badly. The City settled with him by giving him $1,800 as compensation and laid him off for a while since he could no longer work. That $1,800 was quite a bit of money back in the year 1936 when this all took place.

1936 Freeport, N.Y.

With time to spare, dad went into New York City and took a train to Freeport on Long Island. The train stopped right near some docks. With a love for boats driving him, having seen his father design and help build so many, he decided to check the fishing boats out.

He wound up helping a commercial fisherman baiting codfish tub trawl hooks. He was getting paid to do that on the side. He had his injured hand in a cast of course. In those days, casts were made out of Plaster of Paris and when it got wet it turned soft and changed its position. He didn't know that at

Our Freeport parking lot in the mid-40s, at the *Viking* Dock.

the time. As it got soft, he just wrapped it up with friction tape. When they finally cut the cast off, the other fingers on his right hand were all distorted. They had flattened and permanently were crooked. This condition lasted for the rest of his life but he learned to live with it.

My dad had very big hands. His pinky was as big as a normal person's thumb. He could only get four of his fingers in his pocket; there was no room for the thumb to fit in. He learned to deal with that pretty well. Sometimes his hands got awkward, got in the wrong places, but I'll get into that later on.

In the meantime, when he was down around the docks in Freeport, baiting codfish hooks and so forth, he wound up going fishing and he decided he liked that. Later on, he got his Captain's license. He had time, since he was not able to work, and he wound up buying an old boat. It was a "Caliban." The "Caliban" fleet was in Freeport, owned by the Merritt Brothers, Roy and Bud.

To this day, the Merritt name remains well respected and the operation builds yachts in Florida now.

They upgraded to a little better boat and my father sailed right alongside of them at the Tuna Dock in Freeport. This boat was the one that first was to be called Doris, not Adele, but it wound up becoming the first "*Viking.*"

Dad learned by fishing alongside of the Merritt's who had three other Caliban boats, all four operating out of the same Tuna Dock. The Merritt's were expert anglers and were very friendly to him, giving him plenty of help and he learned quickly and well. They had a real big reputation and following and boy, could they could catch! Of course, my father had a leg-up on other boat owners because he had purchased a boat from them.

He started out in business with their overflow and before you know it, he had a business built up well enough to get a second boat.

The tunnels of New York now being nothing but a memory, dad bought that second boat and put a captain on it. Business was going real good and he got a third boat. Soon after, the Merritt boys left and went down to Florida where they started building boats.

The other boats at the dock were complaining to the landlord that it wasn't fair, my father had three boats and he was getting all these charters (they were also charter boats) and they weren't doing anything. That was because my father was a good fisherman.

Building The *Viking* Dock in Freeport

He did so well it wound up that he had to leave the dock. He started looking around for a place to go and a bank in Freeport came after him and said, "You take this place over and we'll make you a deal you can't refuse."

That became the *Viking* Dock, and it was at the head of Woodcleft Canal, right across from Randall Park, and it wound up being the best place on the canal. (It's now occupied by Staten Island Yacht Sales).

My father called it, of course, "The *Viking* Dock," but at first, it was not

Postcard of our fleet in Freeport.
I rowed a photographer out to take this picture after World War II.

much more than a mud bank and a railway. He decided to build his own dock
and move his boats to this site. Remember, he had one hand that wasn't in
anywhere near perfect shape, but in spite of that, or maybe because of it, he
pushed on.

He bought a bunch of old railroad ties someplace. I was just a little kid and
was around the dock most of the time. Dad got a few pairs of ice tongs and a
helper and that is how they handled the ties. They grabbed them by the ice
tongs with a guy at each end, and put them into place. That was the decking
of the dock and part of the whaler system. It was amazing what we could do
with those railroad ties. I remember it clear as a bell!

After building the dock, my father and a few other guys built the Viking
Grill. It was built out of plywood and became the Viking Diner and served
breakfast to customers before the boats sailed. None of the boats had galleys
in those days so the place was very busy.

Freeport Hospital

My siblings and I were all born in Freeport Hospital which is no longer there. It was a small hospital and I remember going in with mom to see dad when he had his ulcers operated on. They took out about three-quarters of his stomach during the procedure. I remember my mother sneaking coffee into him. The hospital smelled like ether, it was sickening. You could smell it everywhere you were in the building; thank goodness they don't smell like that any longer.

Chapter Two

Memories

Some Memories
from my Brother Carl A.

How It All Began

I once asked mother how dad got into the fishing business. She explained that when they were first married dad was employed as an engineer working on the tunnels that were being built from New Jersey to New York; they were building the Lincoln and Holland Tunnels at the time. They settled in Freeport on Long Island and dad kept a small boat on Woodcleft Canal in Freeport. He would go out weekends taking some friends. They would chip in for gas, one thing led to another and he began to get paid in the form of a gratuity. One weekend after a couple successful trips he came home with a pocket of cash and exclaimed to mother, "There's money in this!" It wasn't long before he left his job and was running trips full time, I imagine he moonlighted over the first few winter seasons to make ends meet. The first winters must have been a little skinny as I remember how it was almost a celebration when the first indications of spring arrived and dad could

SPORTS   THE NEW YORK TIMES, FRIDAY, AUGUST 23,

ats Jacomar After Hard Stretch Drive

FREEPORT ANGLERS WHO TRIUMPHED IN ATLANTIC COAST TUNA EVENT
Captain Carl Forsberg of the Viking II, Walter O'Malley, Mate Chet Spivey, Everett McCooey, whose 120-pounder was the largest fish caught in the Belmar, N. J., three-day tournament, and Everett McLoughlin.   Times Wide World

This is my dad on the far left, and next to him is Walter O'Malley, owner of the Brooklyn Dodgers Baseball team with his award-winning tuna.

gather me as a helper, rush to the boatyard where the boat was hauled for the winter to begin making money again. He was so popular as a Captain and so successful that in a few seasons he had a couple boats running. It was during this time that dad won the very prodigious Atlantic Tuna Fishing Tournament. His client was the owner of the Brooklyn Dodgers Baseball team, Walter O'Malley, and that catapulted dad into the spotlight. He was renting dock space for the boats a ways down the canal when an opportunity came up to acquire the Freeport Boat Yard, a sort of run-down facility, but the location was exquisite; right at the head of the canal. Anyone going fishing in Freeport would have to pass right by that location. Dad would have Paul and me out in the early morning darkness waving white towels at the parking lot entrance to get the attention of arriving fishermen. It was at this location that the *Viking* fleet prospered into a fleet of about five charter and two head boats.

The Confiscating of the *Viking III*

At the beginning of the war everyone was expected to contribute to the war effort. The growing *Viking* fleet, about five boats at the time, was no exception. Mom and dad were informed that the *Viking III* would be needed for patrol duty in the New York Harbors. I imagine there was some very welcome financial assistance included in the deal, as even though mom and dad were very reluctant to let the boat go they seemed willing to accept the deal, (actually they had no choice), with calm agreement.

I remember hearing the officials explain to dad how they were going to mount a machine gun to the boat's cockpit deck in place of the fighting chair. I was almost in tears; this seemed so out of character for that beautiful boat. Drill holes in that beautiful wood deck, mount a machine gun? The *Viking III* was a classic sport fishing charter boat. With her gleaming white hull and flying bridge, varnished mahogany topsides, bright red waterline and outriggers poised for action she was something out of a Hemingway novel. She was returned after the war and what a mess the poor thing was. They had stripped her and painted her a drab gray, the deck was drilled full of holes. I don't think they ever cleaned her, she was covered inside and out with filthy New York grime-soot about three inches thick. It made me sick when they took her, and sicker when they returned her. It still churns my stomach when I think about it.

SPAM© on White Bread

During the war, dad made ends meet by commercial fishing. He would outfit the boat to catch whatever was in season at the time. Sometimes flounder and other ground fish, sometimes scallops, skimmer clams, mackerel, sword-fish, etc. The crew would consist of dad, a mate, and sometimes Paul and me. It would be a long day and the crew gotta' eat. The provisions were sparse on board, to say the least. No galley, no cupboard, no refrigeration. There would be coffee, water in jugs, some bread, eggs, a few cans of beans, Chef Boyardee

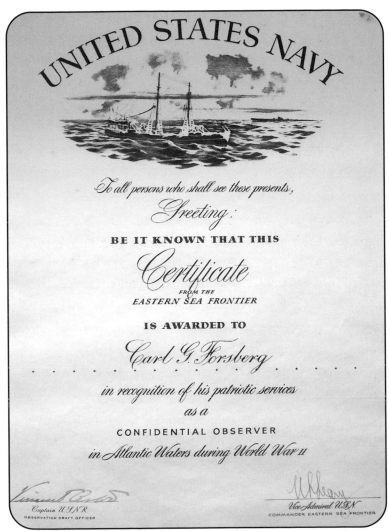

UNITED STATES NAVY

To all persons who shall see these presents,

Greeting:

BE IT KNOWN THAT THIS

Certificate

FROM THE
EASTERN SEA FRONTIER

IS AWARDED TO

Carl G. Forsberg

. . . .

in recognition of his patriotic services

as a

CONFIDENTIAL OBSERVER

in Atlantic Waters during World War II

Captain U.S.N.R.
OBSERVATION CRAFT OFFICER

Vice Admiral U.S.N.
COMMANDER EASTERN SEA FRONTIER

Here's the certificate the Navy gave dad when they gave him his boat back.

and such, and SPAM©. A beat-up Coleman kerosene stove was set up in a corner of the small pilothouse and it was the mate's job to prepare the meals. The canned goods were usually heated and eaten right out of the cans. I'll never forget those SPAM© sandwiches. Two pieces of hot SPAM© fried brown and crisp, placed between two slices of bread and covered with mustard, to die for! The Coleman would hold only two slices and the SPAM© would have to be cooked one sandwich at a time. Paul and I would line up outside the pilothouse door and a nice warm sandwich would be placed in our hands as each one was prepared. I still love SPAM©, with mustard, on white bread!

Swordfishing...
"The Most Pleasant Way to Go Broke I Know Of"

As just discussed, during the war years dad would go commercial fishing for whatever specie was running at the time. The boat, always the *Viking V*, would be converted with the necessary equipment and off he would go. One very interesting method of fishing was harpooning swordfish. Individual fish, usually about 100 lbs., were worth quite a bit of money and five or six would make a trip. The boat would be equipped with a pulpit, basically a long plank with a hand rail extending ten feet or more from the bow out over the water, a mast with a cross piece for the lookout to perch upon, and a hand-held harpoon with several rigged nail keg buoys.

Once on the fishing grounds, the idea was to slowly cruise around at a constant idle speed looking for the protruding fins of the prey relaxing and sunning at the surface. There was a remote steering wheel rigged on the mast so the lookout could steer while the others rested in the cabin below. In addition to the swordfish there also were sharks loafing along and the eye was trained to recognize the difference between the two, and while one crew member rested below another was in the mast looking for targets.

As long as the engine speed remained constant and there were no loud noises on board, the fish were approachable with a reasonable amount of stealth. When one was spotted, a "thunk" on the mast would signal the crew member below that we had a target and positions would be taken. The boat would be maneuvered so the pulpit eventually was positioned above the unsuspecting swordfish and it would be harpooned by the man on the pulpit. The very surprised fish would take off at top speed, unwinding the long line

Here I am bending over the biggest swordfish I ever got. (1950s)

as he went. There was a nail keg buoy attached to the end that would be thrown over when all the line was out. The harpooner had to very, very careful not to become entangled in the screaming line and to jettison the buoy before the line reached the bitter end.

The poor fish would drag the buoy around all day, tiring itself out, while the boat continued looking for additional prey. At the end of the day the buoys would be retrieved with the exhausted fish at the line's end. Usually there was a back slapping, jumping, hugging celebration as each fish was landed as each was worth quite a bit of money.

I remember one time; just as the fish was brought to the surface, the harpoon dart pulled out and the fish slowly began sinking to the depths. Dad, with absolutely no hesitation, sharks or no sharks, immediately launched himself over the rail and into the deep six, wrapped both arms and legs around the fish, and got the gaff inserted. No way was all that money going down the drain.

The fish retrieved that day would be cleaned and iced and the hunt would continue at dawn the next morning. This method was a several day, 24-hour operation, with some trips lasting as long as eight days. This was my favorite form of fishing and, I think, our Dad's too as when he was asked about it years later his reply was "Ah, harpooning swordfish, the most pleasant way to go broke I know of."

Carl A. Forsberg

The following four pages is the *Viking Bulletin*. Dad was very creative, besides the postcards we sent out, he came up with this novel idea about how to publicize what he was catching and where.

VIKING FISHING FLEET

Captains Carl G. and Paul Forsberg
Viking Dock – Montauk, L.I., N.Y.
Phone MOntauk 8-2786

VIKING BULLETIN – Volume 1 – Issue 1
(Published Now & Then)
APRIL 1960

HAVE YOU HEARD OF THE MONTAUK SPRING RUN OF COD?

During the months of March through June 15 the cod are found off Montauk Light and in Block Island Sound. At times, only 20 minutes ride from the Dock. Due to the shallowness of the feeding grounds, the Montauk Cod put up an excellent fight; they can be caught in great numbers from 3 lbs. to 30 lbs. each and larger.

Also – there are other "fighting" fish readily available "for catching" during the same trip. Pollock, Sea Flounders (Snowshoes), Blackfish, Hake and Haddock add an interesting variety to your catch.

Come on "Out to Montauk" – The current (watch your papers for time changes) VIKING Schedule to above grounds is' –

VIKING STAR I	Capt. Carl Forsberg	5:00 A.M.	Fare $8.50
VIKING STAR II	Capt. Paul Forsberg	7:00 A.M.	Fare $7.00
VIKING	Capt. Bill Anderson	7:15 A.M.	Fare $7.00 (Block Island & Local Grounds – Exclusively)

INTRODUCTION FROM CAPTAIN CARL FORSBERG

This is the Viking Fleet's **first** "Fishing News Bulletin." We hope you are pleased with it. The object of this bulletin is

1. To keep in touch with our friends and customers.
2. To inform those of you who have been unable to "get out" fishing what has been happening on our boats during the past few weeks.
3. To let you "sinker bouncers" know what **we** may all look forward to take place in the fishing weeks ahead at Montauk.
4. To print, for your information, interesting fishing topics, pertaining to the **VIKING** boats.

To our knowledge, this is the **first** time any Fishing Fleet Operator has published such a bulletin. We certainly hope it will not be the last. Your comments will be appreciated.

THE VIKING BOATS BALLAD

The Sea Gulls know the Viking boats have fish
    Cause we "make em bite," with our "tastee bait"
Tis tastee – we are sure, but if you're in doubt, taste it yourself
    the VIKING BOATS are ALL WEATHER BOATS
Cause if the sea gull can fly, in wind or storm, our boats will sail
    For when seas are rough, the FISH BITE BEST
When it's CALM, they take a rest.

THE MONTAUK CHAMBER OF COMMERCE REQUESTS

Letters – A short note from you might also help. As President of the Montauk Chamber of Commerce, Carl Forsberg has written many letters to the New York State Highway Department, Albany, New York regarding suitable markers for the Route 25 and Route 58 intersection at Babylon. Your assistance by writing a few letters to Albany on this subject might get some action. So far – the Highway Department has improved road markings and <u>there is</u> consideration being shown for early morning travelers to eastern Long Island.

Oh yes – while we're on the subject of roads etc., <u>don't forget to sign</u> the Chamber Of Commerce petition to Honorable Governor Nelson Rockefeller requesting that better roads be built on Eastern Long Island. All the Montauk boats have these petitions.

The Long Island Expressway is fine as far as it goes. At its present rate of building it will take approximately 75 more years for it to reach Montauk. Long Island should have a Parkway, similar to the Garden State Parkway in New Jersey right out to Montauk and Eastern Long Island.

DRIVING INSTRUCTIONS TO MONTAUK

Regarding roads and the easiest drive to reach Montauk, did you know that on the South Shore there is now an extension of the Sunrise Highway from the old eastern end at Patchogue to Shirley, L.I. This is 20 miles of excellent road with posted speed of 50 mile limit.

Coming from Manhattan, New Jersey, Upstate or from the L.I. Expressway or Grand Central Parkway, ride the Northern State Parkway until you can't go any further. Go on the Jericho Turnpike and turn off and take the Smithtown By-Pass. The following is important and will save you time.

Near the end of the Smithtown By-Pass the road forks to the right to Route 25 or Jericho Turnpike. DO NOT TAKE THIS ROAD. Continue straight ahead on route 25-A through Rocky Point to Route 25 just west of Riverhead. This eliminates going through 5 or 6 small towns with traffic lights.

COXE'S LEDGE

<u>What is it?</u>   <u>Where is it?</u>   <u>Why Go There</u>

Coxe's Ledge is a bank of Rocks, Reefs and Black Mussel covered Feeding Grounds which takes in an area approximately 15 to 20 miles long (East & West) and 3 to 5 miles wide (North & South).

Ok fellows, get the map out, this ledge begins 13 miles S.E. of Block Island and runs in a general ESE direction for 15 to 20 miles toward Nantucket Island. Being 20 to 25 miles south of the mouth of Narraganset Bay, this ledge is bathed by the westerly end of the Labrador current which flows around and over Nantucket Shoals. In addition to the Labrador Current, the tidal flow in and out of Narraganset Bay, Vineyard Sound, Buzzards Bay, Block Island Sound and the Eastern mouth of Long Island Sound produces various rips, eddies and currents each carrying bait and other food to the many different species of hungry fish, especially Cod, Pollock and Haddock, who seem to rest on the slopes of Coxe's Ledge all summer long.

Commencing June 15 to approximately October 15, the VIKING STAR I and VIKING STAR II will be fishing the fabulous fishing grounds known as Coxe's Ledge. The VIKING FLEET fishermen locate the fish every day. Your catch of fish, from this area, will be tremendous; 200 to 300 pounds per man is not unusual. Most Anglers get "arm weary". You had better plan several trips to Coxe's Ledge this summer. You'll still be talking about your "Catches of Fish" when the winter months roll around again.

Rod And Gun

By CARL McKAY

Williams To Lead Anglers

The Bergen County Anglers, at their Past Presidents Dinner, installed new officers for 1960.

Bruce Williamson received the gavel from outgoing President Ozzie Mehrhof who in his term of office saw the Anglers grow into the largest club in Bergen County.

Bergen County Anglers

Installation Of Officers

There are only two other men in the 23-year history of the Anglers to have served more than one term as president. Williamson will now add his name to this list, having also served in '58.

The rest of the slate for 1960 seems to add up to a banner year for the Anglers. Larry Page is first vice-president, Joe Jarmicki second vice-president, Bill Heath recording secretary, Howard Menzer corresponding secretary, Shorty Kraus treasurer, Fred Rexer sergeant at arms, and Pete Staats assistant sergeant at arms.

At this dinner, Captain Carl Forsberg of the Viking Star, out of Montauk, L. I., presented Jarmicki with a $100 savings bond as the winner of the contest run exclusively for the Bergen County Saltwater Anglers. Joe took top honors with a 26-pound codfish, caught aboard the Viking Star.

In a grab bag for prizes at this dinner, Carl Forsberg won a free trip with Captain Les Baletti on The Palace out of Hoboken. Do you think he will use it?

* * *

● **CODFISH** *Gadus callarias*

Also called Bank Cod, Black Cod, Rock Cod, Shore Cod, School Cod.

Average weight 15 pounds; largest on record 211½ pounds; food value, good.

Optimist

Joe: "How many fish have you caught, pard?"

Jim: "Well, if I get this one I'm after and three more, that'll make four."

OVERHEARD ON
THE PARTY LINE

"Hello, Joe ... You're going fishing?!? Must be crazy ... Why? ... Well, it's too blamed windy, cold, wet and miserable out ... Yes, the road to Montauk Point is under a foot of water... I'm busy's a beaver around the house ... No, my wife won't stand for it ... but if you're stopping by I'll be ready in about five minutes."

SPRING FISHING COMMENTS

THE PICTURES TELL THE STORY

The fish are here. All you need to do is come on out fishing on the VIKING Boats and catch them. Our tastee bait will insure you that they will bite.

THE NEW VIKING STAR II
Captain Paul Forsberg

The VIKING STAR II will join the Viking Fleet early in April and Captain Paul Forberg will be the skipper.

This boat has been designed especially for Party Boat Fishing at Montauk; it is being built at a Virginia shipyard. It will be the most modern and best equipped fishing boat in the business, not to mention the fastest.

The power plant, a 275 H.P. Diesel, will get you out to all of the various fishing grounds including Coxe's Ledge in short order. .The equipment, consisting of Radar, Radio Telephone and Fish Scope will guarantee your safety plus finding fish to catch. Lounging quarters, refreshment and snack bar, juke box and sun deck are all included for your comfort. Even the real land-lubbers, who love to chum, will find a few bunks available for their convenience.

Each of you will surely want to make several trips on this new and modern fishing boat. You had better arrive in Montauk early as the VIKING STAR II will be the first of the three VIKING BOATS to leave the Viking Dock; this trip will be known as "The Crack of Dawn Trip" and will go where the fish are; - Block Island Reefs, Ledges and Wrecks; Pollock Rip; Out of this world grounds; Sharks Ledge and Coxe's Ledge. Watch the papers for scheduled sailing time, however, if loaded the VIKING STAR II will sail as soon as final preparations for active fishing have been completed.

TIRED and WEARY

The drive to Montauk, fishing and the return trip home too much for you to do all in one day? I guess it is, for some of you, but did you know that <u>overnight</u> or <u>weekly</u> motel accommodations are available in the Montauk Harbor area the <u>year</u> around. <u>Offseason</u> rates, which means they cost you less, are in effect from September 15 through June 1.

THE VIKING WEATHER FORECASTER

Did you receive our accurate Weather Guide forecaster and calendar for 1960? There are a few left. If you want one, free of course, drop me a line (not fish line). Be sure and include your complete address.

JUST PLAIN FISHING COMMENTS

It takes <u>sharp</u> hooks to catch fish. <u>Hooks are cheap.</u> Why use old rusty hooks attached to used old monofilament line? Keep that tackle in <u>good</u> working order. IT COULD BE THE POOL FISH THAT GETS AWAY FROM YOU.

Fish all the chance you have. If you get into a big tangle - cut the line. Rigs are cheap. Fishing time is not. You aren't fishing for that POOL FISH WHILE UNTANGLING THOSE LINES nor are you just plain "catching fish".

What's the jewelery for? Are you trying to impress the fish or me? I'm not impressed, nor are the fish.

YOU WILL ALWAYS CATCH MORE FISH USING NEW HOOKS, RIGGING UP THE MONTAUK WAY AND USING OUR TASTEE BAIT. (1/60)

• **POLLACK**   *Pollachius virens*

Also called Green Cod, Quoddy Salmon, Sea Salmon, Boston Bluefish.

Average weight 5 pounds; largest on record, 50 pounds;

Want to receive this *Bulletin?* Mail below coupon to Capt. Carl Forsberg, Montauk, N.Y.

Please send me *Viking Bulletin* when published.

Name ....

Address ....

City .... Zone .... State ....

Chapter Three

1940s

Engines, Then and Now

In the days when we were down in Freeport, most of the boats had gasoline engines in them and the most famous gasoline engine was the "Chrysler Crown;" the flathead, 6-cylinder engine, a straight-6. It was a smooth running engine and had a maximum horsepower of 90 hp. It was the sweetest running engine and the soundest engine you ever heard. You could always tell a boat that had a Chrysler Crown in it. There were engines made by other companies such as Chris-Craft, Northberg, and some others but they just weren't as reliable and as sweet sounding as Chrysler Crown was.

Our other boats all ran with gasoline engines but after World War II ended, my dad put Gray Marine 671 diesels that he got from Army/Navy surplus stores in the *Viking V + VII*. General Motors "671's"were known then as "man's best friend." They were really inexpensive, really dependable 2-cycle

Here's our *Viking II*.

engines. A lot of them still run around today. They are very dependable as long as you don't try to take too much horsepower out of them. They stopped making those engines now. They modernized them somewhat as they were going along, the basic engine, but they stopped making the "71" series because they couldn't meet the EPA's new air pollution standards.

Back then, all dad's boats were single screw (one engine). My father happened to purchase a boat named the *Moccasin*. She had two engines in it and it came from Gerritsen Beach. He brought it to Freeport. She had a good following so he felt that he would keep the name the *Moccasin*. She was a very popular vessel among the anglers and with her good following became a definite asset to the *Viking* fleet.

Who Stole the Engine?

The skipper who ran the *Moccasin* loved it because she had two engines and that made for an easier day for him in case one engine happened to fail. He wore an old-fashioned captain's hat and if, for example, the port engine was dead, in order to let people know what was going on as he ran up and down Woodcleft Canal he would turn the cap to the side of his head that matched the engine that was working well. So, a good starboard engine, cap turned to the right. And when both engines were working well, he would wear his hat nice and straight with a big smile all over his face!

But one Friday night, during the busiest of seasons in Freeport, summer as I remember, the *Viking III* was trying to get back and her engine died because she ran out of oil. She had to be towed in to the dock.

Bearing in mind that all of his charter boats were fully booked up for the weekend, this made dad scramble. His Scandinavian ingenuity roots took over right then and there.

Once the boat was at the dock the guys lifted the defective engine out with a giant boom that they had also used to lift huge fish off the boats, swordfish, tuna and the like. They rigged the boom up to the front of an old car, removed the dead engine and placed it on the ground in the parking area and then went to the *Moccasin* and swung the boom over it. They attached it to one of the engines from the "twin-screw" boat and lifted it up and out and over to the *Viking III* and hooked it up. My job was to hold a light for the other guys and pass out tools. I remember that night as "clear as the day!" In effect, we "stole" the engine from one boat and, installed it in the other and closed down the hatches like nothing unusual had occurred at all!

I went to the dock early on Saturday morning to see if they needed me for anything. I went into the office where my mom was checking customers in while dad was giving out the bamboo rental rods with old-fashioned Bakelite "sidewinder" reels.

The office was very small and very full of folks anxious to go out and catch some fish; none of them were ready for what took place then. The skipper of the *Moccasin* came running in, upset and yelling to my father. He yelled, "The starboard engine in the boat is gone. There is no engine in it. It's gone, it's gone, it's not there!"

So dad said "Well, damn it, you've got the other engine so run out on the other one, don't worry about it." But the captain said "Yeah, but it's not there, the engine is gone, somebody stole the engine, it's gone, it was there yesterday and now it's not there!"

Try to picture this scene for yourself as well as how we must have struggled to contain smiles and laugh's because we had really fried this guy's brain, big time.

Dad chased him out of the office, screaming at him, saying something like "most boats only have one engine, what are you, a privileged character, thinking you have to have two engines? You're just like everyone else now that you've only got one engine so get in that damn boat, go down the canal, and take your customers out fishing, they are already on the boat-go!"

I will never forget the look on that guy's face. He was flabbergasted as he boarded the boat, mumbling and grumbling. Of course dad was always right anyway.

Some of the older engines were, to say the least, somewhat unreliable. Generators alone didn't produce the 12-volts needed and so even if the engine started easily in the morning they often would not start again if we shut them down, therefore, we had to leave them running when fishing. Often there would be no spark early in the day so they would take a battery out of the *Viking* truck and bring it on board to jump-start the engine. At times a passenger anxious to go fishing would allow us to take the battery from his car and use it to jump-start the boat engine.

"Botch-Up!"

My father had unique ways of combining vehicle batteries, hacksaw blades and broken down engines to somehow make the engines kick into gear and he taught me how to do so as well.

As an example, my dad, in dealing with a leaking hose, would simply tape it closed with friction tape. There was no such thing as electric tape back then and when on the water, dad simply taped a leaky hose shut and if stopped leaking, he pronounced it "repaired," virtually never actually replacing it when he got back to the dock!

Quite often, even though we loved the old Grey Marine diesel engines, one or another wouldn't start each and every time we tried to leave the dock, or for that matter, when we wanted to head for home. The batteries were often dead or the generators wouldn't work right but as usual if a problem presented itself, dad would break up a trusty hacksaw blade, remove the valve cover of the engine, and put the pieces of the hacksaw blades between the valves and the rocker arms to relieve the compression. In particular, when still at the dock, he'd remove the 12-volt battery from his old Studebaker truck, jump it to the engine batteries, hit the button, and she'd roll. A little spray of ether helped as well.

The engine would start, he'd remove the hacksaw blades, put the valve cover down, and that was that for the day, repair, complete! On days that the engine seemed particularly untrustworthy dad would keep the engine running all day long as his anti-breakdown policy.

Pepper Solution

Yet another "botch-job" repair my dad perfected was the use of, believe it or not, pepper. When an engine developed a leak in the water system, simply putting pepper in the engine would stop the leak. I feel that the use of pepper could be called the best leak stopper we ever had.

I continued dad's use of hacksaw blades to assist myself when a General

Motors, Grey Marine, Ford, M. T. U., Caterpillar, or Cummings engine gave me grief. When I got water up the exhaust and the cylinders were flooded I'd stick a hacksaw blade in to relieve the compression and the engine would start, spitting water out of the exhaust and loosening up the exhaust manifold so the water would not come back into the cylinders. Once the engine was running, I would then remove the hacksaw blade and tighten the exhaust manifold.

If it was cold in the morning and after dad determined that the Chrysler Crown engine wasn't going to work he pulled off a trick that he perfected to make it go. First of all, he would take the spark plugs out. Then he took an old metal quart-sized oil can they used and, with his trusty boy-scout knife, remove the bottom of the can. He pulled the stopper out of the bottom of the carburetor and drained any water and gas that was down there. Lastly he put the spark plugs into the open oil can with the gasoline, and threw a match into the can.

The gas would ignite, heating the plugs, and as the fire went out, my dad picked the plugs out with his bare hands. They were, of course, hot, but he was in a rush to get going. He screwed the plugs back into the engine, hollering and screaming because he simply was too macho to wear gloves. He attached the plug wires and hit the starter button and I don't care how cold it was, that engine would start right up on the first roll!

Ether Solution

It was always hard getting the 671 Greymarine diesel engines started in the cold weather; they just didn't want to start. One way you did it then was to take a blow torch and heat up the air box on the engine. You took four bolts out of the silencer, heated up the blower and the whole airbox and then hit the starter button. My dad would stick the blow torch right in the blower blades itself and the engine would eat the flame and then we'd get her started.

Somebody told my father about using ether to start an engine. At that time the only ether you could get was medical ether and you had to have a prescription to get it from a pharmacy or a hospital.

Well, one day my father said, "I got a prescription, by golly, I can get ether; I got a prescription." Well, his "prescription" was going to the back door of a pharmacy with a big bag full of codfish fillets. He got his ether!

Ether then was very strong. It came in a can the size of a third of a pint and it had a cork plug in it. And boy, it was pure ether. Of course this was before ether was refined to be used as starting fluid; there was no such thing as yet.

He'd throw a little of the ether into the side of the blower box and hit the starter button and boy, she was starting at the first turn. This eliminated the need for the blow torch so with that my father improved on that point.

He took one of those trusty square boat nails and a big hammer and hammered a hole in the middle of the top of the air silencer right in front of the blower box for the 671. In that way he could turn the ether can and just let a couple of drops go in the nail hole directly into the blower. He used far less ether to get that engine started. From then on the blow torches were put away and ether was used. Nowadays we get starting fluid in spray cans but most modern diesels start up, they have a better injection system and they fire off better in cold weather. But in case they don't the modern spray cans of starting fluid comes out!

Now if you already have a headache from these quite complicated explanations, please realize that there are more methods we used but frankly, unless you are a mechanical genius, all you could get from additional discussion is a migraine so we'll slow down.

One of Many Scary Moments

I was involved in many a scary moment, having been on the water just about all of my life in lots of hazardous conditions. But that is just a part of the trade that I grew up in. I was mating on the *Viking III* one day. I was only ten or eleven years of age at the time, but the hired skipper gave me lots of work to do.

The name of the captain was Bill Anderson but everyone called him "Big Red" because of his hair color. Red was quite overweight but still a great fisherman, good boatman. He loved to run the *Viking III*. He would go up and jam himself into the little flying bridge and he liked to stay up there the whole trip if possible.

One day we had a charter out codfishing at the Cholera Banks grounds. We had a mess of cod aboard and before you knew it was time to head back. The usual plan was to go through Jones Inlet but Red noticed that things were looking bad there. The sea was up high and it was very warm out. Red said that he didn't trust Debs Inlet either but felt that it was a better option than trying to get in via Jones.

Hanging back outside the buoyed area Red told his passengers to put lifejackets on. The boat didn't have adequate covers over the engine hatch. He told one customer that if they took a sea aboard to lift the hatch handle so I could use the Pyrene fire extinguisher and spray the wires. Sure enough, as she came into the inlet, a big sea came over the corner of the stern, bringing a couple of feet of water into the cockpit.

Some of the water ran out but much of the water got into the engine area and stalled the engine. Red had already prepared for such an incident. My job was to dry off the engine if and when it was soaked and that is exactly what took place. As the engine putted to a stop, I used the Pyrene fire extinguisher and sprayed all over the wires, spark plugs and distributor cap, drying everything off. Anderson hit the starter button and the engine started! The battery had enough juice and the boat brought everyone back to the dock with ease. Those Pyrene extinguishers were very popular in those days. The idea was that Pyrene evaporates so fast that when you put it on a fire, it extinguishes the fire, but it also leaves off strong toxic fumes. It would dry the wires on the spark plugs and the distributor cap almost instantly thereby enabling us to start the engine up right away. However, because of the toxic fumes, they became unacceptable.

The passengers took their life jackets off, and I cleaned the fish. Even though the people were pretty wet, they still went home happy with quite a story to tell their friends and relatives to boot. As for me, I viewed it as just kind of normal, an everyday occurrence of the fishing life. If you did anything like that in this day and age, it's go to jail forever, but that was just the way that things were done back then.

Swimming, the Hard Way!

I was just a little guy in Freeport when my mom taught me how to swim at Jones Beach. Finally, I talked to my father one day and told him that I knew how to swim and didn't need to have a life jacket on any more. I said that my mother had taught me how. Dad said something like "You know how to swim, do you?" And my reply was "Yeah, I know how to swim real good." Pop came back with "You sure?" and I said "Yeah dad, I don't want to wear this life jacket anymore."

The *Viking V* was backed into the dock in Freeport as dad was working on the bow, building a lifejacket storage box out of plywood. Dad told me, "alright, take your lifejacket off, you don't need it anymore." Boy, I took it off. I was so happy about that. I was watching him there cutting the wood, and I'd turned around. I'm looking out at the other boats in the water and all of a sudden I found myself in the air, flying overboard! There I was, in the air, and then I was in the water right off the bow of the *Viking V*.

I came to the surface gasping for air and I looked up I saw that my father wasn't even looking at me. So I swam to the dock, and climbed up the bulkhead. When I got up the bulkhead my father was standing there watching and he said, "Yup, you know how to swim, son. Here's your lifejacket. Put it on the *Viking IV* over there. That's where it came from. You don't need it anymore. Get in the truck, I'll take you home and get you some dry clothes and we'll tell your mom you don't need your lifejacket anymore.

My father continued, "That's the way it's going to happen. You fall

Here's me as a little guy, around the same time as I got thrown in!

overboard; it's going to be sudden. You're not going to know what's going to occur." So that's when I outgrew my lifejacket. By golly, was I a proud guy after that!

The Old Studebaker Truck

Dad had quite a temper. One time we were driving down the road, heading back to the Viking Dock. We ran alongside Randall Park and came to a cross street. You had to make a left to go to the dock and my father was coming around that corner at a pretty good clip. I was the passenger in his Studebaker pickup truck. My father loved Studebaker pickup trucks. But that one day, it up and revolted. The door flew open and I went flying right out the door and I rolled over, just missing a telephone pole. Luckily, I never got hurt. I just rolled in the grass and over onto the sidewalk, pretty upset, crying my head off.

I got back in the truck and my father screamed and yelled at the Studebaker because it was the truck's fault. When we got back to the dock, dad took out some of the huge nails that were used to nail boats together. Boy, they were monster nails. Square cut galvanized nails that are still used today, particularly in wooden boats built down in the Virginia area.

Swearing and cussing all the time, he just nailed that door shut with those nails. Before he knew it, he had a crowd of people around him, watching him. He put four or five nails in, swearing and hollering saying, "That'll never open up again, damn it." And he turned to me and said "That fixes the door son, we won't have any problem with that damn door anymore." And that was the end of that. The door never did open again under any circumstances until he sold the truck.

Anyway, he had a temper and when he got his temper up, he could get carried away, that's for sure.

Paul — The Entrepreneur

We were youngsters but still, dad realized that he should give me and my brother Carl a jump-start into the business so he bought a 14-15 foot dory for us and equipped it with a Briggs and Stratton gasoline engine, hooked directly to a shaft with no transmission. We named it "Viking Kids." The boat had a little tiller in the stern and I ran up and down the canal in it with my brother Carl. Carl didn't care much for boats but to keep me company, he often went along for the ride. The engine was very hard to start but once it turned over, it would start right up especially if it was a warm day. Allowed to keep running, it worked fairly well.

In order to start it, dad and I took a half-inch drill and made a rig that would fit on the end of the flywheel. To start the engine, we had to pull on the drill's trigger and that was not easy because the drill itself weighed twenty pounds or so and it would almost turn me around in the pulling process. But with enough friction built up around the piston to jump-start the engine, it would eventually work. However, if the bottom of the boat was wet I would often get a big shock. This taught me to either get the deck dry or get my feet up off the deck. Once started, if kept running, it would work okay, but if I let it stall out the process would begin all over again.

One day, someone suggested to me that instead of just joy-riding around in my boat, I may be able to make some money on warm days by going out to the rental boats that were fishing in the bay and sell soda to them. Flounder and fluke were often caught in good numbers but the anglers were hardly ever adequately prepared for heat and hunger.

The boat rentals were usually towed out and back by the livery operator. None of them had their own engines so heading back to buy a cold one was not a good option.

I put a sign up on the dory, something like "Cold Soda for sale" and got myself an old fish box and a big chunk of ice and that's how the business got under way. One of my father's captain's took me to a nearby store and I bought a few cases of soda and put them on ice in the boat. I rode around, looking for business, and sold lots of cold soda that way, pulling up alongside each boat that hailed me.

Eventually, someone suggested that I could sell cold beer too and the same skipper who helped me buy soda also bought beer for me. Still later, I added candy bars to my "menu." Of course I remember eating as many candy bars as I sold.

Still later owners of some of the houses that were built on stilts along the marshes reached out to me to get them chunks of ice from Freeport Cold Storage. Many of the homes were very rustic, with no electricity and I at least helped by bringing ice to them.

One day, I compared notes with my mother about how the "business" was going. Remember, math was, harrumph, not exactly my primary function in life. In fact, I was lousy at it because I never studied much about it. Anyway, it turned out that at the end of a significant period of time, the money she gave me to start my business had not grown at all. In fact when she took the final tally I may have had less. However, mom made a businessman out of me, in part, by teaching me mathematics!

At one time I also tried a paper route but that didn't work out well for me. Besides it was too much like work, and worse, it kept me from the docks so I didn't last too long as a "paper boy."

I wasn't even a teenager yet but my next boat was a speedboat. Don't think though that this was the top of the line craft, far from it. In fact, dad found it pushed up on a mud bank during a storm. He got some crew members and took one of the *Viking* boats, pulled the boat off the mud bank and towed it back to the *Viking* Dock where I eventually got it back to seaworthy condition.

The boat had a V8 gasoline engine and I tooled up and down the bay area in Freeport I felt just like a real skipper. Freeport had a very famous resident at the time by the name of Guy Lombardo, the well-known band leader. I had visions of racing and beating Mr. Lombardo with my little boat. Lombardo had a very big and very pink boat which everyone knew was his because of its color. However, the pink boat was far too fast for me to even keep up with let alone race!

Chapter Four

1950s

Part One

The First *Viking* Boat in Montauk

I told you about dad's ulcer operation earlier. He was able to get mom to understand that the pressure was too great in Freeport and that Montauk would be a far better place to be. One reason was that the fishing was much closer, meaning that he would be home more (hah). Porgies and sea bass were within minutes out of the harbor, right off the lighthouse. In Freeport, he had to go much further and fish area wrecks. She wasn't exactly convinced that this was such a good idea though. One thing I remember clearly was that she knew that there wasn't even a traffic light in Montauk.

But one fine day in 1951, off we went with the *Viking V* to Montauk. My speedboat was on the back deck. The rabbit cage and the rabbits were down below in the cabin. Also on board were the dogs, the cats, my little brother Jon, and my older brother Carl. My mother and sister went by automobile.

We had all kinds of stuff loaded on the *Viking V*. There wasn't much room but what an exciting trip that was. When we came into Montauk Inlet, boy, I fell in love.

School Days

After moving to Montauk, school became something that I had to spend some serious time thinking about. Until then, with my school in Freeport being terribly overcrowded, I played hooky most of the time and rarely was caught. We had fifty-odd kids to a class and with split sessions of about twenty minutes per class before moving to the next room, all the teachers could do was take a roll call and hand out homework assignments. I was usually at the dock or on a boat but because of that, didn't even know the alphabet by the time I was in the seventh grade. When we hit Montauk, I couldn't even read road signs, I was that far behind.

However, partially because we went from 50+ kids to two small groups in our class, 7th grade with a girl and six boys and 8th grade with seven boys and two girls, things got better. But this was mainly because I had a teacher who cared! Mr. Ross was the teacher of both classes and the School Principal at the same time. He smoked in the room and answered the school phone too but still managed to handle it all well. Not being invisible any longer, I had to attend class daily and after class was over, Mr. Ross would tutor me. It was quite a way from school to home so I would either walk or ride my bicycle.

I remember a few trips I had taken to Montauk with dad to go sword-fishing before we left Freeport. I used to harpoon swordfish with him in those days. At that time we went all the way to Montauk and up and around Block Island for the swordfish. The first time we actually pulled into Montauk Harbor I remember telling myself, "Boy, this is where I want to be. This is me. I like this place!"

My father called me "eagle eye" then because I had a good way of seeing the swordfish. He would send me up in the mast to be a swordfish lookout. He paid me a dollar per swordfish I spotted, a lot of money for a kid who was barely a dozen years old. I would guide him to the fish with my eyes so that he could harpoon the fish. If it turned out it wasn't a sword but a shark or something else of large size, there was no dollar to earn. But if my father agreed that it was a swordfish, even if he missed the fish with his harpoon, I would still earn the buck.

Unfriendly People

When we first moved to Montauk the town was very small and kind of unfriendly to our family. We were outsiders. I remember my mother coming home from church and she had been crying and said the people wouldn't talk to her. My father had a dock sign up on a piece of property he owned on the corner of West Lake Drive and sometimes when we used to go down to the boat in the morning, it would have been knocked down. My dad would get out of the truck and nail it back up, saying that they'd tire sooner or later, once they find out that he was going to keep putting it back up again. He owned the property and there was nothing illegal about the sign, it was just that the other boatmen didn't like him having that sign there.

The town was very small, and we only had a half a school bus. Marshall Predo, Sr. drove the bus. He had one hand missing at the wrist but he managed to drive with the stub of his arm and the other good hand. Gee, you'll never find a bus driver like that again, that's for sure. He also owned Marshall's Gas Station.

There was a man everyone called "Stinky" King who hooked up the oil burner in our house. Before that, we had coal-fired heat and had to bank the fire at night. My mother rented out four of the bedrooms in our house. The people from Montauk Manor would call and give her any of their overflows. When that happened we'd all move to the other side of the house. My mom's goal was to make one thousand dollars a season and she usually did it and when she had all the money she made an improvement to the house. That's how we got storm windows and the oil burner to replace the coal. The oil

[Top] Cattle round-up in town.
[Bottom] Cowboys at the train station in town.
Both photos courtesy of the Montauk Library.

burner never did work right but at least we had oil fired heat anyway when it worked. The next year, she had the roof re-shingled.

Dad kept running the boats and my mother would be renting rooms and running the business in the summer too. To survive, we really had to scrape to make a living with four kids in the house. I also made some money trapping.

Other than my hunting and such, the town was dead in the winter with little to do. If I wanted to go to the movies I had to hitch-hike back and forth to East Hampton and that was a big deal on Friday or Saturday night. I did have a friend who was older and had a senior driver's license. I was able to drive to the movies in the daylight in his car and he drove us home but other than that, it was hitch-hike or walk, period! And there weren't many cars on the road at that time of the year so it more often than not, was shoe-leather. For that matter, I didn't get into sports at East Hampton High School because I could hardly ever get a ride home afterwards and in the cold and nasty weather each winter, it just wasn't worth the effort. Besides, I would rather hunt and trap.

I also had an old 1946 Ford jalopy that wasn't suitable to take on the roads but we could drive it in the woods. We'd drive right off the road in many places through the woods and brush via dirt roads, as long as we could keep it running. We brought it into the garage at night and worked on it. We would get it running for a while and then it was time to fix it again. For sure, it was an interesting life.

Meanwhile, Back in Freeport

Dad eventually shut down his operation in Freeport and moved it all to Montauk but for some time, he continued to have boats in two ports. The smaller and older *Vikings* remained at the Viking Dock in Freeport with his boat partner Frank Dorman managing the business, aided greatly by Captain Al Lindroth who originally trained under dad. After Al was licensed he ran one *Viking* or another for many years. A few other *Viking* boats were moved later to Montauk.

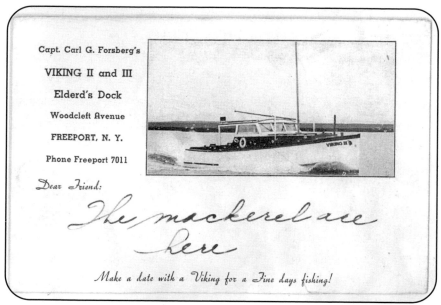

Capt. Carl G. Forsberg's

VIKING II and III

Elderd's Dock

Woodcleft Avenue

FREEPORT, N. Y.

Phone Freeport 7011

Dear Friend:

The mackerel are

here

Make a date with a Viking for a Fine days fishing!

Here's a typical postcard we mailed weekly to all our customers.

Captain Al Lindroth

I guess the one person that I speak of with the biggest of smiles on my face of all is Captain Al. Hardly a sentence ever ends about Al without me saying one nice thing or another about him but in kind, Al praises the Forsberg's equally as highly.

The 60-foot long steel party boat, *"Captain Al"* sails daily out of Point Lookout. Al had the boat built for himself in North Carolina and even though now in his 80's, still takes over the wheel every now and then. Wintering in Tarpon Springs, Florida near me, he and his wife still spend most of the year up north in Freeport.

Al ran one *Viking* or another out of Freeport. He started there on the *Viking* I and eventually pushed east to join my father in running the *Viking VI* out of Montauk, working his way up to Captain.

At one time or another Al operated each of the seven *Viking* boats that had

**Captain Al in the foreground on the *Viking Freedom*.
To his right is mate Joe Flapjaw.**

numbers instead of names. He remembers a few specific trips that he ran that involved me being on board. You see, I really, really loved to fish. While I knew and understood that as a little guy my "job" was to do whatever dad wanted me to do, I really preferred to have a rod in my hands rather than a broom or swab to clean a deck with. So every now and then, I would hide in the head of the boat that Al was to take out that day. The head was behind the wheelhouse and no one knew I was there until Al would set up to anchor on a spot and up popped me with a pole in my hands.

Lindroth told Manny that I was always thinking of ways to make money. On the days that the porgies were flying over the rails, and there were many such days, I convinced customers not to throw the smaller ones overboard, asking them to give the little fish to me instead. I was well liked by the passengers who tossed the small fish down and I picked them up and put them into a big cooler. There were no bag or size limits at the time, and I would bring them to a wholesaler at the dock making as much as $25 for a mess of fish, quite a lot of money in the 50's!

Al went into the Army but when he was discharged he rejoined the *Viking* crew. At that time my father asked him to operate one of the Montauk boats. Still living in Freeport, but knowing that the daily ride from Freeport to Montauk was too long, he was invited to live with our family at our place in Montauk. We had a little unheated upstairs room at the north end of the house and that is where Lindroth slept in on the night before each trip he made from Montauk. He remembers how cold it was there but still it beat the long nightly ride back and forth from Freeport to Montauk.

With eight great-grandchildren at last count, Lindroth credits my dad as being the one person who helped make him what he is today and I credit Lindroth as being the guy who taught me well, second only to my father, about fishing and boating.

Lindroth took a few non-fishing trips with the family also, telling Manny about one such trip to Key West with his wife to visit with me. We stayed on the *Viking Freedom*, the 60 foot sail-assisted commercial boat that I love to operate.

On another trip, he joined my dad and our mate Dick Dose on a trip to Price's Boat Yard in Virginia to get some repair work done on the *Viking VII*.

But underway they ran into pea soup fog and with no radar that was tough for sure. Worse, down around Barnegat, N. J., they noticed that the recently rebuilt single 671 engine wasn't sounding too good so dad shut it down and went below to try to fix things.

He taught me how to fix engines with any and all tools we could put our hands on and I did so many a time by myself. This time, it was dad who took two knives, a hacksaw blade and somehow got the engine up and running again. But during the repair work he got his hand caught in the gears and ground it up badly. When they got to Price's a day or so later, Mr. Price got an ambulance to bring dad in for emergency aide.

1950s Part Two

The *Pelican* Tragedy

A terrible accident took place on 9/1/51 when the 42 foot headboat, "*Pelican*," turned over causing 45 passengers and crew members to die.

One person who was there and told what he saw occur was the man who has come to be associated with shark fishing, probably the man who made the most fame seeking and catching huge sharks, including the World Record "Great White." I'll tell you several true stories about that man, Captain Frank Mundus of the *Cricket II* in a little while. For now, let's hear from Frank himself. Manny found the account of the incident on line when he typed in "The *Pelican* Tragedy."

Captain Mundus reported that the "*Pelican*" was hit by rip current waves which began washing over the starboard side. Most passengers panicked and stampeded over to the port side to escape the waves. However, this caused the boat to list far to one side and she quickly rolled over, throwing nearly everyone into the ocean. 45 people including the Captain drowned and only 19 were rescued by the boats that had been nearby.

He said that his boat had been docked alongside the *Pelican* that morning at Fishangrila on Fort Pond Bay in Montauk. A Long Island railroad train had pulled into its station loaded with folks who wanted to go on one of the party boats. It being an extremely busy day, many of the boats had already been boarded by anglers who drove out by car. The train passengers were so numerous that there simply was no room for them on any of the boats.

The *Cricket II* was fully loaded and Mundus started to leave the dock as he heard his friend, Captain Eddie Carroll on the *Pelican* shouting "no more, no more" to the people who were trying to board his boat but he saw them throw their tackle onto the deck and jump the five feet so that they could catch the boat before it left.

Eddie was the last boat to leave, minutes after Mundus. Frank said that the weather had produced a flat calm sea, with no breeze as the day began. The *Cricket* had engine problems though and he was slow to reach the fishing grounds, an area southwest of Montauk Point.

His passengers quickly got into a load of porgies and sea bass and all the boats in view were also bringing many fish in. But the weather got bad and, since his passengers had all caught quite a mess of fish, he opted to go home as did most of the other boats besides the *Pelican*. The wind blew hard out of the north east and the biggest problem of all was an ebb tide, putting the wind directly against the strong tide, making for rough seas.

Mundus had already reached his dock when he heard a little girl crying and screaming, putting her arms around him, and she said, "The *Pelican* turned over at the lighthouse!" He quickly took a few people, including his mate, out to the scene. When he got there, he saw the boat on her side, drifting towards the rocks that were near the lighthouse. There were no people visible in the water. Apparently those that made it away from the undertow were picked from the water by a few boats that were in the area earlier.

Captain Mundus realized that the boat would shortly smash against the rocks and since there might have been some passengers trapped in the boat; he wanted to at least tow her away from the rocks. He reached my father who had gone to the scene as well, doing whatever he could do to help. The two agreed that they would each tie lines onto the bobbing boat and try to tow it in to the harbor.

The wind cut back and with only slow rolling swells to contend with, they headed slowly in against the tide. The weight of what they were pulling was extremely heavy, imagine a 42 foot boat filled with water, but they had a mission to accomplish and moved on. They wanted to at least recover as many bodies as they could for relatives of the deceased.

Meanwhile, the 83-foot Search and Rescue Coast Guard Cutter that was based in New London, Connecticut, had gotten a call to come to Montauk to help in the proceedings. It was windy when they came to Montauk and instead of heading to the scene, they tied up and waited. Dad felt that the boat rolled pretty good and maybe the crew got sick, but instead of heading to the *Pelican,* they remained at Gosman's Dock and stayed there.

There were people on the dock screaming at them; there were kids throwing stones at them. The Coast Guard claimed that they were waiting for orders before heading out. By the time they finally untied their lines the weather had improved. The few survivors were plucked out of the water by nearby boats and my dad and Frank Mundus already had the submerged boat in tow!

Dad and Frank reached the Shagwam buoy which was quite close to the jetties and the 83-foot Coast Guard Cutter that was based in Connecticut finally appeared and told them that they were going to take over the tow.

Mundus refused, telling them that the *Cricket II* and *Viking V* had the issue under control and felt that they could bring the *Pelican* in by themselves. However, the Coast Guard skipper insisted that he be given the tow line that was being used. He had a sailor throw a "heaving line" to the *Cricket,* telling Mundus to attach the tow line to its end. But the *Cricket* mate, cold, tired and wet, cut the line and tied the Coast Guard heaving line onto it so that they could begin the tow by themselves with the larger vessel.

Frank said that instead of going forward with the pulling of the *Pelican*, the cutter "backed down (put both propellers in reverse) and got the *Cricket's* tow line tangled in both his propellers. When he saw this, he called over to my father and told him what happened and suggested he go home because he knew that dad couldn't tow the *Pelican* all by himself. He tried though and broke his line, and came home.

The bigger boat now being out of commission because her engines were enmeshed in the towing line, they radioed for a tow and a smaller Coast Guard boat came out and towed the big boat in. The smaller boat then went back out and put a line on the *Pelican* and brought it home. An incoming tide had actually pushed the submerged boat almost right to the inlet anyway.

Skipper Mundus said "In the newspaper, the Coast Guard got all the glory. Forsberg and I got no recognition at all for doing all this work. The only thing we wanted from the Press was one word: "Thanks," but never got it."

Needless to say, actually being there and living through the tragedy was something that could produce a very factual accounting. Mundus was displeased to read a report from the Coast Guard that differed considerably from what he witnessed.

Among some probable errors he found was a statement that said that "The *Pelican* was rated for 20 passengers but took on 62 that day." Mundus wrote that the *Pelican* was less than 15 tons and as such was not subject to any passenger count restriction. He went on to say that the report had shown that the *Pelican* "set out at mid-morning for a day of blue fishing off Block Island." Further, that she took a fearful pounding by heavy seas all the way back from Block Island and that ten miles east of Montauk Point, her port engine flooded and eventually, she rolled over. Mundus said that the boat had been nowhere near the area reported, only fishing in an area nicknamed "Frisbees," and that neither the *Pelican* nor any other boat had been fishing for bluefish. Also, that the boat's problem was a wind against the tide matter, compounded by the out of control passengers who aided in causing the boat to roll over.

Unfortunately, all 86 life jackets that were stored in two deck lockers remained in place because the incident took place so quickly that no one was able to reach them before the tragedy occurred.

Filling in yet more detail, I remember that a boat that managed to save 15 of the people who had been thrown overboard when the *Pelican* capsized was the *Bingo II*, run by Captain Les Behan. In fact, in their hurry to bring as many on board as possible, a *Bingo II* mate actually gaffed a few people in their clothing to lift them on board and even got the gaff stuck into the arm of one of them who was so grateful that he thanked the mate, not even realizing that he had been gaffed.

I think you can still find a written account of the tragedy entitled "Dark Noon" which also reported on an additional terrible part of the day. It seemed that a red haired youngster died on board and his father had apparently tied him to a railing on the boat so that later on, at least the kid's body could be recovered. But what with all the horror that took place, in the tow process, the rail that the boy was tied to was apparently knocked off and he floated away. Years later, his floating skull was recovered and identified at Shelter Island, miles away from the scene.

My father was really pisssed off, he was so mad he screamed, "Those bastards, if they had only left us alone, Mundus and I had it under control; we would've had the boat in. He blamed the loss of that boy's body on the Coast Guard boat.

Whether it happened that way or not I don't know but that was his feeling.

If you remember, earlier in this chapter I told you about the kids that were throwing stones at the Coast Guard boat that was tied to the dock. I can personally swear to that part of the story because I was one of the kids throwing the rocks!

When my father got home that night he was naturally cold, wet and weary.

He sat at the kitchen table and asked for a cup of coffee. My mother made him some and then he started crying, the only time I can ever remember seeing my father cry, he actually cried!

Commercial Swordfishing

My father rigged the *Viking III* up for sword-fishing but she turned out to be a little small so later on he rigged up the *Viking V* instead. He put a Leilin diesel in the III. It was a British industrial engine and consequently he couldn't find a transmission to fit it. He solved the problem by hooking the propeller shaft right to the fly wheel direct drive which meant that he had no reverse and no neutral. When he started the engine it was already in forward gear.

He put a long pulpit on the front of the *Viking III* to harpoon the swordfish and a mast for spotting them. Phil Rhule was working for him then, a young man of about 18. Phil worked for my father for quite a few years and I knew him as a kid, he's about twelve years my senior. We got very friendly later on in life when he moved his family to Montauk. He told me this story:

It was a dark night and they were on their way from Freeport to Montauk. In those days, they didn't have any kind of equipment; the only instrument they had on the *Viking III* was a compass. When they came around the lighthouse they cut Shagwam Point a little bit too short and "boom" they crashed aground. Luckily there were no rocks there, just sand, but there was no way of backing off because they didn't have reverse.

They had to shut the engine off because it was pushing the boat further and further up onto the reef. The tide was kind of low and they stayed grounded on the reef for hours in the darkness, waiting for the tide to flood. Finally, near morning, Phil and my father jumped off the boat and got around the bow. With the both of them standing on the reef and pushing against the bow they managed to push the boat off the reef. Then they climbed back onto the pulpit stays and back onto the boat when she drifted down and finally, continued on their way to Montauk.

I got this big swordfish on a rod and reel while mating for Doug McCabe on the Francis Ann in the 1950s (that's me on the lower left).

My father often said, "Boy, you gotta be fast with that spring line when you come to a dock." That was because you had this twelve foot pulpit sticking out past the bow of the boat and since there was no reverse if you didn't get that spring line out there to stop the boat whatever was in front of you would have been crashed into.

He told that story one day as they were coming into Montauk and Phil got that line on there on their first pass, by golly, he put it on the bit and the boat pulled in sweet as can be. Phil was so proud of himself he said, "Wow, that's unbelievable; how I did that I don't know, but we did it!"

There were about a dozen guys sitting there on a long bench, all sword fishermen, disgusted because the weather was not good for sword-fishing. My father pulled in to get some stock and ice on the *Viking III* and when he and Phil walked out the guys were still sitting there. My father said to them, "how's the sword fishing?" No one answered, they all just kept looking straight ahead so my dad repeated it a little louder, "how's the sword fishing, guys?" Still no answer; they all just kept looking straight ahead so my father repeated it a little louder and still, no answer. So he turned and looked at Phil and said good and loud, "Friendly bunch of bastards, aren't they?" Fortunately no one got up; they just sat there and stared straight ahead. They stayed at the dock overnight and sailed the next day for swordfish and then headed back to Freeport.

My father wound up taking the Leilin diesel out of the III and putting in a Chrysler Crown gas engine again which had a transmission with a reverse. That was when he swung the swordfish gear over to the *Viking V*. She held lots more fish and ice and was a bigger and better boat for that type of fishing.

People often ask me what kind of fishing I like to do the best. I answer just about everything you can do on the east coast of America, from tub trolling to lobstering and dragging; party boat and charter boat fishing, and so forth but my favorite type of fishing has always been harpooning swordfish.

We no longer have that in America but there is still a small harpoon fishery up in Canada. Swordfish are now mostly caught long-lining but harpoon fishing was always my love, my favorite fishing. My father loved it also.

When you read the comments from my brother Carl you will see that dad had a great saying, something like: "It's one of the nicest, most exciting ways I know of to go broke."

It is very, very exciting fishing. You're up in the mast or up in the high part of the boat looking for fish and it could be hours or days before you see it. Suddenly you'll see something clip out and you don't know if it's a swordfish or a shark or ocean sunfish so you go over in that direction. Well, it's most likely a shark or sunfish or something else but when you see the fins of a swordfish come out you just see its' clip, they don't have to come fully out, just the clip, and you know it's a sword! There are no ifs, ands or buts about it, something just tells you inside that's a swordfish and with me it's just a very exciting moment.

I swear my heart must stop beating because it just hits me like a sledge hammer and there he is, and the thing is, when you see one and you point at him so the other crew can see it and they start running the boat up on the fish, man, that's wild!

Now when you're up on the pulpit and you're coming up on that swordfish, it's you and that fish; that's all there is, just you and the swordfish. You're looking down at the fish that's worth hundreds of dollars, weighing hundreds of pounds, swimming along nice and easy in the water and you're gonna' see that big monstrous eye that a swordfish has and it looks as if that eye is looking right up at you.

You have this harpoon gripped in your hands and when you throw that harpoon, it's the most exhilarating feeling you've ever had in your life. It's one-on-one and a hell of a challenge. It's awful, awful exciting and that's my favorite fishing of them all; it's just an absolutely great feeling. Unfortunately there wasn't much money in harpooning because there were just too many hours spent at sea without ever seeing a swordfish. But it was an awful lot of fun and very exciting and challenging, no doubt about it.

Our first boat with a name, the original *Viking Star.*

The First *Viking* with a Name, Not a Number —
The Last Price-Built Boat

The first *Viking* with a name and not a number was the "*Viking Star*" which was to become the biggest and last boat ever built by Price Shipyards in Deltaville, Va. Mr. Price was very well known. He built the "Cadillac" of boats. To this day, there are many boats still fishing that are called "Price-built" and one thing that some are famous for is their closeness to the water from their hand-rail. Some refer to them as "over the rail and into the pail" boats because lifting a fish up and over is easy to accomplish. He really had nice workmanship in his boats.

The *Viking Star* was 65-feet long and 22-feet wide, designed, of course, by my grandfather. He designed every one of dad's new boats and dad named the first seven with a roman numeral until he got the first one with a word, the *Viking Star*.

This boat was to head to Montauk and as our three generations of Forsberg's (my grandfather, father and me) started to bring the vessel up from Deltaville to Montauk we saw Mr. Price standing at the dock, holding himself

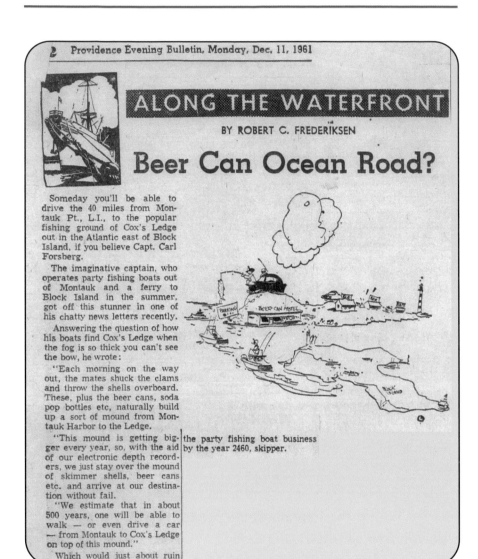

Providence Evening Bulletin, Monday, Dec. 11, 1961

ALONG THE WATERFRONT

BY ROBERT C. FREDERIKSEN

Beer Can Ocean Road?

Someday you'll be able to drive the 40 miles from Montauk Pt., L.I., to the popular fishing ground of Cox's Ledge out in the Atlantic east of Block Island, if you believe Capt. Carl Forsberg.

The imaginative captain, who operates party fishing boats out of Montauk and a ferry to Block Island in the summer, got off this stunner in one of his chatty news letters recently.

Answering the question of how his boats find Cox's Ledge when the fog is so thick you can't see the bow, he wrote:

"Each morning on the way out, the mates shuck the clams and throw the shells overboard. These, plus the beer cans, soda pop bottles etc, naturally build up a sort of mound from Montauk Harbor to the Ledge.

"This mound is getting bigger every year, so, with the aid of our electronic depth recorders, we just stay over the mound of skimmer shells, beer cans etc. and arrive at our destination without fail.

"We estimate that in about 500 years, one will be able to walk — or even drive a car — from Montauk to Cox's Ledge on top of this mound."

Which would just about ruin the party fishing boat business by the year 2460, skipper.

Another article about Captain Carl
in the *Providence Evening Bulletin*, December 11, 1961

up with two canes. He was dying of cancer and had tears running down his eyes as we removed the mooring lines and pushed off.

Mr. Price was very proud of *The Viking Star*. I firmly believe he fought long enough to get that boat completed and see it go down the river. Sure enough, some time later his son called my father and told him that three days after we left, his dad had passed away.

The Viking Star was also the last boat that my grandfather designed for my dad. He passed away shortly after.

The boat was less than 15 ton. Tonnage in the marine industry is not weight. It is measured in space, measured inside usable space in a cabin and below deck. My grandfather was pretty good with tricks involving tonnage; you had to be in those days. If you were less than 15 ton, you could go out in the ocean as far as you wanted to go and put as many people on a boat as you wanted as long as you had one life jacket for each person on board plus three fire extinguishers.

That was it. If you were over 15 ton, you had to be inspected by steamboat inspectors and you weren't allowed to go more than 20 miles away from land without a special permit.

The steamboat inspectors were used to walking on ships instead of wooden boats, and that was always a problem. Everybody worked very hard to stay under 15 tons. They weren't regulated that way with the Coast Guard. Later on, that all changed to 100 tons, which we have now, and we have marine inspection which isn't steamboat inspection. Marine inspection was designed in the 50s and that is what we go by now.

Captain Chris Mahlstadt

I'll talk again about Chris later on. But now, let's hear directly from him. Manny interviewed Chris who told him a thing or two about our relationship.

"I was a few years younger than Paul when I began working for the *Viking* fleet as a deckhand for a few summers many years ago. He and I became close friends and we worked side-by-side as mates for his dad and then I worked the deck once Paul got his Captain's license. Some years later, I went into the insurance business and, with my son, now operate two agencies that specialize in insuring boats and, of course, we insure all of the *Viking* boats. Our business

Here's my friend and insurance man, Captain Chris Mahlstadt with the two biggest sea bass he ever caught. I only wish I had a better picture of him.

is called "Island-Wide Marine Insurance," out of Ormond Beach, Florida, and Setauket, N. Y.

I also got my Captain's license at the early age of 18, the same as Paul did. I kept the license active until 2008 when I acquired mesothelioma, a cancerous disease of the outside of the lung. The diseased tissue was removed but it weakened me to the point that I can now say that I have an excuse for not being able to hit a golf ball as far as I used to.

One day, on one of the older *Vikings* that I was working the deck on, Paul was up topside in the wheelhouse. Folks were catching loads of fish that day but as people tend to do, they still complained that the fish were too small. Now there we were, anchored south of Montauk in November, and codfish from 4-7 pounds were flying over the rail, but they wanted bigger fish and started making noise. Paul took care of that! He came down from the wheelhouse with one of those old bamboo rods mounted with a "sidewinder" reel and then took one single cast. The sinker took his clam bait down and a moment or two later, I recall him swinging skyward. Soon after, I was alongside of him, holding a gaff and I stuck a 50-pound plus codfish for him. Paul promptly retreated back to the wheelhouse and that shut the complainers up for sure."

Signed: *Chris Mahlstadt*

And from Alaska, Some Words from Andy Mezirow

We've heard from Captains Al Lindroth and Chris Mahlstadt; let's also hear now from a guy in Alaska who sent me a nice note on Facebook on March 3rd, 2011. His name is Andy Mezirow. Here are some of the things he wrote:

"Hi Paul, you probably barely remember me. I worked for you and Steven in the 1980's. I have been in Alaska fishing for the last 23 years.

I wanted to take a minute to thank you for teaching me so much during those early years in my fishing career. I learned that to really be a fisherman, you needed to be a marine engineer, biologist, politician and master of marketing. You were all those things and even if you didn't know it, I was watching and learning from you and Steven things that I have used every day over the last 30 years to rise to the top here in Alaska.

I know you have had great success and you must be proud to have so many of your children and grandchildren in the business."

Signed: *Andy Mezirow*

Memories From My Younger Brother, Jon
Paul's Balloons

"It was back in the 50s. Paul was 15 and I was 10. He was always at the dock or working on a boat, he lived down there. Montauk had little for young kids to do in such a sleepy fishing village at the end of Long Island.

My friends and I would basically hang around each others houses. Paul and I shared a bedroom for several years and one day, we came across Paul's wallet in the bedroom.

We looked in it and found what we thought were balloons all wrapped up in very hard to open plastic wrappings. We really thought that they were balloons as we blew into one end and created a long blimp with a nose at the other end.

With a secured knot at the open end we went to the garage to enjoy hitting the balloon back and forth in the open space. This went on for months. Every time we found Paul's wallet we would wipe him out of his balloons. Only years later did I realize what they were and could only imagine the frustration he and his girlfriend (now my nephew's mother) went through at a passionate moment.

I think my friends and I may be responsible for my being the uncle of their beautiful first child and subsequent wedding!

Our Mom

"Everything happens for the best." We had a special mom. Whenever anything had happened to any of us kids, Carl, Paul, Audrey or me, mom would always say "Everything happens for the best." We all heard these words many times while growing up. For some reason, when our mother said those words, it always made us feel better.

Back in the 60's, the last 65-foot wooden *Viking* boat was tied up to the dock and it burned almost all the way down to the water line! It was a black, charred mess. I found Paul at the dock, looking down at this awful sight of water, oil and black muck. I put my arm on his shoulder and we spoke for a while and then Paul said "I'll see you later, I'm going up to see mom and if she says "everything happens for the best," I'm going to kill her!

A few days later, I ran into Paul and asked him what mom said. And his response? "Everything happens for the best."

Jon Forsberg

1950s Part Three

Passenger Carrying Captain Paul (Sort Of)

I had my own boat at a very young age and as Captain Al Lindroth told us a few pages back, I always was looking for a way to make a buck. I would operate my little speedboat in Lake Montauk, now called Montauk Harbor. My dad allowed me to go as far out as Shagwam Reef and with a compass on board, I could always find my way back to the southwest and beach the boat if need be. Aided by the horn on the jetties, at an early age, it was okay with dad.

Again, I was only in the seventh grade but still, with a friend, we would go out and catch a mess of porgies and sea bass. But the boat was too low to the water so I sold it and bought an ex-Navy 24-footer with a small cabin on board. It was powered by an old but reliable 4-cylinder twin ignition Redwing engine with a Model A Ford carburetor.

I had a bit more range with that boat and fished several other sea bass and porgy hot spots, increasing our catch well. I also did drift fishing at the Inlet, catching a mess of fluke before the sun came up too high.

And my own "business" continued to grow! One particular Memorial Day weekend, the docks were loaded with fishermen with no room for some to board any of the boats, they were all sold out. I was about to go out with two friends for a day's fishing when four anglers asked me to take them out fishing. That's when the "business" really got jump started!

The 24 footer had a good sized cockpit but it wasn't big enough for seven people to fish from so as we were into a load of porgies, one guy actually had to stand on the toilet, fishing out of the hatch in the bow, and he threw his fish down between his legs for a buddy to pick up. We were only three miles out and everyone caught a load of fish.

Back at the dock, one of the four anglers handed me twenty dollars, or five bucks for each, the going fare at the time, and, wow, all of a sudden, I was in the charter boat business. Me and my friends cleaned the catch and the boat and I gave each of them a couple of dollars and that was how I began as a passenger-carrying-captain, sort of.

It was still early and Teddy, the mate on the nearby *Margaret IV*, came over and said that he had a man, his wife, and their little boy with them who wanted to go fishing in calm water. They didn't want to go offshore but would be happy to get some inshore flounders.

So out we went and as we were underway, the man handed me ten bucks; this took place in view of Salivar's Dock where a few party boats were tied up. Needless to say, at a dozen years of age or so, with no license, of course, this was quite illegal. A guy saw it and started yelling and screaming at me that he saw me take the money and that he was going to report me to the Coast Guard. I was so proud of the fact that I was going to make two trips in one day, making lots of money, but this really messed things up.

Later on, after dad brought the big boat back in from a day offshore, another skipper told him what took place and said that he feared that the Coast Guard would give him grief about it. Sure enough, the Coast Guard showed up before I got back to the dock. My father was able to convince the Coast Guard that his son was just a little kid who didn't know he was doing anything wrong and they let me off with just a warning.

Dad told me that from then on, "Don't take money from the people directly. If you're going to take people out fishing just tell them to leave the money on a bunk down below. You should say that the money just fell out of a pocket there and you didn't see it until the folks left the boat. That way, you can't get pinched!"

Former Run-Runner

One of the funniest things that happened along the waterfront involved a boat called the *Helen*. It was a wooden boat lapped straight like a skiff. Before she was converted into a party fishing boat she had been a rum-runner with two big gasoline engines. The former owner used to run illegal alcohol in from Canadian boats and ships twelve miles offshore. The smaller fast running boats would haul the alcohol to land to be loaded onto trucks to go into New York City. But that was during prohibition.

George Glas obtained the boat and he painted it red on the outside to cover the rust. He gave the mate a five-gallon pail of gray paint purchased at a navy surplus store and had him take it down to the passenger cabin that was below deck in the forward part of the boat. At that time most party boats had the wheelhouse aft and the down-below cabin was forward for the passengers.

He told his mate to paint the inside of the boat gray. The guy did a great job but the next day when the boat went fishing there were all these gray streaks running down the side of the boat. The gray paint leaked down between the lapped-straight joint planks and there she was, a red boat with all these gray drips running outta' her! Well, I wanna' tell you something, on the radio, everybody was laughing and giggling.

That paint job was talked about for months. Now, after he painted the inside, of course he had to go around with a raft and paint the outside again to cover over the gray streaks. That gives you an idea what shape some of those boats were in.

Anything Legal to Make a Buck
"Armstrong"

Back in those days I did anything to make a buck. Anything legal that is. The winter was tough. The first two years I was married I was tub-trolling with the *Viking IV*.

One day I went to Montauk marine basin and got a job there painting boat bottoms, sanding hulls and so forth. They also had a dock building operation and one morning the owner, Carl Darenberg, told everyone to line up so we all did and just stood there.

I didn't know what was going on; he was looking at us and started picking people out one by one. My name was called and I stepped forward. I didn't know what it was all about until he said he had picked out the biggest guys as a crew to go and build docks, do the tough work. We didn't have hydraulics, we didn't have winches; it was all "Armstrong." that was a term in the boat industry meaning strong arms. That was why he wanted big, strong guys. Well, I was the littlest of the big guys. Dave McMann was six-foot-five; Jesse Scott was six-foot-four; I'm only five-foot-eleven and three-quarters but I later found out that the guys who were in the know slinked down and bent their knees a little bit and made sure they were shorter than everybody else 'cause they knew what was coming-those guys had been in the yard a few years. It was tremendously hard work but we were paid two dollars an hour and were sure glad to get the money.

Whether we were painting the bottom of boats or building the docks we earned two dollars an hour, sixteen dollars a day. We rebuilt the Montauk yacht club dock and that was one of our biggest jobs. When that work wasn't available I always signed up for snow plowing.

The town hired private contractors and they hired some of us locals. We'd go snow-plowing at night and salted and sanded the roads. We'd jump into the back of the truck and shovel the sand back to the spreader and, boy, that was cold. One year when we got a lot of snow in town we had to pick it up and take it to the beach and dump it. Anything to make a living, anything to make a dollar.

"Northern Dawn"

One winter later on I got a job on the boat *Northern Dawn* with Lenny Babin. *Northern Dawn* was a commercial dragger, forty feet long with a 671 Graymarine war surplus engine, man's best friend, 125 horsepower. We took the net over the side in those days; the spool in the stern was not invented then. We were three handed, Lenny Babin, Eddie Conklin (nicknamed "Bubbles," I don't know why, but that was what we called him), and myself.

We'd go offshore and drag haddock and codfish, but mostly yellowtail flounder in the inside hole, fourteen miles off Montauk. We'd fish one day and night and the next day and we'd get up to 20,000 pounds. Then we'd go to Greenport and get paid three cents a pound and come back to Montauk. Believe it or not I made anywhere between $125 and $135 for the trip and that was good money.

When I was not working on the *Northern Dawn* I gave my dad a day or two off a week.

The way you dragged in those days was you brought the net up and grabbed it with a rope called a taggle, which was a rope and a hook. That went up to the pulley on the boom and back down to the winch head and the captain would pull the line up, get the net up as high as he could and then drop it real fast. It was my job to jump on the net and hold myself down with my hands underneath the cap rail on the bulwarks, hook the taggle around the net as the boat was rolling underneath.

Of course all boats rolled in those days but the *Northern Dawn* was really a round-bottomed boat and as I tell you elsewhere about one of our older *Viking* boats, that boat too could "roll peanut butter off of bread!"

Bubbles would hand me back the hook and I'd put the line around the net again just outside the boat and lift. It took three lifts before we had the bag up high enough so we could swing it aboard. When aboard I'd then pull the puckering string and let the fish loose on deck and then tighten the string again on the bottom of the bag and throw the whole thing overboard and set up for another tow.

Well, it was real rough one night and the boat was rolling really hard. Lenny was yelling at me to pull down harder because some of the net webbing was going underneath my feet and overboard. It would take four or five times to get the bag up if we lost too much of the net so each time we caught it we dropped it faster so we could get the hook unhooked and re-hooked and get it lifted again so we could lose less in between.

That particular night he was yelling at me real loud "pull down on that damn thing, would you?" Well, I got the bright idea to turn and face the net and put both my hands under the cap and that was a mistake. I didn't realize it 'til later and he didn't notice it either otherwise he would've stopped me. The boat was rolling so much, the webbing caught the heel of my boots and I went head first, catapulting overboard.

It was the fall of the year, the first part of November, and one of the problems we had at that time of year was the blue sharks. The blue sharks would be biting the bags, biting the heads off of fish through the bag, whatever they could get.

Once in a while they would bite through the bag and put a hole in it and more fish would come out. Well, as I said, I went face first overboard. My fingers were caught in the web. I spun around in the water and started pulling myself back up into the boat. There wasn't anybody standing on the webbing and the net kept coming overboard as I was pulling.

I started yelling at Lenny Babin and Bubbles. I was heavy in the water as they ran towards me. The net kept coming overboard and my boots were filling with water and that water was cold as the devil. I could feel myself getting deeper and deeper. I'm pulling on the net like crazy and it still kept coming overboard towards me into the water.

Finally, I felt it start to tighten. Lenny got on one side and Bubbles on the other. They grabbed me under my arms and pulled me back into the boat. I looked down and those blue sharks were swirling in the water chewing away at anything they could get. Why they didn't chew away at my legs I don't know, just lucky, I guess, but boy, was that a close one.

I went down below and changed my clothes. Lenny couldn't talk for a while; he stayed in the wheelhouse just staring. It was probably a half-hour before he said, "Damn it boy, you scared the living Jesus outta' me. I looked there and you were gone." "Yeah, I won't do that again," I said. Then I told him what I had done. "Oh boy, that's a mistake," he said.

Sears and Roebuck

Yet one more way to earn a buck involved Sears and Roebuck! When we first moved to Montauk, I had a trap line. I set the trap for three years as a very young teenager. I'd trap muskrat in Montauk Lake in town and also trapped foxes and raccoons in the woods around town. I did pretty good on the golf course too. We used to buy the traps and spreaders for the pelts from the Sears and Roebuck store through their catalogue, "the wish book."

It was quite interesting. I would skin the animals, put them on stretchers and stretch out the pelts and then salt and clean them and let them dry out real well. Then I would send them to Sears and Roebuck and they would mail me back a check. Depending on what kind of condition the pelts were in, some pelts were worth more money than the others. I raised some nice dollars with my traps!

Trapping for Sears and Roebuck is all over with now, of course. I don't know exactly why it ended but I had a few good years with it. I'd carry my 410 shotgun with me when I ran a trap line and I did pretty well. I did this on weekends in the off-season. In the winter I had to chop holes in the ice to put traps into the lake to get muskrat. It was a lot of fun and good experience for me. That was just part of growing up, I guess, part of the great thing about moving to Montauk. It was open with very few homes around. It's built up quite a bit today but, gee, it was a great experience moving from Freeport and coming to a place like Montauk. I'm very fortunate for having experienced that in my lifetime.

Sudden thought. I wonder what folks would think now in this day and age if they saw a twelve year old boy walking down main street in hip boots and heavy coat with a shotgun over one shoulder plus a couple of dead muskrats over the other? I'm sure that would cause quite a commotion today!

We made it through the bitter winters by eating venison, pheasant, rabbits, and of course lots of fish. We ate clams when the water was without ice and that was how we survived.

My First Car

When I was sixteen I was all about getting my junior driver's license and my first automobile, a 1939 Chevrolet which I bought from the sister of a good friend of mine, Frannie McGlaughlin's sister Joan. I paid seventy dollars for the car and gave her twenty dollars down and ten dollars a week until it was paid off. In order to meet the expenses of an automobile I had to make some money. I was going to high school and my father was tub-trawling codfish on the big *Viking*. He and Dick Rade were fishing together and I would come down at night and bait some gear with clams. I got paid three dollars for each tub of gear I baited. I did that for a few hours every night and went to school the next day. If I had the weekend off and there was bad weather and my father didn't sail with passengers I would go down below in the cabin of the boat and bait some gear and that worked out pretty well for me.

Before I got my car, my driving consisted of taking the garbage to the dump in dad's truck via a back road to avoid getting pinched. Dad taught me how to drive the Studebaker and once a week, I'd haul the garbage to the dump.

In those days, there were very few motels in Montauk; they were just starting to build some. Montauk Manor was up on the hill and was just about all that a visitor could find, the local yacht club had a few rooms too but besides those two, our home was the only place where an outsider could rent a room.

There weren't very many trees in Montauk way back when. In old photos of Montauk you see mostly grass with some very short shrubbery. We used to burn a lot of the area in the early spring and we were always told it was to kill the deer ticks but the real reason was to have grazing land for cattle. This went on for many years. Back in the early 50's the train used to come to Montauk to unload cattle and they used to have a cattle drive, with men on horseback just like you see in the western movies. They would drive the cows right through Montauk town and go right up the hill on Montauk Highway to the dude ranch, which went all the way out to Shagwam Point and East Lake Drive.

There were cattle all over the place out there. Eventually there were less and less cattle coming and not as much grazing land was needed so of course we didn't have to do as much burning. Montauk has changed a lot since then because we now have lots of trees. My father blamed the lack of trees on the wind, saying that it blew so hard that trees couldn't grow but the real reason was that we couldn't have any because of the need for grazing land. It's funny, really, now that we have the trees folks complain that they had purchased homes with great views but now the growing trees block them!

As I said, Montauk was very small. We had the Shagwam Restaurant and Johnny's Tackle Shop. Across the street was White's Drugstore. White's is gone but now a liquor store is in its place. A small post office was next to White's but as Montauk kept growing, the post office had to grow too. We now have a separate and larger post office. The Circle Restaurant was just being built but other than that, for food, to the west end of town, you could find Boller's Restaurant, which has since become John's Pancake House. That's about it, other than a gas station next to Boller's. On the other side of the street was Marshall's Service Station, owned by Marshall Predo, the one-handed bus driver we discussed earlier. Marshall's has since tripled in size.

Discussed earlier, there were few if any places for travelers to stay back in the early 50's, but now motels are lined up all alone the beach. Montauk Manor has since closed down because it couldn't compete with the lower prices being offered then by the motels and now the Manor has become condos.

Near-Death Experience

I outgrew my smaller boat and my next one was a 28 footer named "*Marie.*" Powered by a relatively modern Chrysler Crown gasoline engine, the boat was beat up but still was a considerable improvement over the 24 footer. I bought it from Captain Rade who got quite famous later on as the owner of a head boat called the *Marlin*. You will see the Rade names often throughout this book.

Dick Rade often ran a *Viking* boat for my father in inshore waters when dad was out at Cox's Ledge. Dick knew his ranges well and when he could see land, he was excellent at finding where he wanted to fish.

Captain Rade told me right up front that the boat wasn't worth anything but the engine was excellent. But I was too headstrong to listen and was determined to make a good boat out of that rotten, old hulk and it almost cost me my life!

I painted the boat but she was still somewhat leaky. Nonetheless, one early May day I decided to go out and net some mackerel for the market. I took out my father's old World War II cotton gill nets. They were all dried out and in awful condition but that didn't bother me. Off mackerel netting I went with my friend Billy Brockman.

Maybe six miles outside of Montauk to the South, I put the nets out and drifted all night. When we hauled the nets we saw to our dismay we had only a few bushels of mackerel in total. During the haul-in, the boat labored too hard for its condition and the exhaust broke. I decided to use some of the skill dad taught me to deal with emergency repairs.

Using a rag at first to block the broken exhaust, I took a length of pipe and some wire and rigged a temporary dry exhaust between two five-gallon cans of oil sticking up two feet above the deck. With the engine cover off the hatch I rigged a temporary wash-down hose to try to cool down the engine, running the water out overboard from the deck.

We brought the net on board, as noted previously but the net was so shot that many of the mackerel swam through it. Maybe 14 years of age by then, I was dead tired and as we headed back in I asked my pal to take the wheel so that I could go down below and take a nap.

It was a beautiful day and as the boat came around the lighthouse, Billy tried to wake me up. But the exhaust fumes that resulted from my repair work found their way down below and it was difficult to get me kicked into gear. I asked my friend to let me sleep more. Not knowing it, I was deeply under the influence of the fumes. Finally, my buddy forced me to wake up, maybe saving my life, as we got past the jetties. My friend had no skill in operating the boat and as I stood up, I promptly passed out! Worse, I fell against the exhaust pipe, burning through my shirt, but I was so out of it that I never felt the burn until later that day.

Billy managed to get the boat in without me, tying up at Gosman's Dock with some help from people at the dock.

Those around pulled me off the boat and someone called Dr. Kirk, a local physician, who called an ambulance as well as my mother even before he got to the scene. Burt Tuma, another well-known Montauk name, was manning the ambulance and got there before Dr. Kirk arrived. Burt worked on me, pumping my chest, but I was unable to even talk, even though I heard the doctor speaking to me.

Mom arrived and she screamed and hollered as Dr. Kirk did his best but he told her that I didn't look good, my color was terrible. I said to myself, "Oh my God, I'm not dead, I'm alive here!" But no one could hear me as Burt Tuma put an oxygen mask over my face as they drove me to the Southampton hospital.

I remember looking up once in the ambulance and then falling back into an unconscious state, waking up next in the hospital with nurses asking each other how many shirts and sweaters I had on as they undressed me. I had my arm patched up and stayed in the hospital overnight before being released. I had nearly died of asphyxiation but because of the team that worked on me, I managed to survive.

Another Big Scare

Not yet ready to realize that the boat was doomed, I fixed the exhaust and decided to go out and catch some of the big snowshoe flounders that were available near Block Island. Rigging a few "set-lines" (a very long and heavy tarred line with hooks tied on at sufficient space from each other to avoid getting tangled), off I went with two other kids.

It was blowing out of the southeast and the boat started to leak and then it leaked even more. Reaching the lighthouse, the set-line thing wasn't being thought of any longer, instead, the goal was to survive because the pumps weren't keeping up with the water that was filling the boat. I had my friends put on lifejackets with me and as I turned the boat around, we hugged the coast as best I could near the former number three buoy, thinking that at worst;

I could at least beach the boat.

Just then, the engine conked out because too much water had been flying up onto the spark plugs. There we were, adrift, bailing with five-gallon buckets, when a boat came around the Point and threw a line to me. The Good Samaritan was Captain Frank Morse of the charter boat *Kuno II*.

He towed me to White's Shipyard. As he hauled us out, Bill White told me that the boat was going to kill me if I didn't get rid of it. During the process, the boat was leaking like a sieve!

Knowing, or at least thinking I knew, more than anyone else, I still kept the boat for that summer and stayed near shore anyway, doing commercial dragging by hand, with no winch at all, but again, a teenager. I did put an extra pump on the boat but still, the *"Marie"* was just an accident away from a tragedy that might happen.

So, after the season, I pulled the engine out of the boat and sold it and gave the boat itself to the local fire department to torch so that they could have a practice session with it. They set it ablaze and did their thing, and that ended the life of the *"Marie,"* which I had since renamed the *"Penguin."* Picture the floppy side-by-side walking of a penguin and perhaps that was where I got that name from.

After getting rid of the boat, I got a job briefly with Captain Zef Anderson on the *Marlin II*, a party boat which did lots of porgy fishing around Montauk Point during the day. My mom had insisted that I get a job with someone other than dad so that I could get more experience that way. I remember that summer with a smile when I recall how nice a person Captain Zef was and how well he treated me.

My Father had his Scary Days Too!

One particular trip my father decided to go down to fish Cox's Ledge. He and Dick Rade caught some nice big fish. On the way in a northwester came up and he had a head sea all the way home. Dad took a hell of a shellacking coming in. I kept going down to the dock but he wasn't there yet. The wind was blowing and it was bitter cold, and I wanted to bait some gear. I kept going back down and my mother was starting to get a little worried.

Finally, he came into the harbor at one o'clock in the morning. Boy, the boat was just covered with ice. It was an eerie sight watching that ice-covered boat silently slide into the dock. My father had to have the window open about four inches so he could see over the top because they were all iced up and he couldn't keep the ice off because of the spray.

Dick looked really mad as he put the spring line on. My father had the boat in gear as she came tight to the dock. Dick said, "Oh, you tie the stern line up, I quit!" He went home and didn't show up at the dock for a few days.

When my father came out of the pilothouse he was just covered with ice from the wind blowing in over the window opening. His eyebrows were all iced up and he had this blanket wrapped around his head and body. He stepped out of the pilothouse and went down below in the cabin up forward and sat down beside the pot-bellied stove. He didn't say anything for quite a while, just sat there shivering until he reached over and pulled out a can of beer. He opened it up and put it on the stove to heat it. Then he drank it to warm himself. Finally he said, "Damn it, son, this is no boat to be offshore with in the winter weather. I can't wait until the *Viking Star* gets done; this is no boat for this type of work, this kind of fishing.

To make a long story short, when the *Viking Star* was built he sold that *Viking* and it went up to New Hampshire. That boat ran for another 25 years or so, back and forth through some islands. She didn't have a hard life as the runs were not very long and she wasn't in a lot of bad rough weather so she lived a good long life.

The Sawdust Solution

Quite a few of the wooden boats of the day had leaking problems. One of our boats would leak so bad that we had to get up in the middle of the night and go down to the dock and start the engine up and pump her out. But my dad came up with an unusual solution.

Dad used to take some codfish to give to Clem at the Montauk lumberyard. Clem, in turn, started saving all his sawdust for him. My father would take a couple of bags of sawdust and throw them into the water. He took a scrub brush handle and put an extension on it and pushed the floating sawdust down under the boat. Naturally, the sawdust would float up and into the seams, swelling up and slowing down the leaks. That way we could sleep all night long without starting the engine up and pumping the boat out.

Once the word got out what dad was doing, there was quite a rush on sawdust at the Montauk lumberyard.

The Harp was owned by the Hegner brothers. She was down at Gosman's Dock and people joked about how bad she leaked with the pump running on her all the time. Gosman made a remark one time; he said, "That's the only boat I know of where you can go down in the engine room and check the oil and water and look in the bilge and know whether the tide is ebbing or flowing. All you had to do is look to see which way the killies were swimming in the bilge. In spite of all that though, Montauk boats still had very good safety records.

The Telephone Pole Solution

So we brought the *Viking Star* up to Montauk, but somewhere along the line my father didn't get a transducer for the Bendix DR9 Fishfinder so we came up to Montauk without one. My dad took the Bendix out of the *Viking V*.

Spider Hegner was running the "V" for fluke fishing at 9:00 a.m. He could see the rips that time of day and therefore didn't need the machine; he never even turned it on.

Dad got a hold of me and said, "Son, I need your help here, we've gotta' get the transducer out of the *Viking V*." I said, "Alright, okay, how we gonna' do this, dad?" Well, someplace in the road he found a piece of a telephone pole and took an axe and a hatchet and shaped it into a big plug about three foot long with a tapered end on it. One night he took a big roll of canvas and hung it on the side of the boat. This canvas was about four feet wide and must have been at least forty feet long. He let it hang in the water underneath where we were cutting the transducer out in the hopes that once we had a hole cut in the bottom of the boat the canvas would float up covering the hole and help slow the water down. However, it didn't quite work out that way. We took a brace and a bit and cut a small hole in the bottom of the boat. Then he took a keyhole saw and started cutting around the wooden bottom where the transducer was. He knew exactly where it was because the wire came up through the bottom of the boat.

He started cutting a hole as round as he could, marking it first with a pail. The water would squirt up around and behind the saw. He'd saw a little and then he'd take out some corking cotton and cork right up to the back of the keyhole saw. It was a slow process and took hours.

We had the engine and pumps running. He got just about all the way around and we only had a little bit of wood left. He looked at me and said, "Now son, we're gonna' have a lot of water coming in here all of a sudden and I'm depending on you not running off on me because the water's gonna' be pouring in and I need your help. We gotta' make sure we get the plug in this hole."

He looked at me very seriously. "We can sink this boat doing this, ya know." I was like, "Dad, no problem. I'll be here, I'm okay." And boy, when he cut that last little bit of wood that transducer blew up into the boat and I never saw so much water rush into a boat so fast in all my life. I'm telling you, in no time, we were up to our waists in water. My father and I grabbed the telephone pole plug and were fighting like crazy to get it into the hole, he was swearing and cussing and the water was rising and, man, it was cold!

We finally got the plug in and were stomping and jumping on it, swearing and hollering and yelling, "I've got you, you bastard now." Dad pushed that plug down and took a two by four, measured it and cut it off and jammed it in against the top of the plug and bottom of the deck of the boat. Then he toe-nailed the two-by-four into place and it held the plug down into the boat nice and tight.

However, the hole was not exactly the same shape as the plug so he took cedar shingles, stripped them down and hammered then down in between the hole and the plug. Then he took corking cotton with a hammer and pounded the cotton wherever the water was leaking in. Finally, the water stopped!

And there it was, done and repaired. The canvas never did come up and help us with all that water. All the while the water was rushing in my father was yelling, "Where the hell is that canvas?

Anyway, we took the transducer over to the *Viking Star* and laid it inside the bilge. We used it that whole summer but because it had to send the signal through the bottom of the boat I believe it could only utilize about fifty percent of its power. You couldn't see the fish that well but it did give you a bottom line. You had to turn the volume up higher on the machine to get a reading but as long as the transducer was submerged in a little bit of water it would work. When we hauled the *Viking Star* out later we had the transducer installed outside the boat.

During the summer season, Spider Hegner came back to run the *Viking V* and do some fluke fishing off Montauk Point. He didn't know anything about us stealing the transducer; he noticed the machine was gone but he couldn't care less because he never used it anyway. Well, somewhere along the line it comes time to haul the *Viking V*, clean and paint the bottom and give her hull a nice coat of paint. It's in the spring of next year and spider brought the boat over to Montauk Marine Basin which was then White's Shipyard. When the boat was on the railway the plug was sticking out past the keel and just luckily that plug was in-between the rails. Gee, if the boat had sat on that plug it probably would not have pushed that two-by-four right up through the deck.

Well, anyway, they hauled the boat out. Bill White was walking around the boat getting ready to get the ladder so Spider could come down when all of a sudden Bill saw this plug sticking through the bottom of the boat.

He and his assistant started laughing. Pretty soon the two of them were laying there rolling on the ground laughing. Poor Spider didn't know what was going on; he was still stuck up on the top of the boat waiting for them to pass the ladder over to him.

"What the hell are you guys laughing at?" he said, and after some time went by Bill White passed up the ladder and said, "Wait until you come down and you see this." Spider came down and when he saw that plug sticking through the bottom of the boat, he took off. "I quit, I can't run a boat like that." Well, of course my father hired Bill White to cut the bad plank out, put in a new plank and close the hole up properly. I'm sure my father had forgotten all about that telephone pole plug and Spider never knew anything about it 'til the boat was hauled. He ran the boat a year after the repair was made. That was an incident I remember very clearly and will never forget and it was the talk of the town for a long time.

Chapter Five

2013

The Current *Viking Fleet*

We've discussed the seven boats that began with the word "Viking" and ended with a Roman numeral. I also touched upon the time when we changed our routine with boat naming and instead of the name ending in a Roman numeral; they ended with a word instead of letters. Currently, there are, once again, seven Vikings. They are:

Viking Star

She is 104 feet in length and it replaced the original "*Star*." I built her to navigate and fish the waters of Montauk in comfort, (with heated hand rails-much more on that later!) the boat is licensed to carry 149 passengers. It has 110 rod holders and her heated cabin itself is as long as the prior "*Star*" at 65 feet. Seating is available inside for 76 passengers.

The boat has a full galley, serving hot meals and beverages, plus a tackle store. She can seat 76 people on the main fishing deck. The "*Star*" has a huge

(Top) Here's a cabin shot of the current *Viking Star*.

(Left) Here's my publisher's grandson, Joe Morea, holding two beasts that he caught on a special offshore trip on the new *Viking Star*.

Here's the *Viking Starship* — the biggest boat on the coast.

upper observation deck also, which can seat 75 more people.

Needless to say, the boat has plenty of room to hold customers coolers, and for offshore fishing, she can bunk 44 passengers and even has a hot water shower room. As with all the *Viking* vessels, she has a pilothouse that is equipped with top of the line technology.

Viking Starship

Licensed to carry 300 passengers, this boat, which I believe to be the longest party boat in the entire country, is a sight to behold at 140 feet. Equipped with 70 Navy-style bunk beds below deck, she can take you out and back to far-offshore areas in comfort. With reclining cushioned chairs at cabin level, as well as a hot shower room, and an 80 foot long heated cabin, just imagine yourself taking a trip on this super-boat.

I've sailed her out of several ports besides Montauk. They include Key West and Tarpon Springs, Florida, plus Puerto Rico, and elsewhere.

The *"Starship"* has 150 rod holders and of course, has a full galley and tackle store.

This is our beautiful *Viking Superstar* — after we finished all the work. It's our Montauk, Block Island and New London ferry.

Viking Superstar —
With Thoughts from my Friend Chan Stone

The *Viking Superstar* is a boat we salvaged and hauled up from Belize but my friend Chan Stone will tell you lots more about it in a little while. Redesigned by yours truly this 120 footer can be used as a fishing vessel of course but she was built to mainly accommodate the needs of folks who want to just take a boat ride. She is a triple-decker high-speed ferry as well as a sight-seeing boat. Make sure you bring a camera to take pictures from her upper deck.

Two hundred twenty-five passengers can be seated inside and out. Heated and air-conditioned, the *Superstar* has Australian made extra comfortable seating as an unusual "plus" and with special stabilizers she is well-designed providing this soft anti-seasickness feature.

Snacks and beverages are available. The boat has adequate storage room for bicycles and surfboards to accommodate the people who are being taken to an island vacation spot.

The *Superstar* mainly travels as a ferry from Montauk to Block Island and from Montauk to New London, Connecticut.

Back to my friend Chan Stone. Chan lives near me in Tarpon Springs, Florida. He was a pipe fitter and then a Union President for ten years in the state of Michigan until he moved to Florida and we met when each of us was out shopping with our lady friends. We've been good friends ever since. Here's what he told Manny about the *Superstar*.

"The prior owner of the *Superstar* had it built in Louisiana. All aluminum, she had four powerful 1271 Detroit diesel engines. The prior name isn't important but what is of extreme interest is the history of how Captain Forsberg acquired her.

The boat was operating out of Belize, a very poor place indeed, but still, it catered to the wealthy folks from America and elsewhere who simply loved to go deep-sea diving. The boat took seven day trips to less known areas so that its customers could see first-hand what the wonders of the sea could reveal. Unfortunately, in 2001 or so, the boat was tied to her dock when Hurricane Hugo suddenly appeared and made a direct hit on Belize without warning. In fact, the boat had lots of customers on board waiting to make a trip and in the violence of the storm flipped the boat over and 17 of her passengers were drowned.

The boat was eventually beached and the owner collected what ever he could from his insurance policy and the insurer took over ownership. However, the boat was resting in sand and clearly, was no longer in any manner of operational condition.

The insurer finally gave up with salvage attempts and put the boat up on E-Bay for sale. Paul and a partner bid on it and acquired ownership with a payment of only $25,000 but then, once they owned it, the question was what could they do with it?

Captain Forsberg found a tug boat near him in Tarpon Springs who quoted a price of $50,000 to remove the boat from her sandy grave and bring it back

The *Norther* — not pretty, but it did the job.

to Florida in tow. However, Paul found an old wooden shrimp boat, a single engine 65-foot boat named *Norther* that gave him a much better price, only $10,000, and the deal was signed. The *Norther* first had to be stripped and made ready for the long trip to Belize and this took quite a while to finish.

With the skipper of the *Norther* at the wheel, plus Paul and several helpers (including me) he brought with him, we set out for Belize. There was a terrible current working against us and the trip took four days at only 3½ knots to reach Belize City and that was still a long distance from where the boat lay, filled with water, in sand.

Paul carried two small boats on the deck of the *Norther* to help get the craft afloat. Once we finally made it to where the boat was resting, the small boats went to her with lots of equipment to pump it out and get her afloat.

Brought to a dock in Belize, the crew put the boat into tolerable shape so that she could make the trip to Florida in tow. The boat sat at the dock for quite a while until Paul was able to convince the local authorities that he actually owned it. Lots of cash exchanged hands between Paul and the local government guys but that was a "cost of doing business" that he was stuck with.

Finally, we set out in tow. The prior four-day trip on the shrimp boat became a seven day trip and once in the Tarpon Springs area, yet another ordeal was staring us in the face and that was bringing such a big boat through some rather small spaces. You just cannot turn a boat in the same manner as you can do with a car!

Once brought to Duckworth Boats in Tarpon Springs, Paul removed the old engines which were of course, ruined, but he outreached to folks in need of spare parts and sold the four G. M. engines for a few thousand dollars. He eventually added four new German Deutz engines which can certainly push the boat now at high speed.

Of course it was no easy task to get the boat operational. She had to be completely stripped of everything that could be removed and new material had to be added. I was charged with the responsibility of ripping virtually all the metal out of the craft since it was so badly weather-beaten and we replaced everything.

This entire process took two whole years but once finished, it looked like a brand new 120-foot yacht! She operated out of Tarpon Springs for a while as a fishing boat because Paul wanted to be sure that she was fully operational. Once convinced that it was as good as or better than a newly built craft, it was time to head north. The boat currently operates as the Block Island Ferry, as noted above, and chances are that virtually no one that makes the trip had any idea of her storied past!"

Chan Stone

And here are some more details from my memories about the terrible problems we had getting the boat!

That shrimper tow-boat, the *Norther,* was 35 years old, wooden, and beat up badly. The only thing holding it together was its fiberglass section over the area from the waterline on down. You could actually almost see through the rotten planking, and in fact, if you went to the shower in the engine room, you could see daylight through the hull above the rub rail! But she had a good engine and generator and the price was right! I still can't believe that we made a 1,400-mile trip each way with it but since we were in good, calm water, it worked out okay. But if you asked me if I would even take the boat past the Montauk Lighthouse now, I'd say never!

On the way to Belize the rigging came loose and we had to tie it down with a rope. The Captain had the boat booms out to steady the boat and as the boat rolled one way, the rigging was rolling the other. We had to tie a tow line to a two-by-four and twist it up tight to the rigging to get it all to hold in place.

Chan told you earlier about some of the money miseries I was put through. Here's still more, in greater detail! I paid one guy to pump the boat out because it was filled with water and then I had hired another guy to work on the boat as it sat on its side, removing stuff that wasn't usable anyway, like the water-sogged paneling and insulation. The boat had no glass left because the locals were so poor that they took everything removable away. Many of their homes had no windows at all so that satisfied some of their needs, courtesy of my boat. Everything of value was removed that could be put to some use on land.

But my guy had the job to protect the boat and in his spare time, get a truck, remove the junk and cart it away to a dump site. However, I discovered that while he removed it, he just chucked it all over the side into the mangroves and never did get a truck. On top of that, when I gave him grief about it, he said that I owed him seventeen hundred dollars and I had to pay him, regardless of my complaints. I told him that I paid him for a truck and since he didn't use one the bill should be lowered and that I still wanted the mess he left cleaned up.

He told me that he didn't care about the mess, that he just wanted his money. We argued back and forth and I told him I wouldn't pay him until we got things straightened up. With that, I went back to the dock with my crew and began making preparations to tow the boat off the mud bank away from the mangroves. As we were running lines out, two police cars suddenly came pulling up. "You're under arrest," they said, and put me in one car and took me to the local jail. To make a long story short it was Friday and they told me that the Judge and Chief of Police were away until Tuesday and I would have to spend my time in jail until they got back to hear my case. I told the assistant chief of police my story but he didn't care much about it (because he was a cousin of the guy who claimed that I owed him $1,700!) He said that I had to pay or go to jail!

With that, they allowed me to go the only Western Union Office that had so much cash, 50 miles away, and that office had a "special" back room where bigger money transactions were conducted. I had hired a wonderful guy named Elvis who had his own small ferry boat operation with which he took a small group of workers back and forth to nearby Nicaragua.

He and his brother took me to the Western Union Office and when I came out the two of them were standing at the door waiting for me. They stood alongside of me and walked me back to the car. Once in the car, Elvis told me, "Mr. Paul, you went into the back room and when a man goes into the back room that means that he is going to come out with a lot of money and we just wanted to protect you."

We got back to the police station and I paid the Assistant Chief the money and then as they were letting me out, I watched the two cousins counting the money and splitting it up!

When I got to the boat, I found out that this mess still hadn't ended. A local guard came up and said, "Customs man wants to see you at the end of the dock." I went to the Customs guy who told me I owed another $750 before we could leave. He gave me some papers which had everything all misspelled but at least, it was time to go.

The next morning, Elvis came back to help me still more by towing me down the river. We got underway towards international waters, the *Norther* pulling us, and once I reached my office to say that we were en route, my assistant Carol (who has since passed away) told me that the Belize Coast

Guard was looking for me. It seemed as if I still didn't have all of the papers needed.

I had finally had all of that nonsense that I could handle. Knowing the Belize Coast Guard had no way to find and reach me, I decided to just push on towards Tarpon Springs and once we got there, our customs guys did what was needed. Sure, we had to pay for their overtime but it was well worth it. The only thing that they had to do was go through our

Here's Manny with a big red snapper caught on the *Viking Gulfstar*, June, 2012.

garbage (I guess just being careful we didn't have anything on board we shouldn't have.)

And that is the whole story of how the beautiful 120-foot *Viking Superstar* ferry boat came to be. Looking at her now, you would never believe what she looked like when I first saw her.

Viking Gulfstar

The *Viking Gulfstar* is the first all-fiberglass *Viking* and at 65 feet in length and 18 feet in width is a very comfortable ride. Her two big engines can produce speeds of 20 knots, which can take you to offshore fishing areas quickly.

She can carry 44 passengers for regular fishing outings but when out on her special far offshore adventures the *Gulfstar* is limited to 18 passengers and can sleep16 in bunks below deck in air-conditioned and heated comfort, as well as another group up on the second deck behind the wheel house.

Here's the *Viking Stariper* at sea.

The main cabin has the usual *Viking* full-service galley and a tackle store as well as being air-conditioned and heated. The state-of-the-art pilot-house has the finest of electronic equipment, bet on that. The *Viking Gulfstar* sails mainly from our dock in Tarpon Springs, Florida. She is Coast Guard licensed for a range of up to 200 miles offshore.

My partner in this boat is Capt. Rich Castellano, an expert skipper himself.

Manny has taken two special far offshore trips on this boat and can attest to the fact that they produce incredibly excellent results for all kinds of fish from snapper to grouper to huge amberjacks.

Viking Stariper

With a name like that, you can be sure that this boat produces some wonderful results when she heads out after striped bass. But stripers are not all she seeks.

This is the only wooden head boat remaining in the *Viking* fleet and is a classic in appearance and performance. Built from mahogany on oak, she has two big Caterpillar engines to bring her out and back. Licensed to carry 72 passengers, the *Stariper* is often chartered by large groups to give them the "personal" touch. She has plenty of seats, in and outside.

Viking Freedom —
With Thoughts from my Friend John Badkin

Not at all a "party-boat," this one is a commercial sailing vessel that I designed and built right across the street from the Viking Dock in Montauk with the help of my friend John Badkin and his son Robert. Construction began in 1982. The keel was laid in the parking lot and the boat was finally completed in 1990.

Robert used to fish on one or another of the *Viking* boats and while attending college, volunteered to help with jobs that involved tools of any kind. He ultimately became the Marine Maintenance man for the *Viking* fleet.

Here's John Badkin on the main mast of the *Viking Freedom*.

Known as a "sail-assisted" commercial and research vessel, this unique boat presents a most unusual and attractive picture to folks who have never seen her on the water. Imagine a 60 foot long fishing sailboat!

I consider this boat to be my personal "baby" and I am most often seen at the wheel, heading out to sites unknown in quest of a mess of fish. The "*Freedom*" has sailed to places as far away as the Canadian Hague Line to the north and down south, to the island of Trinidad next to Venezuela.

She has commercial fished out of Montauk for tuna and swordfish in the summer, but most of the year, she sails out of Tarpon Springs, Florida and targets snapper and grouper out at the fabled "Middle Grounds" region. While I was writing this book, I had just come back from an outing in which we were seeking tuna so she doesn't only go after bottom dwellers. In fact, in that trip just referred to, we produced 32 yellowfin tuna in a two-day stretch off the Louisiana coast.

60 feet long and 15.3 feet wide, she has a six-foot draft and has the capacity to hold 3,800 pounds of iced fish. When not actually fishing, the boat is found at sea, always in quest of some new fishing areas for her sister *Viking* ships.

My office manager suggested that Manny speak with John to get further details and the following is some of what he wanted to share with you readers —

John was a service engineer in the Aerospace industry and lives in three locations, depending on the season and how much he is needed with the *Viking* boats. He and his wife Marilyn can be found in Amaganset, N. Y., Franklin Lakes, N. J. or within a residence that Paul provides in Holiday, Florida, near his Tarpon Springs site.

The Badkins, John, Marilyn and son Robert went to Florida to help finish the boat and Marilyn recalls actually helping paint the deck! Paul had given Robert a book on building boats and he read it cover to cover before lending assistance, first up in Montauk and then, later on, in Tarpon Springs. They first built a "floatable shell" in the yard in Montauk before putting it on a trailer, to be finished in Florida.

John keeps a daily journal of all of the work that he has done for Paul and he told Manny that "Paul has more ideas to the square inch than anyone he has ever met!"

For far more about the "Freedom" move ahead to Chapter Thirteen.

Viking Fivestar

Newest of the fleet, this all fiberglass boat is 65 feet long and has two 600 horsepower diesel engines. Custom-built in Alabama in 2011, I traveled often from my winter home in Tarpon Springs, Florida, to Alabama to be certain that the boat was being built to my specifications.

I'm a perfectionist, and during one of my many telephone conversations with Manny, I recall having to interrupt the call to yell at one of the guys who was building the boat because he had left the site but was returning in his car to pick up the cigarettes he left on the boat. The parking area was dusty and I gave him hell because the car's tires were kicking up a cloud and I feared that the boat's newly painted surface would be damaged by the dust. You can bet that this guy never did that again.

Pool winner on the *Viking Gulfstar,* with the *Fivestar* in the background.

The primary purpose of the *Fivestar* is as a Premium charter boat and she can sleep 12 passengers below deck on her offshore ventures. She has luxurious accommodations of all kinds.

We spent countless hours putting in all the finishing touches to this boat at our dock in Tarpon Springs before bringing her north to Montauk in 2013.

Other *Viking* Boats

There have been other *Viking* boats, for sure. Forgetting boats that once had other names and were changed to a *Viking* plus a Roman numeral, there was the *Viking Starlite*, another *Viking Star*, and several others.

Back in the 70's, I was in Florida and saw the success that some headboats were having by taking customers out on half-day trips and when I got back north, I started operating the *Viking Starlite* as a half-day boat too. To the best of my knowledge, she was the first headboat in the northeast to do half-day trips and it was quite a success for folks who didn't want to spend a whole day at sea.

One of my other boats was called the *Viking Star II*. She was a converted

Army T-boat. With a rounded bottom, I still refer to it as a boat that "could roll peanut butter off of bread" so you know she rocked and rolled quite a bit.

I took any excess passengers out on the *Star II* when there was no room for more customers to get on the *Star*. I followed dad out to Cox's with her when the need was present and while only able to achieve nine knots, with a single diesel engine, she was kind of out of her league and after two years; we sold it. It became the Captain Bill Van in Belmar, N. J. Billy Van Wetering bought her and for close-to-shore trips, it was enough boat for the task. Little Bill Van wound up with beautiful aluminum 75 footer later on.

Referred to a few paragraphs back, the *Viking Starlite* was built in Virginia to become the first Block Island Ferry. As my father started to slow down and let me move into the primary role I was to reach, I talked dad into letting me take over the *Starlite* for fishing. The *Starlite* was fast, twin-screw and a good fishing boat. I was only 20 years of age but with a captain's license for two years by then, I certainly was able to handle the additional responsibilities my dad turned over to me. The competition had grown older too and that left room for me to march right in through the open door they left for me.

I put sonar on the *Starlite* and in those days, it was quite a thing. I took that same machine off the *Starlite* and put it on the *Viking Freedom*, my sail-assisted commercial boat and even though parts aren't available for it, I still will never get rid of it because it works so well in finding wrecks. It reaches out for a full mile or maybe more if you use it just right. Referred to as an "ELAC" sonar and with bearings taken just so, it was the state of the art at the time, true modern technology.

Our Biggest Ferry that Never Was!

Way later on, I'll tell you in detail about what would have been our biggest ferry boat but it never did take a single passenger out because of the trouble given to me by my own neighbors in Montauk. Briefly though, she would have been the Queen of our fleet at 154 feet but government gave me so much grief that I leased it out for use as a gambling boat. We had difficulty with several prospective buyer and lessees but at last look, we have a very good deal with Sun Cruises. The boat sails out of Port Richey, Florida, and offers her customers virtually cost-free opportunities to gamble at sea in extreme comfort. The boat has been called the *Royal Casino* and *Ella Star Casino* among other names.

Chapter Six

4 Generations

The Forsberg Empire

In addition to dad and I, there are five other Forsberg's that have or are wearing Captain's hats and that is why Manny came up with the sub-title, "Forsberg Empire." After all, with four generations and, who knows, maybe a fifth one day in the future, what other name could so well describe this operation?

Paul B. Forsberg

My son Paul B. ran several *Viking* vessels. But now he seems to prefer dry land, working in the Real Estate business. Before that, he and his brother Steve did commercial fishing each winter in the 80s. However, he also helps out with the operation of the *Viking Gulfstar* in Tarpon Springs, Florida.

Carl Forsberg

Carl is young Paul's son and he has the great love for the sea that his great-grandfather had so giving him that name was a very good fit. Carl grew up in Montauk and from the day that I took Carl and his cousin Steve out overnight codfishing, he was "hooked" permanently. As soon as he was old enough, he worked the deck when not in school.

After graduating from high school, he took classes in business in California during the winters and came back to Montauk to work on the boats each summer. After college, he got his Captain's license at age 20 and started running the boats.

Carl has run the all-day fluke and sea bass trips, and was second captain on the offshore tuna and cod trips. He then went to Tarpon Springs, Florida and ran the *Viking Superstar* trips to the offshore grouper and snapper grounds where they also caught king mackerel, amberjacks, and lots of other species. The lure of Montauk drew him back and he currently sails one *Viking* vessel or another up north.

Steven D. Forsberg

My son Steven is as close to a "clone" of me as anyone can find. Born and raised in Montauk, what he calls the "fishing capital of the world!" He said that "as a small child, I grew up fishing with my father Captain Paul Forsberg from the time I could walk."

Steven spends a lot of his time in the office in Montauk but his true love remains being out on the water. He pioneered offshore party boat tuna fishing out of Montauk and he really prefers being way out offshore, after tuna, tilefish, or whatever is in the deep blue water. However, he has spent countless hours below deck too, sweating it out in the engine rooms. He loves marine construction and enjoyed designing and building the *Viking Fivestar* with me, and his son, Steven, Jr.

Steven N. Forsberg

Steven D's son, young Steven proudly calls his family a four-generation one. And since his great-grandfather Carl designed many of the *Viking* vessels, one can even say that it could be referred to as a five-generation Empire.

Steven took his first two-day tuna trip at age five! By age eight he was working as a mate on a charter boat and by age 11 or so, he was already a regular mate on one of the *Viking* vessels. At age 18 he got his captain's license and a year later, he upgraded it to a 100 ton license.

The fall of the year he got the offshore license, he began running two day tuna trips and as he said "I never looked back!" He took two trips to Alabama to help me with the construction of the new *Viking Fivestar*.

Elizabeth Forsberg

The distaff side of the family is well represented by Steven D's wife, Elizabeth. She is licensed as a captain and at times, will operate a boat. She prefers inshore fishing and you can bet that she has taken passengers out often for stripers and bluefish.

I can feel my chest sticking way out as I proudly talk about them. About son Steven, he was in the engine room with me when I broke down, working all night and of course his mother would argue with me that he wouldn't be able to get up and go to school the next day. He was right there when we went fishing and always asked to steer the boat, not being able to wait until he got his hands on bringing it into the dock.

I feel that Steve Jr. and his cousin Carl will make equally good skippers; cut from the same mold. They live, eat, sleep, and drink fishing and riding the boats.

Captain Paul G. Forsberg

We have spoken about me as an author; now let's discuss me as an angler. Born in Freeport Hospital, I grew quickly into one of the most enthusiastic anglers of all time, not wanting to be in school, preferring instead to learn about life on the water. This was to create a few problems for me eventually, among them being able (or not being able) to spell and make change.

My mom was the business person in the family. Dad was a true fishing and boating expert but as for running the business? He left that up to my mother. She helped me learn how to improve my spelling skills for sure, but I remember that when we moved from Freeport to Montauk, as a 12 year-old, I didn't even know how to spell "Montauk." A teacher of mine had to teach me how to do that.

When it came to math, I hadn't learned much at all about that in school, mainly because I wasn't there most of the time. This was eventually fixed, but not before I started my own business and had considerable success with it but didn't earn any money at all. Mom though, got me up to date on such matters.

The *Viking* College of Fishing Knowledge!

Without all of the many other folks who keep the *Viking* fleet performing smoothly, there would be no success at all. In fact, there are some people who have spent more than 25 years working with the *Viking* fleet! In addition to the mates and office crew, we have a gang of licensed skippers running the boats that have over fifty years, maybe more like seventy five years, on the water between them.

For example, Capt. Dave Marmeno has been with us since 1988! Eleanor has been with the company just about as long. Orla started with *Viking* in 2003. It's great to know that, while the work is hard, when the chips are down we're right there by each other's side. The *Viking* fleet is successful because of the people that work in it. We are a team, not only working together but we socialize together too. We all get along together and that's what it takes.

Over the years *Viking* has employed thousands of mates, some locals, some not, who have subsequently gone on to successful careers in a variety of occupations. Some have become doctors, some lawyers, others teachers, etc.

Still others have continued in the fishing business becoming hi-liners in the industry as far away as Alaska. Many have become party boat captains and mates up and down the East Coast. One of our former mates and Captains is now a prominent spine surgeon in New York City! I like to think the *Viking* has been a good training-ground for all of them.

Chapter Seven

Licenses

Getting My First License

I was to become what might have been one of the youngest licensed captains in America, earning my ticket at the early age of 18. At the time, licenses were both for mileage offshore allowed as well as how much tonnage the boat the captain operates can carry. The Coast Guard soon changed the requirement to be age 21 but eventually, they settled on age 19 to be licensed. Because I was so young, they watched me more carefully than the other skippers. They did give me a 100-ton license though at the start but due to my age, even though the *Viking* I was operating was within guidelines, they bounced my ticket down to 50 miles instead of letting me sail up to ONE HUNDRED miles out.

This came back to give me trouble later on when I searched for and discovered the wreck of the *Andrea Doria*, which we discuss much later on.

Getting the license itself though was a very interesting experience. I had a choice to either go to New York or New London, Connecticut to take my test

Here's a copy of my first license. I got this in 1957.

and chose New London because it was easier to get there by boat. My father gave me the *Viking V* to go there with.

My friend John Lyke and I studied hard together after school. He had been a mate with Frank Mundus on the *Cricket*. We went to school together and on the way back on the bus, we'd get off and go to his house and break out the Chapman's book and study. There weren't license schools in those days. So we would memorize the book as best we could. In those days, you didn't even need to know how to read or write. The test was oral, but still pretty tough so the Chapman's book was very important to us to learn.

John and I worked for months after school to memorize the book. One day, a friend from school, Richie Rade, came along and said he wanted to go take the test with us. I told him we'd been studying for quite a while and he said that he had also been studying so the three of us decided to go to New London.

My father gave me the *Viking V* to take to New London but first said I shouldn't turn her up over 1200 RPM because she had thrown a blade right at the end of the season, one of the blades off of the propeller. She only had two blades left and if you turned her up over 1200 she would vibrate like hell. He told me to just hold it down. I should be able to make about 4 knots and New London was only 18 miles away.

She had Larry Johnson wheels on her, the only propellers known in those days to rust and they were also known to throw a blade off every once in a while but they were made right in Freeport and my father loved them.

He was special friends with Larry Johnson so we got Johnson Wheels. They're very good propellers now but in those days it was what it was.

So anyway, I started up the trusty 671 GM in the *Viking V* and there was no oil pressure, very little at first and then after it was running for a few minutes there was none so I changed the oil and the filter. I thought that maybe the oil was contaminated.

My father came in from fishing and I started the engine up but I still didn't have any oil pressure. I went to my dad and told him about it and he chewed me out, big time. He yelled that I had wasted seven gallons of oil, good oil. He said that that engine hadn't had any oil pressure in two years; it had been running fine without oil pressure. He added that the oil flew around enough in the engine to keep everything lubricated!

Anyway, back to the story. We took off the next morning, nice and early. I had my future wife Muriel with me, plus John as well as Richie Rade. Off we went, towards New London due north of Montauk Inlet. We got to the New London Harbor and tied up at the city dock in downtown New London. We could see the Coast Guard building so we three guys walked over there. Muriel went shopping. It was a great chance for her to do some shopping, by golly; it was the city of New London so she spent the day doing that.

We went upstairs and signed in. We flipped a coin among the three of us to determine which one would go in first. Richard won the draw. He went in and, boy, he was only there a few minutes when all of a sudden there was some screaming and hollering. Richard came running out the door and ran right by us and down the stairs. Then this big Coast Guard guy came out and, boy, he was wearing a white shirt and puffing a big cigar as he was yelling. He hollered, "If you don't know any more than he does then you're wasting my time and your time and I'm not going to waste any more time!

He went back into his office and slammed the door shut and, boy, John and I just looked at each other. We didn't know what the hell to do. The secretary came over and asked, "Well, do you guys know what you're doing? Do you feel good about this or what? The commander's in a very bad mood and evidently the other fellow didn't know that much."

The two of us told her how we had studied very hard and that the other guy hadn't really been with us but that we had studied very hard and felt very confident and we wanted to give it a good go. She said, "Okay. We're gonna' let him cool down for a few minutes." She waited about ten minutes and gave us each a glass of water. She went into the backroom a couple of times and then finally came out and said, "Okay, who's next?"

In the meantime John and I had flipped the coin again and this time, he won so he was next. He went in. It must have been about half an hour I guess before he came out. He gave me a thumbs up, wearing a big smile on his face, and signed out and left. I was next so I went in. It was an oral test in those days, nothing in writing at all. The way you had to do it was make a mark for your name; you didn't even have to know how to read or write.

It was a lot different than it is today. However, this commander didn't seem to like the idea that we young guys were applying for our licenses already. I was the youngest, having just turned eighteen and John was almost nineteen and I had a feeling he just took offense to that a little bit, probably thinking we were a little young to be running boats and taking people out for hire.

He started firing those questions out one right after the other; he really let me have it. John told me later he did the same thing to him. I was, like, three questions behind on the answers. I could hardly get them out fast enough but anyway I made it all the way through.

We got to the absolute end and he's smoking his cigar and asks me, "Now, your boat's tied up overnight at the dock; what's the first thing you do when you get aboard?" I sat there for a minute and said, "Well, I'd pull the boat in so I won't miss my footing as I step aboard and then I'd lift up the engine hatch, go into the engine room and check the engine.

He starts blowing smoke in my face and says, "Come on now, you did a good job here. It's the last question; don't mess up on this." As he talked he kept blowing that smoke in my face! Finally, I answered, "Well, if I had a gasoline boat I would extinguish whatever I was smoking first before I had gotten aboard and lifted up the engine hatch." "Well, that's right," he said, "But what is this about if you had a gasoline boat?"

So I pointed out the window and told him that we came across that morning on the *Viking V* and that it had a 671 diesel engine in it. Well, he backed up a bit and said, "That's a mighty big boat. Who owns that boat?" It was the 48-foot *Viking V* and I told him my father was out fishing with the other boat and he had told me to take this boat over to get my license.

"Well," he said, "He must have some confidence in you, don't run anybody over on the way back, will you?" And then he told me I had passed okay and that I'd get my license in a couple of weeks in the mail. Then he repeated, "Be careful now going back. It's gonna' get dark out pretty soon and you be careful, don't run anybody over." And then he shook my hand and off he went.

The four of us boarded the boat and he was right, it was starting to get dark. I was rambling around in the engine room and found some wires to connect to the battery to make the running lights work. I used vise grip pliers to put the wires on the batteries and finally got them working.

Ii came up out of the engine room and we were just getting through the race when I got a radio call from Frank Morse on the charter boat *Kuno*. He's the same fellow who rescued me a few years previous when I had the old *"Marie"* when I was sinking off Montauk Point. Anyway, he called me and said, "You're dad just stopped by and asked me to give you a call to see how you made out." "Well, Richie Rade didn't do so good; he has to come back," I said, "He missed a couple of questions but John and I both did okay, we got it, we're on our way back."

Then I asked him which way the tide was running in Montauk. It was flooding over in New London and we were going real slow against the tide. I didn't tell him I had one blade missing from the propeller. We were just paddling along at three, four knots and, boy, it was a long way home. He said, "Alright, I'll let your dad know."

We were about three quarters of the way across and Richie Rade was lying down below. John, Muriel and I were up in the pilothouse, happy that we got our licenses and all of a sudden, Richie comes running up yelling, "We're sinking, we're sinking!" "Yeah, Richie," we said, "And good night to you too." "No, no," he said, "I'm not kidding, I don't kid like that."

We had a flashlight and we shined it down on his pants and they were stuck to his legs up to his knees.

"The waters up to the bunk," he said, "The sloshing woke me up. John took the wheel and held it while I went down below and, oh my God, sure enough, there was water splashing back and forth all over the place.

I turned the valves over and got the engine cooling pump to pump water out through the engine. A little piece of daylight out the side of the hull caught my eye; there was an opening there about an inch-and-a-half and the water was coming in every time the boat rolled down.

I realized it was the overboard discharge thru-hull fitting for the salt water cooling discharge. The salt water cooling pump was pumping water into the boat instead of overboard. I found the discharge hose and re-installed it on the thru-hull fitting. However, there was no clamp on the hose to keep the hose on the fitting.

Just then, a two-by-four came floating by and I grabbed it. One part of it had a notch in it and I thought, well, that's convenient and I stuck it up underneath the hose and got out of the engine room. Now I'm pumping water through the engine and overboard. I'm also using the trusty ¾ inch Jabsco bilge pump that ran automatically all the time.

We'd check it from time to time to make sure the water was going down and it was slowly but surely doing just that. However, we still had plenty of water in the engine room.

Well, we finally came into Montauk Harbor later that night. At the time my father was President of the Montauk Chamber of Commerce and was on his way to a chamber meeting, all dressed up in a three-piece suit and a fedora standing on the end of the dock waiting to congratulate me for getting my license.

The dock that the *Viking V* used was the same one that Fred E. Bird's *Flying Cloud* uses now, however, the dock wasn't as strong as it is now. We had light weight pilings and it was the same dock that we had built by hand.

Anyway, I had to make the turn to get the dock on my port side and bring her into the slip. I took the engine out of gear. The transmission in those days was a Borg Warner and because it had no clutch plates it was quite an art to pop the engine into gear. However, I learned how to do it. So there was my dad and as I got her out of gear and into reverse and put the power to her, she caught it okay but the boat kept going forward and made a slight right turn portside of the bow and slammed into the end of the dock real hard and sprung it over. When it sprung back my father fell backwards right on his rear end and almost went overboard. Luckily he didn't but his fedora went in and he yelled at John, "Gaff that fedora, quick!"

Then my dad got up and started yelling at me, "You god-damned jackass; you may be getting a piece of paper that says you know how to run a boat but you sure as hell don't know how to stop one!"

I told dad that we had a load of water and it was over the floorboards and she would not stop with all the extra weight of the water. Dad asked where the water came from. I answered that the overboard discharge hose came off the through hull. Dad said there is a two by four with a notch in one end that holds the discharge hose up. You must have knocked it over when you were hooking the running lights to the battery. Make sure the two by four is jammed in place good and tight and pump her out completely before you leave.

With that dad got in his Studebaker truck and drove away!

The next day, when dad cooled down, he shook my hand and put his arm around me and congratulated me. Wow, I felt like a million bucks!

Chapter Eight

The Coast Guard

Rules and Regulations

F ar earlier, we talked about the *Pelican* Tragedy, let's discuss this subject in greater length now. For example, boat length. The Coast Guard has regulations that apply to boats based on their overall length as well as their tonnage, plus what manner of life-saving gear they carry on board. In addition, they measure how much usable space the boat has.

Before the *Pelican* Tragedy, if you were under 15 tons you didn't need a marine inspection, all you needed were life jackets for everyone aboard plus three fire extinguishers. However, after the disaster rules changed for everyone who carried more than six passengers for hire in America and all such boats must be inspected and post a certificate of such inspection. Each boat has to be inspected topside every year and be removed from the water for a dry dock inspection every two years.

Captain George Glas was quite involved with the national party boat alliance with John Suydam and they worked with the Coast Guard to get the regulations passed that we have today, ones that we could all live with.

Before that work the requirements called for so much safety gear that a boat could hardly float but the combined effort produced fine results. Inspected boats are the safest vessels in the world today.

Of course the inspectors differ from one to another as well. You know that if the boat is older than the inspector that boat owner may be in for trouble. The older I get, the younger it appears as if the inspectors are. But when you have a kid right out of the Academy you could wind up with way too tough an inspection. Far and away, the best inspectors are the guys who are wearing the uniform the longest, warrant officers who came up through the ranks to wear the highest rating an enlisted man can wear. He knows his stuff, knows how to get his hands dirty, and what to look for.

They know where to make rule changes that will never sacrifice safety but still save the owner a lot of grief.

Once upon a time, many years ago, what was probably the most commonly used method to determine weight had nothing to do with most things in use today. Back when they had sailing ships that carried cargo, tonnage was measured based on how many barrels of wine they could carry! And they didn't use length or width of the boats, simply what a load it could transport.

This is so complicated and technical a subject that I don't want to give you a headache going over it all so please, just take my word that there are and were more regulations than you could shake a stick at. And they have changed too from time to time.

Of interest to many would be the fact that boats are measured at the water line, not by overall length. So when you read that a boat is 100' long, it could only be an 85 footer. You see; the Coast Guard measures the distance from bow to stern of the boat. And a skipper may measure it from the tip of the pulpit all the way back to the overhanging railing in the stern. This easily could add another 15 feet to its overall length. The pulpit on some boats is 10 or even more feet long and clearly, it is out of the water. In fact, in years past, a pulpit or two has been snapped off of a boat in heavy seas.

I firmly believe that vessels that are licensed to carry over six passengers for hire in America are the safest boats afloat in the world today and that's due to the inspection system the Coast Guard has. Nothing is 100% and some things are a little ridiculous but all in all it made the industry a very safe one. The following are but three examples of some different extremes in use today.

Reflective Tape

Some of the things we have to have though are from lobbyists in Washington pushing new and expensive products, several of which becoming a regulation requiring us to have them on board. One such item is the use of reflective tape on our life jackets. It's a great idea! You can see the person in the water at night if a light flashed on the person wearing such a jacket, however, when the regulation came into being there was only one company in the world that was approved for such a tape. That meant that the price was very high and worse, because the demand became so great, that provider couldn't make the tape fast enough. A few months after the due date a few other companies were approved and that made the tape cheaper and more available.

EPIRB

The acronym EPIRB stands for Emergency Position Indicating Radio Beacon and this device is used to alert search and rescue services in the event of an emergency. A similar thing took place when EPIRB radios were required for offshore boats. Again, there was only one provider and that made the price sky-high and the product difficult to get because the demand exceeded the supply. We had to pay a $500 deposit which gave us a letter stating that we had made a deposit and that we would get one as soon as the supply was increased. That allowed us to fish offshore while waiting for our EPIRB.

At first, the cost was more than two thousand dollars but once competition came in, it dropped to as low as three to five hundred dollars. As with reflective tape, I feel that having an EPIRB is a very good idea.

Inflatable Life Rafts

On the other hand though, at least as of 2012, the Coast Guard put in a new rule that I really disagree with, requiring that life rafts carried on our boats have to be inflatable, and this makes me think of that expression, "If it isn't broken, why fix it?" The hard rafts that we all carry float and once people get inside them, they continue to float. Using them creates a perfectly safe system and better, no one has to take the time in an emergency to inflate them. They have a 100 percent safety record, they work. They are launched off the boat, they float, and people get into them. Inflatables don't have the safety record current ones have and worse, they are terribly expensive. Worse, they have to be taken off boats once a year to be repacked in the factory and then sent back to the owner.

The cost of repacking the rafts runs between one thousand and fifteen hundred dollars plus the cost of transporting back and forth to the boat. More: The life raft's official number has to be sent to the Coast Guard telling them the raft is off the boat and being tracked, meaning that we have to carry a spare raft to take its place so that we can continue to sail. Still more: After five or six years of this procedure the rubber in the raft has to be replaced and the cost of doing this can be as high as replacing the entire raft. And even more: I feel that the lobbyists pushing this regulation in Washington don't much care that these rubber rafts aren't as safe as the hard ones, that they also don't care that demanding their use on boats licensed to carry more than six passengers takes up lots of extra room, are very heavy and cumbersome, leaving less room for passengers due to stability issues created.

Basic Coast Guard regulations are good, but I disagree with this one. As said earlier, the mindset of the inspector is key. A capable inspector, working with the boat owner, is most important of all.

Chapter Nine

Captain Mundus

Captain Frank Mundus
and his Pranks

Discussed a little while back with the attempt he made with my dad to pull the capsized boat "*Pelican*" back to shore, Captain Frank Mundus was indeed among the most famous of all the captains who ever sailed out of Montauk Point. In fact, he was often considered to be the skipper that the movie "Jaws" was based upon.

Mundus passed away in Hawaii on 9/10/08 at age 82 but the year before, he was still seeking and catching sharks, his number one favorite opponent. He made fame in 1986 when his boat produced what was then the largest fish ever caught on rod and reel, a 3,427 pound Great white shark! There was also an account of one far bigger, 4,500 pounds or so; that he got while commercial fishing, via a harpoon in 1964.

But I remember Frank more as a great person, a wonderful jokester, than just as a superb fisherman. Here are just three of many Mundus pranks I actually watched take place:

The Outhouse

I was quite young, operating a boat named *"The Penguin"* (formerly called the *"Marie"*) in Montauk. I fished all day and slept on the boat most nights, going home every now and then to take a shower. One night I was on the boat and heard a disturbance and saw a pickup truck pull up to the dock.

Capt. Mundus was in the truck with Ted Stevens and Doug McCabe, and an outhouse was standing up in the back of the truck. Doug's wife Lucille was following them in a car and with her was Ted's wife as well. Needless to say, they had been partying and may have had a few tastes of fermented berry juice within them.

I watched in quiet, not wanting to be seen, as the five people removed the outhouse from the truck and stood it up right behind Captain Bob Yule's party boat *"Rex,"* laughing and giggling. They wrote *"Rex's Office"* on the outhouse which had the usual half-moon cut in its door.

But, laughing hysterically as they were, Mundus was still able to spot me watching all of that! He came over and said to me, "Hey Paul, you didn't see this!" It was 1:00 a.m. and the boat *Rex* was to sail at 7:00 a.m.

I swore myself to secrecy and Frank told me that there was going to be some noise about this.

I remember that Bob Yule always spoke in a very rough voice and seemed like a very grouchy guy, with a German accent, tough-sounding indeed to a young man like me. He scared me at our first meeting but I grew to really like him, even though he scared most people.

I stayed up all night, not wanting to miss anything. So Yule came down that morning and passengers had already boarded the *Rex*, while the outhouse was sticking up right behind the boat in the parking lot.

Captain Yule boarded his boat, removed a fire axe, and went to the outhouse and began to chop it up, screaming and hollering all the while. The police came and a huge crowd began to form. The entire waterfront heard about it, of course, and for months no one knew who had left the outhouse behind the *Rex*. Some might have speculated about who did it, because Mundus was known for being a prankster, but I never revealed what I knew and no firm proof was ever found.

The Fighting Chair / Toilet Seat

Yet one more joke that Captain Mundus pulled off was when he took an old toilet bowl and seat and snuck onto the head boat *Helen II*, putting it down in the dark of night in the stern. The *Helen II* was owned by Captain George Glas whose son Brad now operates the family's current boat, *The Hel-Cat* out of Groton, Connecticut.

George Glas was famous as an open-boat tuna fisherman and Mundus had painted a huge sign, erecting it behind the toilet bowl, with the words "*Helen II* tuna-fighting chair" above it. Once again, no one ever found out who put the "fighting chair" on the boat and everyone in Montauk talked about it for the entire rest of the season.

The Wooden "Swordfish"

I talk warmly about Mundus to this day, considering him to have been a great fisherman, a nice man, and a good friend. I recall a day that I got a call from Mundus on the radio, at sea. This was most unusual because Mundus hardly ever called anyone; he wanted radio silence all the time as a rule. No one could ever even get him to respond to a radio outreach (unless it was for an emergency of course).

Therefore, when I got such a call, I was surprised, and perhaps, knowing Frank's well-deserved reputation as a comic, a bit suspicious. I had been having a great swordfish season on our boat "*The Viking IV*." In 1957, I had harpooned 14 big swords and 13 a year later. One day, a mate and I stuck five of them alone. And the next day, we took a charter out and harpooned three more, losing two that had been hooked via rod and reel.

The call came in though, with Mundus telling me:"Hey *Viking IV*, I saw a fish out there, Paul, a swordfish. He's in here someplace. He keeps coming up and going down but he's in here."

The *Viking* and *Cricket* were in the middle of a big bunch of other boats and I remembered that the first thing another boat doesn't do is call someone nearby to tell them that a single fish is nearby and because Frank never called anyone, I grew quite suspicious of the call.

Captain Mundus had conceived of a way to pull the prank of the century off on me, a guy who had become so well-known as a swordfish expert, or so he thought. Mundus had taken a two by eight foot board at the dock, painted it black, and nailed swordfish fins and a tail onto it from a swordfish he caught the day before, adding a bill, creating his own wooden "swordfish."

I suspected the worst, and prepared for what kind of gag was to come. Mundus went near a few other boats and while no one was looking, quietly slipped his "sword" into the drink.

I saw it before any other boat and with passengers on board, told my mate what I saw, instructing him to not only look elsewhere in the water but to also tell the passengers to "look to the left," knowing that the object floated to our right. I went past it to the right, about 400 feet off that side, and Frank called me again saying that "you know, that fish is in here, Paul, and you know, you gotta' look around."

I made like I believed him and took three or four circles around, going right past the "fish," telling my passengers about the gag. Finally, Mundus caught on and came by and picked his creation up. Later in the day he tricked another boat owner into going after his make-believe swordfish so at least he got someone with his prank.

More about him — I really loved the guy as a wonderful man who taught me how to splice fishing lines as well as how to have fun. I also worked for Captain Mundus when he was short a mate.

In September of 2008, we were about to leave our *Viking* dock in Montauk on board the *Viking Freedom* for a tuna-fishing trip. I shook hands with Frank who told me that he was flying home to Hawaii in a few days. He had moved there with his wife some time back. I told Frank that I would see him again when he returned to Montauk the following year and then we parted. That was the last time I would ever see my good friend and mentor who I remember looked absolutely dreadful, ashen and pale, when we said goodbye.

Mundus was 82 and as we separated, he shook hands with me and placed his second hand over the other saying "You take care, Paul" and off the *Viking Freedom* went to sea.

The next day, Mundus got on the plane and as he got off in Hawaii, he walked to get his luggage and his wife went for the car that was in the parking lot. Frank passed out in the airport and was taken to a hospital where he and his wife were later told, "You have a 60/40 and the 60 is not in your favor. If we operate on you, you have a 40% chance of you surviving. If we don't operate on you, you're going to die, there's 100% in favor of dying." Frank took the chance and agreed to the surgery but he didn't make it, he died.

Mundus was far from being popular among the charter and party boat captains because of his success while shark fishing. They felt, as the Chamber of Commerce had, that to promote such fishing, he would also be letting the world know that sharks roamed the waters off of Montauk which, although being true, also applied to most ports up and down the Atlantic.

That to the side, there was a day in the early 50s when Frank asked my father if he could become a co-tenant of his at the brand new dock that we built. My father wasn't exactly winning any popularity contests either among the other Montauk guys because, plain and simple, he had "more boat" then they had! His *Viking V* had a powerful marine diesel engine in her while the other boats ran on gas, and he often produced more fish than any of them too.

So when he finally moved away from the other boats that were at the

Town Dock, most weren't sad to see him leave. When dad accepted Mundus as a tenant that made the other owners even happier because both of them would be out of sight, out of mind. Through the years, the *Cricket II* occupied several different docks but for the last two years of Frank Mundus' life, she again wound up moored at the Viking Dock. Now Captain Fred E. Bird, who I talk about elsewhere, occupies the *Cricket* space with his famous *"Flying Cloud."*

Chapter Ten

Viking Land

The Viking Dock and Grill

irst, The Dock: During World War II, dad was not able to serve his country due to the terrible injury he had in the subway tunnel. Instead, he did commercial fishing. He wasn't able to take paying passengers fishing due to fuel shortages but to produce food; that was another story. He made the *Viking V* into a commercial boat, dragging a net to produce large catches of fish. Sailing out of Freeport, he brought the loaded boat in at Montauk to sell his catch. He made friends with a local Realtor who reminded him of what he already knew, that Montauk was where the fish were, and offered to sell a choice piece of land to him to build a dock at.

The Realtor's name was Jack and one day, as he was unloading his catch in view of Jack, after being again politely pushed about the offer to sell, my father suggested that they make a verbal deal right then and there. Knowing the catch would produce a good-sized check via the Fulton Fish Market in

New York, dad suggested that, instead of the *Viking* name being placed on his catch that day, Jack's name should be written on it and that whatever the fish sold for, that was to cover the down payment on the land.

So that was how my father acquired the land for The Viking Dock! The papers were signed and soon after, the deal went through and then one day, dad had to tell the "Money person" about it, my mom! After the war was over, one day a bill came to the house from Jack and this was her first knowledge that she and my father had purchased anything at all! She balked, carrying on really badly but knowing that he already had money in it, even though "they don't even have a traffic light out there!" she started making payments on the land.

The land went down to the water's edge, maybe 100 feet or so in length. Later on, he obtained far more land and the dock is now at least 400 feet long. But it wasn't at all fit for use, especially to be used to pull big boats up to. There was simply too little water to handle a party boat and there was no dock either, for that matter, and there wasn't even any electricity available there.

The road to our land was Wells Avenue and as it turned left, it went to Gosman's Dock and came back. There was no road south of our dock, nothing but beach. The town dock was nearby and Duryea's Dock was being built also.

So dad wound up heading out to Amagansett eventually and met with Frank Bistrian who owned a construction company. The Bistrian family owned a 100-year old barn on their property and my dad bought the barn with all of the really big timbers that were inside. The barn was torn down and, at low cost, the start of the Montauk Viking Dock was just around the corner, at least he hoped so.

We've already touched on the old Studebaker truck that my family had. Well, dad would drive the truck out with me riding "shotgun." Several of us would load the back of the pickup with as much timber as we could carry, and repeat the process over and over again dropping it all off at the edge of our property.

The *Viking V* was operating out of the Town Dock and when she came in from a day's fishing, as well as on any days she didn't sail, dad put his crew (my brother Carl plus me and the mate) to work with him, building the new Viking Dock.

With a crew of five or more, he got a mess of large oak poles to be used as pilings and with the *Viking V* moved up against the shore, he got each pole upright. They hauled them up one at a time and plopped them down right into the mud! They then took the boat engine pump, rigged it with pipe and, using the powerful Gray Marine boat engine, pumped each pole into bed rock, one at a time.

As you can imagine, this took quite a bit of spare time! With no electricity available, we started to cut the timbers into three-inch decking for construction of the dock. We used planking for sheathing the bulkhead. With a two-man saw, one at each end, we cut them to proper size. One-by-one, each board was laid and each nail was driven in by hand. We had hand-powered Brason bits to drill the needed holes because, again, no electricity. My father, my brother Carl and I worked together with a few guys to do all this.

Remember, this was just a lot of mud with a little water and not much else, no docks, of course, just the most rustic of all plans but it wound up working out anyway. There were some boats sailing out of the Town Dock and a few more out of Gosman's Dock and maybe a couple more but at the time, Montauk was nothing like it is now for sure!

After operating out of the Town Dock for two years, it came time to try to move to his own dock but there wasn't much water to be seen. Dad managed to bring the boat in to assist in the dock work but to go in and out on a daily basis, especially in low tide conditions, would have been impossible. So using Yankee (or we should say "Viking?") ingenuity, he set out to deepen the water himself!

He pulled the boat in as close as possible when the tide was at its peak height (maybe only three feet), and working the boat propeller, he dug a trench back and forth to produce a little more depth for himself. He even did this on days he had taken a load of passengers out to sea. He'd bring the customers back in, drop them off, and head over to his place.

My father called the operation "digging the clams" as he dug his own channel.

Next, The Viking Grill

Once the dock was finished and the *Viking V* was operating out of it, it wound up that he wanted to have a coffee stand. So again, dad used his creativity to get one, at low cost. Dad bought a garage at the Star Island Coast Guard Station and we took the trusty old Studebaker truck over there to cart it back. We opened the garage door, backed the truck in, and jacked the garage up about ten inches off the ground, nailed two-by-fours across the bed of the pickup truck and drove that around from Star Island to our dock. We kept backing it up, and bringing it in until my father said "O.k., that's it, that's where we want it boys, let her go!" We cut the two-by-four stringers off and let that building come down on the ground and that became our coffee shop, serving coffee and doughnuts in the morning. That was the start of what is now known as "Dave's Grill," but at that time, we called it the "Viking Grill." Eventually they started cooking eggs and bacon, etc., but you had to stand outside to eat, there simply wasn't any room to sit down.

Dad bought a tin building in Freeport that had been a tackle shop but it went broke. Dad took the old Studebaker there as well as another truck he hired and the guys took the building apart with wrenches. It had been bolted together and with the use of the two trucks for transport, the sections were moved to Montauk where we reassembled it all into what became the new Viking Grill. For a number of years, it was the place to go for breakfast in Montauk. Some called it "The Greasy Spoon," especially those who got seasick. But if they didn't get sick it was known as the Viking Grill where you could get a good breakfast.

Everyone needs an excuse, I guess, so blaming their sea sickness on our food was their excuse. By now, most boats have their own galleys on board but back then, it was our grill or nothing.

Chapter Eleven

1960s

Part One —
Discovering New Grounds

The Pinnacle / Inner Wreck

Elsewhere, you'll see how I searched for and later found the wreckage of the *Andrea Doria*. Both me and my dad simply loved to explore and find new grounds since such work was so challenging. One of the wrecks that he discovered is called "The Pinnacle Wreck" now but dad referred to it as "the Inner Wreck." The ranges he used to get over the wreck were tricky. Using the *Viking Star*, you could walk the entire length of the old *Star*, all sixty feet, and the range would change depending on your angle of approach. He had the exact ranges perfectly figured out for getting right over it and for years, no other boat could locate it even though The *Star* was fishing right near them. Finally, modern technology came into play and with better gear like GPS, etc.; the location of the *Pinnacle* Wreck became common knowledge.

The website: www.ecophotoexplorers.com says this location is "one of the most interesting dives in New England, being comprised of boulders left from the ice flow 15,000 years ago! It's only 75 feet deep, with some structure that reach up to as little as thirty feet from the surface, its no wonder that fish, fishermen, and divers all love it. There are countless hiding places in the boulders and tunnels at the bottom over nearly an entire acre."

The *Grecian* Wreck

Lying just west of the old Fairway Buoy, also called "The Intermediate Wreck," Dad, and then me, pulled loads of fish off of this near home site, the *Grecian* wreck. According to, www.ecophotoexplorers.com, "The *Grecian* was a 290-foot steel freighter that was sunk after being struck by another vessel in 1932." At times used as a dive site, dad found it and caught loads of fish there. Only 95 feet down, this is a great depth for fishermen.

The Apple Tree Wreck

Another near-Montauk spot, held in my back pocket by me just in case all else failed, was what I called The Apple Tree because of what my sonar view of it looked like. Each winter, it held loads of small pollock, maybe 18 to 20 inches long and a mess of smaller cod also. Used as a bale-out site if I couldn't produce good catches elsewhere, I came into the zone and still managed to produce some fish for my fares there.

When the fish were present, they piled up near bottom on my paper machine depth recorder; the stylet burned the paper into what appeared like branches near bottom. The branches formed what looked like an apple tree, and that's why I gave it that name. The Apple Tree remains a great spot to head to when the need arises.

The Lumber Yard

This one involved quite a bit of trickery. My dad found a chunk of bottom that was situated southwest of the southwest corner of Cox's Ledge. There was a big sharp piece of bottom that stood up and fish were all around it. In order to keep this a private spot but also to make it easy for him to find, dad took a bunch of twelve ounce sinkers and tied them onto a length of line just longer than it took to reach bottom and then added a good-sized piece of driftwood at the other end, dropping the sinkers south of the spot. He put an anchor in about four boat lengths to the north of the spot and they had this site to themselves for quite a while.

This site was a little bit off course for most of the more usual Cox's Ledge spots and since it was only "marked" by a length of driftwood, no other captain noticed it for what it was, a "buoy marker" of sorts. For two weeks, dad fished the same spot with no one realizing what he was doing. From that point on, he would change the wooden "marker" from time to time so that no one could know that the same chunk of wood was in place and not moving. This was generally done when no other boats were close by, and each visit produced some nice catches for his fares. That peak remains right where it was and it still coughs up some nice codfish catches.

The Old 40 Line / Martel's Mountain

I fished an area down the east end of Cox's Ledge that I called The Old 40 Line at first, and then I changed it to Martel's Mountain. Ed Martel ran a headboat out of Point Judith and more often than not, Martel hit this chunk before going elsewhere, thinking he was the first boat on the site that morning. But most mornings, before Martel set sail, I stopped there first and I would trim the best part of what was there before Martel had even untied his mooring lines.

Old Faithful

As one could easily imagine, I gave this discovery the name "Old Faithful" because just about every time I put my passengers over it, they caught a mess of fish. I found it in an area that was between the east and west side of Cox's

Ledge. We fished it hard for nine years before anyone else found it and it still carries that same name today.

It was just south of the course that boats ran going from the southwest corner of Cox's to the east end. I ran to this spot often. We had been fishing the eastern end of Cox's more than the western end because the east end held more fish, but they were smaller than those cod my customers caught at the west end. So if we wanted 40-50 pounders we went west but if I wanted to fill everyone's sacks up, we sailed to the east, even though it was a longer ride from Montauk.

The pool was closed this day, but the blue glove side took first prize!

One day, we were exploring a bit and stumbled onto the place I was to name "Old Faithful." It was tough to read at the bottom on an east to west ride but if we rode from north to south, I could see that it had about an eight-foot drop-off and held loads of fish. Old Faithful was only 400 or so feet long by 150 feet wide and I kept it my own secret spot for nine whole years, never anchoring up on it when any other boats were in view.

I would hit the spot at the end of some days when our customers hadn't really beaten up the fish as well as I would have liked them to. I would get to the spot and tell my fares to get ready, with baited hooks, and wait for the word. As I saw that we were right on my spot I yelled for everyone to release their lines and I held the boat in place with my engines. Just about everyone on board hooked up instantly and fish came flying over the rails. I became an instant hero and with everyone yelling for a gaff at the same time, I was wary that someone else would discover our spot but we were able to avoid that for nine whole years.

A few of my customers also fished boats out of Point Judith, Rhode Island, and they asked those captains if they could take them to "Old Faithful," because everyone by then knew that the *Viking* had a secret spot by that name but no one knew where it was. I had guarded the spot so well though that no normal means of discovery was available.

Another day though, as I was in the wheelhouse, holding the boat over the spot, watching to the usual north or northwest direction where other boats would have been coming from, with fish flying in, it happened! A little private boat got in behind us from the south and anchored up, right on the site. Nearby, the *Super Squirrel* out of Point Judith had found our two boats sitting in place with binoculars, and he came roaring over at 20 knots, right at the *Viking*. I moved away but the Point Judith boat saw the little boat anchored up and catching fish so right then and there, the *Squirrel* skipper realized that he had found "Old Faithful."

Al Jarmon was the captain of the *Super Squirrel* and on the way back in, he radioed over to me that he found Old Faithful. Of course I still had private use of it for nine years. I warned Jarmon that he shouldn't abuse it, to only fish that spot from time to time when he needed it so that the population wouldn't be cleaned out. But the next day, there he was again, bragging on the radio that he was sitting on Forsberg's Old Faithful. I decided to mess things up by putting two anchors in, preventing Jarmon from drifting over the spot but for quite some time after, the *Super Squirrel* and other boats fished the spot real hard and simply killed it, removing darn near every fish nearby and it may never build up again since so many folks have the "numbers" of my former top secret spot. Oh well, I got nine years out of it!

The *Suffolk* Wreck

Again, quoting, in part, from the t on-line source, www.ecophotoexplorers.com, "This 365 foot long ship lies upside down in 180 feet of water, 32 miles southeast of Montauk. Broken in two, it rises 25 feet off the bottom." Here's yet another of the spots that probably was first fished with hook and line by one of our *Viking* boats. We clobbered loads of codfish on this wreck, along with pollock.

For far more details about the *Suffolk,* go to Chapter Eleven — 1960s — More About the *Suffolk.*

U-853

Not for sure, but this may be the number of the German submarine that I found in my exploring. We located it to the east of Block Island. Our favorite web site for dive locations, www.ecophotoexplorers.com, said that, "This 250-foot long wreck lies on bottom in 130 feet of water, victim of an American depth charge. She was sunk on May 6, 1945, and remained intact for many years."

The *Bass*

The *Bass* was an American submarine that I found lying on the bottom southwest of Block Island. It was supposedly sunk by the Navy during World War II to be used as a Sonar target. But in checking the wreckage with divers, I found out that the sub was broken in half and it looked like it had been rammed.

We checked the existing records and found out that, in fact, the sub had recently come out of the yard. Repainted and upgraded just before it sunk, that really made the story about intentionally sinking it seem unlikely to believe. I sent divers down and they tried to get in at one end but the hatch was blocked. So we took the *Viking Starlite* back to land, got some explosives, and went out again.

The divers went down with the explosives, attached them to the hatch, lit them off, and got back onto the *Starlite.* I started the engines up to get out of there but the divers told me that there was no rush needed. However, they were wrong and all of a sudden, there was a big BOOM. The *Starlite* jumped a foot or so off the water. Everyone was scared silly but still it was fortunate that the divers had at least gotten back on board.

In a few moments the air around the boat grew to be smelly as the stagnant air pushed up from the submarine below. A minute or two went by and a bunch of dead codfish came floating up, victims of the blast. The guys gaffed them and took them home for dinner.

The water had gotten so dirty that the divers weren't able to go back down to check things out for a few days but eventually, they did and found all kinds of spare parts, new ones, wrapped securely in gauze. The sub looked brand new inside with mattresses on the bunks, not at all appearing as if it was a boat that had been intentionally sunken.

The story I heard was quite different. That version said that the sub had actually been rammed by accident in the fog by a U. S. Navy ship and the sailors on board were killed. Allegedly, Navy divers went down and brought all the bodies up and it being during the war, they didn't want anyone to know what actually took place so it was kept strictly hush-hush.

In asking the Navy about the details though, I was confronted with a push-back. The Navy found out about the blowing up of the wreck by my guys via underwater hearing devices and that could have produced far more trouble for me than it would have been worth to find the real truth. So I dropped the whole matter quickly and still had another new wreck to fish.

Year's Later — "No-Man's Land"

I suppose I can write an entire book just about the sites that have been discovered by members of the Forsberg family. But that may be for another day. Clearly though, besides the ones just listed, and the ones that follow this site, Cox's Ledge and "Gateway," and later, the *Andrea Doria*, there's one more that I would like to tell you about. My dad and I and later, my kids and grandchildren found plenty more but for now, let's discuss "No-Man's Land," a place we found in the 1990s off of the Buzzard's Bay Tower. It lies within sight of land and is often called "The Horse." Buzzard's Bay Tower is called the horse because it stands so high up on its legs.

It sits in 90 or so feet of water and, in season, the bottom is paved with enormous numbers of porgies. We sail one of our boats to this area and customers truly load up on what are called "Scup" in New England. What is not as well known though is the

This is one of our customers, who fishes out of New Bedford, Massachusetts, holding a huge porgy.

fact that I started bringing green crabs out on these trips and frankly, I don't think the resident blackfish population had ever seen a green crab and while some customers were lifting double-headers of porgies on deck, others were tonguing blackfish galore on the crabs. I call it "blackfish haven."

Pioneering Cox's Ledge

Not truly "new" to all, but clearly, new to head boat anglers was the vast area that lies 40 or so nautical miles out of Montauk called "Cox's Ledge." My father was the first head boat skipper to take customers out to these fabled

Notice the sign says:
"Cox's Ledge, Tues. & Fri., 3 AM, A 12-hour Trip for $10."
Dad spelled it *Coxe's*, and I spell it *Cox's*. His father is in the upper left.

grounds and it created lots of headaches for him, caused by other boats that complained about it.

It all began one day that he was offshore dragging nets for codfish during World War II. He ran both party and commercial boats over the years but during the war, since fuel was limited mainly to the guys who were seeking fish for the market, he stuck with commercial fishing. On that day, he saw a bunch of commercial boats at what some called "Cox's Ledge." He came up close to a few of them and saw that they were hand-lining codfish into their boats. It was the summer and everyone "knew" that codfish were mainly a cold weather fish. But Cox's was deep enough and the kind of water that held cod even during the summer. He made a mental note that "you don't have to freeze to catch codfish," and was determined to go back one day and get some himself. He called it "Pioneering Cox's Ledge."

Dad started the business up in Montauk because, as he told mom, "Fishing was so close," but that all changed in 1952 when he took the first trip to Cox's with paying customers on the *Viking V*. It was a tough ride because he was going on memory, not on the kind of gear available on party boats today like radar or GPS, the current "gold standard" for finding a site. It was compass, memory, and his depth finder with which he could "read" bottom.

The *Viking V* had one engine, a 671 Detroit diesel, a World War II surplus marine built by General Motors. That engine pushed the boat along at about ten knots. The boat was a converted commercial fish boat with its pilothouse back aft and there was a small down-below cabin that people used.

There was little room down below for passengers to sleep and lots of them got sea sick due to the boat rocking and rolling and to top that off, there was usually bilge water sloshing back and forth, creating a terrible odor. We had a pot-bellied coal stove down there to help beat away cold temperatures. It was tight quarters and the fumes were terrible. The toilet was down below too so of course, we had those smells to deal with too. It became known as the seasick chamber. That's why all of the boats that have been built in many years now have above-deck cabins and heads. Passengers no longer have to feel all closed in since all the boats also have windows.

At that time, the "V" held forty to fifty passengers and if they didn't want to go near the "Seasick Chamber" they could lay around outside on the deck while riding to and from the grounds. If it rained, you got wet, that's all there was to it. And if it was rough and spray came over the side, you got wet again, so without foul-weather gear, it made for some seriously soaked anglers.

With the pilothouse back aft, it could only hold two people, captain and mate, so everyone else was on the outside most of the time. But once the "V" started hitting Cox's Ledge and producing sacks filled with big codfish, no one cared much at all and since most of this fishing was in the summer months, they could handle it pretty well. The boat had a small generator and most of what he had was old WW II surplus and unreliable. But off he went anyway. He found the area and the rest of the story is history because eventually, others made their way out to Cox's as well.

Most of the other Montauk skippers stayed far closer to home. To them, a long trip was to Block Island and at that, they didn't go much past the western side of Block, the closest point to Montauk. Catching cod in the summer was never heard of on a headboat with only a single 671 engine; that was unique indeed.

Once the crowds became too big to be handled by the *Viking V* dad also brought his old 65-footer out to Montauk from Freeport to take care of that.

As noted above, dad had seen commercial boats out there, some from nearby Point Judith and Block Island but none from Montauk before he perfected it. The commercial guys would anchor up their "mother ship," put one guy on each of a few dories they had towed out, and the crew would then row away to set their own anchors, but staying close to each other. Using two hand-lines in each small boat, they began at daybreak and fished until noon or so, and brought their catch back to the mother boat; usually a 35 or 40 foot lobster vessel, tie off, and then the big boat would tow the little boats back home.

A "good-day" would produce 1,000 pounds of cod per dory and that produced a nickel a pound or so back then, meaning that $50 would be the days "take" per dory. If the weather was okay, on the way back in, one mate would climb high up into the rigging and try to spy swordfish on top. While the rest of the crew was in the stern icing the fish for market, one man went way up in the bow with a harpoon. If a sword was spotted and they nailed it with a harpoon, the market price back then was a dollar a pound. Of course getting a swordfish wasn't common but still, just one fish would produce twenty times per pound what the cod would bring in.

Since gasoline only cost ten to twenty cents a gallon or eight to ten cents for diesel (believe it or not), that meant lots of money for the guys who stuck a sword from time to time.

My father never fished close to those boats, feeling that they were making a living and he didn't want to compete for the cod they were catching since the area was filled with them. Every now and then though, he would pull up alongside of one. I recall that Ollie Olson who ran the *Ingrid* out of Block Island was one such commercial skipper. Olson was highly skilled with a harpoon but most of his fishing was for cod. Every now and then, if Olson was running out of bait, dad would tie up to the *Ingrid* and pass over some clams. He wouldn't let his customers drop their lines over though, of course, until he pushed off and motored a quarter mile or more away from the *Ingrid* before giving his customers the green light.

Many of the older boats (and some still to this day) were restricted by the Coast Guard to stay not more than twenty miles "out." But "out" really meant no more than twenty miles from a point of land and Block Island was, more or less, twenty from Montauk and Cox's was another twenty from Block Island so, even though he was about forty from Montauk, he was still technically, within the law, by a hair. However, in order to be sure that he had no problem with this distance, my father got permission each year from the Coast Guard to be 21 miles out from any point of land instead of 20 and that solved that matter. In order to get this permission, he was required to put empty 55 gallon drums under deck in most compartments which would theoretically make the boat unsinkable.

His equipment included an old Bendix DR9 black and white paper depth recorder which served him well. (Color machines were not invented at the time). He was able to determine depth and fish volume with it as it sent a signal to the bottom and readings would bounce back up onto the paper on the machine. It would first show some fuzz above the bottom line and then, if fish were there in numbers, he got a second signal which indicated their presence.

At times the machine would break down but as with so many other problems at sea, my father was able to fix it with a complex system involving a light cable, similar to a guitar string, with which he got the defective recorder to work well, and change the 2D21 tube.

He became a true expert in reading bottom with his machine and he taught me to do so as well. To this day, I feel that I may be the only man alive who can take a boat out to the southwest corner of Cox's Ledge without Loran, radar, or GPS, just using my compass, my memory, and a depth recorder.

The fishing was so good at Cox's Ledge that my father restricted his customers to the use of just one hook. Call that the first of the voluntary restrictions that may have been used way before government decided to take the matter into their own hands.

I was still quite young and dad told me that the passengers should lift nearly every fish into the boat without sticking it with a gaff, unless it appeared to be at least twenty pounds. With only one mate on board as a rule, large fish on each of two hooks would have been impossible to deal with and since the ocean was loaded, dad put in his own rule.

While heading out to Cox's at 3:00 a. m. daily, nearly everyone was in the cabin trying to stay warm or maybe to grab some sleep and that time was spent by me going from rod to rod, cutting off a hook if any had two of them on. The four hour trip out, plus four hours of fishing, and add another four heading back in, made for a very long day. Often, we stayed out to produce more fish for the customers, and technically, that kind of broke a Coast Guard rule. You see, then and today, if a boat stays out over 12 hours it had to have two licensed skippers on board. More on that a little later on.

A Cox's Ledges Trick

I guess because he had started it all, and maybe too because he truly felt that it was worth it, dad charged his customers $10 for a day's fishing at Cox's Ledge. Again, this was when fuel cost a dime a gallon and all other charges were far lower than today. But the other guys who eventually began heading way out there cut their fares to only $8 in order to try and compete with the *Viking*.

All other boats were charging $5 to fish locally, near Montauk, for porgies and bass but again, Cox's was a 12-hour outing, not just a short hop from the dock. One day, another boat named *Falcon* took the overflow crowd that the *Viking* had no room for. That didn't bother dad, of course, but what got his goat was that the *Falcon* was cutting his price by 20 percent from the start of the morning, not just to take overflow! In fact, the owner got to his boat at midnight and hawked customers to board his boat because he was charging less. Some customers told dad about this and on the way out, he had a chance to get more than even with the *Falcon* skipper!

The *Viking* headed out that day and the *Falcon* followed, maybe three miles behind us, in the dark. A scallop boat was heading to the southeast but the way to Cox's Ledge was east by southeast. The scalloper came across our bow by a half-mile or so, continuing her course and my father turned off all of his lights and continued on his east by southeast course. The scallop boat was therefore the only thing the *Falcon* could see and as the scallop boat headed southeast, thinking it was the *Viking*, the *Falcon* followed her to, literally, nowhere that fish lived! There was no radar at the time and after a while, the *Falcon*, never finding the *Viking* again, returned to Montauk with no cod aboard.

When they got back to the harbor all of the *Viking* customers walked off with smiles galore and full bags of codfish while the *Falcon* fares had little more than a boat ride. This trick became the talk of Montauk for quite a while after. Other skippers were upset because *Viking* was loading up at Cox's Ledge and they couldn't make such a long trip. Again, it was twelve or more hours away.

"The Gateway Fishing Grounds"

First, the way gateway was found: The gateway was on the west side of a big gully between Block Island and Cox's Ledge. The gully runs basically north and south and originally, we called it Gully; now we call it the Gateway. In those days, it was the last reference point to Cox's Ledge. We did not have Loran, or radar, or GPS. Once we got to the gully with our trusty Bendix depth recorders the gully went down off the paper and came up on the other side and up the two edges were an inch and three quarters to two inches apart, making us right on course. If they were closer together we were just a little bit north of the course; if they were too wide, anything more than two inches wide, you were too far south.

You took your time from the west side of the gully. It was forty five to fifty five minutes to the southwest corner of Cox's Ledge compass course to the east southeast so you had to have the west end of that gully to set your time and you could start zigzagging to the south corner of Cox's Ledge.

One morning, I'm the first boat out, a four o'clock in the morning boat, and I passed the west end of the gully, came up on the east end, and the starboard engine overheated. I was in thick, black fog. I turned around and went back to the west end of the gully. I didn't want to lose my reference point so I had to turn around and go due west for a few minutes and get to the west end. With that, I told the crew and passengers that this looks like a good spot, folks, let's see what's here and I went down to the engine room to change the impeller. While I was down in the engine room I heard all this commotion going on up on deck and the mate lifted the engine hatch and yelled to me, he said, "Hey Paul, there are codfish coming in this boat in all directions, big ones." I said, "Well, throw the anchor out."

I kept working on the impeller, got it changed, put everything back together again and went on deck and sure enough, we had codfish laying all over the deck. These were twenty-five, thirty-five pound fish all over the place and poles were still bending so I went up in the wheelhouse and I called my father who was coming out. Surprisingly, he had his radio on and I told him I burned up an impeller and wanted to know if he had a spare impeller aboard.

Well, the first thing he did was yell at me and chew me out over the radio for not having a spare impeller. "What the hell's the matter with you; you know better that that." I said, "Yeah, I know dad, but I'm right here on the west side of the gully and it will be easy for you to get to me. If you blow the horn I'll hear you and talk you right into us." He said, "Alright, for crying out loud, but you know better than that." With that, I went back down below to help gaff fish. I didn't want to say what was really going on. The *Peconic Queen* and the *Helen II* passed us in the fog. They didn't know we were catching any fish; they couldn't see us catching fish because of the black fog.

Well, my father came up alongside of me. We're still baling these codfish; we've got them all around. He yelled out of the pilothouse, "Where the hell do you want this impeller." I said, "Dad, I had a spare impeller, I put it in. We're catching all these codfish." He said, "Well, why the hell didn't you say so." I said "I'm not gonna' say anything on the radio. I don't want any of the other guys to hear it." He finally commented, "Oh, alright."

Anyway, to make a long story short we fished there for over six weeks and since I was the first boat out in the morning, I would go past the gully, make a big circle, and wait for the *Peconic Queen* and *Helen II* to pass me en route to Cox's Ledge, and then I'd go back and we'd fish the west side which is called the gateway now. My father named it the Gateway to Cox's Ledge and the name stuck.

We fished there for a long time. My father was always the last boat out and we would catch so many fish that we would be out of there by the time the boats coming back from Cox's Ledge were returning home. We had that spot for a long time, my father and I alone. Eventually though, a lobster boat from Point Judith was in that general area setting lobster pot trawls, and he kinda' ratted us out to the Point Judith boats and before you knew it we had company from Point Judith but anyway, it lasted a long time and that's the story on the Gateway.

1960s — Part Two

Weight Problems

In those days, a headboat couldn't be more than 15 tons. The *Viking V* was a converted commercial boat that my grandfather, Carl Sr., the naval architect, designed to be a commercial dragger. Eventually, we converted her into a party fishing boat and still managed to contain her weight at below 15 tons. We talk elsewhere about the way that boats were measured over the years in order to obtain licenses for specific distances, etc. To stay at or under 15 tons, they had to measure usable space and this, from the inside of the frame in the boat and that is why some frames are four feet deep in some boats. It was not for strength; it was to use up space below deck.

Later on, the rule changed from 15 tons all the way up to 100 tons, meaning that far larger boats were going to start operating. But because some competitors harassed the Coast Guard into thinking the *Viking V* was overweight, they actually confiscated both the V and the *Viking VI* as being "overweight!" The boats were brought to Sweet's Shipyard in Greenport and they remained there for the entire winter. This had been the first time the Coast Guard had ever seized any boats for being over tonnage. They may have actually been a wee bit heavy, but while at Sweet's, we had them cut a few holes in the side of the below-deck cabin and put a temporary window in which could be kicked out. That made it a semi-complete enclosure meaning that the weight load estimate was cut back.

During that mess, my father and his friend Captain Al Lindroth realized that the *Viking VII* might be facing a similar problem. She was still in Freeport while the *V* and *VI* were operating out of Montauk. Fearing this, they took the *VII* down to Price's Shipyard in Deltaville, Virginia, where the boat had originally been built. My grandfather met dad and Lindroth at the yard and with Price personnel, made the necessary calculations and measurements. A few very minor changes had to be made to get the VII down to 15 tons and back she went to Freeport, all problems solved!

Unfortunately, while heading to Price's, the engine broke down. The belt had worn out and Lindroth told my dad to stop the boat and replace what appeared to be a broken V-belt. Dad felt he could fix it right on the spot while running. Telling Captain Al that they had traveled off course by a substantial distance he was sure he could handle the repairs underway.

However as my father began the work he miscalculated a maneuver and as he put his hands into the pulley one hand got all torn up! As Captain Al told me later "he just wrapped it up, blood all over the place, in a wet rag!" After a tough ride, they reached Price's where they saw Captain John Larson and his dad from Barnegat Light, New Jersey. The Larson's were at Prices at the time looking to have a new boat built. More than once for years after John reminded me about the mess he saw because he was shocked that dad wasn't bothered by the "hand in a bloody rag" as he should have been.

Years later I developed quite a friendship with John Larson. After the VII was fixed up, dad and Al went back to Freeport and made the necessary changes to get the V and VI in compliance. Back at Price's dad discussed construction of the new *Viking Star*. Construction began and the total price for the boat only was $54,000, a far cry from today's costs. She had three World War II surplus Grey Marine engines in her that were purchased for $750 each. A wooden boat at 65 feet long and 22 feet wide, that made her one of the first "triple-screw" boats around. Even better, she only measured 14.9 tons, what I call a "rule beater" because she wasn't restricted to the same rules as a 15 + ton boat would have been.

At the time, if you were less than 15 tons you could go wherever you wanted without inspection providing you had a life jacket for everyone on board as well as three fire extinguishers. The frame went all the way up to the deck in all compartments except the engine room. That meant that we could go to Cox's without anyone giving us grief, even if it may have been a little bit beyond the twenty mile distance from a point of land. Two years later, the weight matter changed to 100 tons from 15, also making distance traveled more important than overall weight. Additional regulations came into play when a boat was to be allowed to go 100 miles from land. Good and appropriate ones, like the need for an EPIRB system and large life rafts were added in. The more safe a boat was made, the easier it was to get permission to go 100 miles out. I think that our *Viking Gulfstar* which sails out of Tarpon Springs, Florida, is the only over-six passenger carrying boat that is licensed to travel 200 miles! Therefore, when we head way out for swordfish and such in the Gulf of Mexico we are one of the few within guidelines.

Currently, the larger boats can go to 100 tons and because the weights are still taken by measuring the inside framework, what most people consider the very biggest party boat in the entire country, the 140 foot long *Viking Starship*, is actually rated at being under 100 tons because of her superior construction.

If this was helpful, we're glad. But if it gave you another headache trying to understand, sorry!

The Last Old *Viking* to Leave Freeport for Montauk

It was 1957, and I decided to move the *Viking IV* from Freeport to Montauk to join the rest of the fleet. I had just married Muriel McTurck who was the daughter of another boat captain, George McTurck, a well-known charter boat man. Muriel and I had three kids, Paul, our oldest, then daughter Patty Ann, and last, Steven. As noted elsewhere, Paul Jr. eventually moved away from the business to become a successful Realtor but Steven jumped in with both feet, as did I with his grandfather, and now is every bit as much a dedicated waterman as both prior generations were. As an aside, Steve's son Steve Jr. is also a guy who seems to breathe through gills! Ditto with Paul's son, Carl.

Bringing the IV to Montauk was no easy job at all. When I finally decided to do so I sought aide from Captain Al Lindroth who was running the *Viking VII* in Freeport. We got coffee at the Viking Diner and I worked on the engine all night long before heading out. The Chrysler Crown gasoline engine needed some help and my mate and I got the water out of its carburetor, put new spark plugs and points in, and got it running pretty well, good and loud. Next came the trip itself.

I hadn't sailed out of Freeport in quite a while, in fact, Freeport didn't even have a jetty in the last time I did so. I told Al I wanted to follow him out with the IV as he was operating the *VII* and, while in the Viking diner full of people, Captain Al said something like "You're taking that boat to Montauk? By God, I'm buying your coffee. I'm buying your breakfast. Of course you can follow me out and I'll go slowly so that you can keep up with me but that boat is a one-way boat! Get that boat the hell out of here; I'm tired of towing in that boat." I guess we must have done the preparation work fairly well because I made the trip to Montauk without incident.

Very Expensive Skimmer Clams!

While fixing the *IV* up further in Montauk, more sanding and painting, etc., a skipper named Lenny Babin came over to me and said that some of the commercial fishermen out at Block Island needed some skimmer clams for bait and he asked me if I would take them out to the island for him. Babin said that he would go to Freeport to pick the clams up for me to put on my boat to be transported to Block and after he offered me 75 cents a bushel for the trip, I agreed, thinking that this was pretty good money (at least at the time it was). So Babin went to Freeport and got the clams from Billy Gurneu who, himself being a commercial guy, loaded the big coffee bags to the top for his friends, making them more like seventy five pounds per bag instead of the normal fifty.

So we filled the whole deck of the *IV* up with eighty sacks of clams. There wasn't room to be neat; in fact, I even had to put them over the engine room hatch. Lenny warned me against this because the hatch should have been easy to open to get into the engine but, it was impossible because of the load. The entire back of the boat was covered and in fact, part of it was even a little bit under water due to the cargo so I simply had to move some of the sacks over the hatch.

The hatch was level to the deck, a big problem. So out to sea I went, all by myself, fully loaded, with a northwest wind blowing as I left the harbor. As I headed towards Block, it got cold and when I reached a point just north of Southwest Ledge, I caught a heavy sea on my port stern corner. I had a potbelly stove burning below, but being by myself was only able to go down below for seconds at a time to warm my hands.

After the first wave came over I took another sea right behind it over the stern and with wind against tide this was a problem that could only get worse before it got better. The water came in at its worst point near the Submarine Buoy and as I reached a spot just west of the Southwest Ledge, I realized that I had deep water in the cockpit. I remember it being as much as three feet deep running down below into the cabin.

The engine started throwing water up in her V belts. The bilge pumps were running but after a while the engine flooded and stopped. There I was, adrift, with a belly full of water. The pot belly stove was steaming so badly I feared that I might have a fire below deck! I got a five-gallon bucket and started a one-man baling job. There was stuff floating below, pieces of wood, all kinds of flotsam, and all I could do was continue to bale water out.

The boat drifted along as I continued to remove more water and as I got into shallower water, big waves kept coming, but they melted under her belly and I remembered an old saying that went:" Captains sink boats. Boats don't sink on their own. The boat will take care of itself if you just let it do so." And it did just that. I got the volume of water down enough so that I could try to start the engine and sure enough, it sputtered but started. She cleared herself up and the pump got the rest of the water out in a few hours.

I headed in to Block Island and went to dock #3, Payne's Dock, a really high one, and tied a line around a piling to make it secure. Guys were standing there, the commercial guys waiting for their bait, and they weren't in a good mood either because they had been waiting for hours and were themselves very cold. But I was frozen with soaked pants, etc. and in no way ready to listen to complaints. So I said "Good morning, gentlemen/oh, I guess it's actually afternoon now" but no one answered. They just stood there so I went below and started a fire to warm up. Finally, one of them hollered down, "Hey Cap, you gonna' pass these clams up?" I came back out and said, "No Sir, they're your clams now. If you want 'em, you come down here and get 'em. I did my part, that's as far as I go. They didn't even say good morning to me and I was so frozen I was in no way going to cooperate, no sir!

They got on board and passed the clams up from one to the other and gave me an envelope with cash in it, without saying a word, not thanks, not goodbye, nothing. Block Islanders at the time weren't a friendly bunch to begin with and not knowing any of the grief that I had gone through, they didn't feel much like being nice anyway.

With money in my pocket, I headed back to Montauk; the wind had died making the return easy to manage. Going through that experience with no other boats around was harrowing; if I had capsized, I would have drowned. I got back to my house with a bunch of cash and that took some of the sting out of the day. But I sure swore that I would never put any cargo over an engine hatch again!

Risking Death Via a Hook!

At one time or another, just about every angler who fishes often gets a hook stuck in a finger, past the barb, and it truly is an unhappy angler who has that painful experience. One such terrible incident took place one day out at sea on the *Viking IV* while I was commercial cod fishing with two mates.

There were no fancy electronics back then, nothing that could determine depth beyond fifty feet down. The sonar then was a simple flasher that could tell me how deep it was but only if in shallow water. We had a radio and a compass, and that pretty well made up our equipment. So, armed with the knowledge I learned from dad and Captain Lindroth, this helped me learn ranges which could assist me in finding areas that held fish.

I was down south of Block Island one day on the *IV*, setting a "tub-troll," which involved the use of a stick to pitch the baited set line hooks over the side. We used a big tub-full of nylon line, almost ¼ inch thick, with a clam-baited hook every six feet, with a 16-inch "snood." A mate was setting the gear out behind me and the wind caught some of the gear and pulled some line and a batch of hooks into my mate's sweater. He started screaming and I immediately threw the boat into reverse to ease the tension on the line and got my Dexter knife out and cut all of the hooks out of the sweater because, otherwise, the mate would have been dragged over the side.

I cut a hole in the sweater and the hooks all came flying out. But as this took place, the line wrapped around my hand and one of the big hooks got its barb deeply imbedded in the back of my hand, right around a blood vessel! I grabbed the knife with my other hand and sawed through the line, cutting the "snood" and letting the gear go into the water. Had the hook torn through my hand instead of staying buried, I think that I probably would have bled to death.

There I was, with this huge hook in my hand and we had no clippers on board or anything normal that could have been used to push the hook through my hand and out the other end to then cut it off once the barb poked through. Can you just imagine the pain right now as you read this stuff? Well then, now try to imagine how it felt as I remember it too. We had a hammer and a few bricks that were used as weights and those things became the difference between life and death for me.

I put my arm and hand down on a hard surface and they pounded on the top of the hook with a brick to make it go through the other side of my hand so that the hook could be cut off the line. My hand swelled up like a balloon. I couldn't even bend my fingers.

Fishing ended right then and there and all I could think of was getting back to land for emergency medical aid.

Under normal circumstances, we would have spent the day at sea and headed back to Block Island instead of Montauk to tie up before heading out for a second day of commercial fishing. The goal was to average 1,000 pounds of cod per day. We would bait the gear once again overnight while cooking up a mess of spaghetti and/or beans on the pot-belly stove. "Dinner" finished, hooks baited, a few hours of well-deserved sleep followed before going out again. This was impossible now.

When we tied up at Block Island I saw a few commercial fishermen nearby and I remember saying "good evening" without getting a reply, and asking them if there was a doctor nearby, showing them my swollen hand. One clown actually laughed and went back to talking to his friend, but did at least say that the doctor was "off island." Needless to say, the Block Island commercial guys didn't want anyone fishing their area from Montauk or anywhere else. After fishing the next day, we returned to Montauk where I finally got some aide.

"Get Ready to Give Out the Lifejackets!"

One day, aboard the *Viking Starlite*, we were heading back to land after a nice days fishing on the Suffolk wreck. The southwest wind that was blowing kicked the seas up pretty well and something caused the bilge alarm to go off. As it turned out, the bolts came out of the stuffing box in the starboard engine all of a sudden. I had an oil temperature alarm in the crank case of the engines and that produced an alarm if water sloshed up and hit the crank case. The gauge would flicker on the panel, letting me know that we had water in the boat. That simple little creation might have saved the boat and everyone else on board that day. I feel that, at the time, it was the greatest invention ever.

I didn't care much about the oil temperature of the engine since it was always cool but the idea that the water would splash against the lowest part of the engine, making the gauge respond, worked as an alarm. Now, of course, there are true bilge alarms but back in the day, this was all we could have and in the 60s, it sure beat having nothing.

Heading back in with a load of pollock and codfish on board that fall day we suddenly started taking on a huge volume of water in the stern and it was coming in fast. I turned on all of the valves and got all of the bilge pumps working at top speed but I was barely keeping up with the volume of water invading the boat.

We managed to get into waters inside of the lighthouse but were still far from being safe. I had Cummings engines with electric switches but I knew if we got a short the engines would die. I went down below into the engine room and with water up to my knees climbed around to get to the other side of the engine. With the screwdriver end of my Boy Scout knife I turned the screw that made the shut-off manual instead of automatic thereby preventing the engines from conking out even if water was slopping onto them.

The customers knew nothing about there being a problem but I told my mate, John O'Connor, that we had a major problem. I said that we would hug the beach on the way back in and if one of the engines died, I would have to make a left turn and beach the boat. Just in case, I told O'Connor to pull the covers off the life jacket boxes and stand ready to pass them out if necessary.

Avoiding scraping bottom with the boat wasn't easy because we had gotten fairly close to the beach but I finally made it safely into the inlet and then the harbor. The stern deck was just about level with the water. Pulling into the dock, I told my mate to get the stern line on first instead of the spring line and as soon as I got the boat alongside of the bulkhead to start unloading passengers as quickly as possible.

Another skipper, Carl Darenberg from Montauk Marine Basin saw what was going on and ran over to try and help. He brought a submersible bilge pump on board to cut down on the volume of water. At that point, noticing the huge volume of cod and pollock all over the boat, he asked me "where the hell were you fishing?" We forgot for a moment what was going on and instead began discussing the day's catch, believe or not! Of course I kept my secret spot, The Suffolk, still secret and shortly we got back to the business of unloading people and their catch all at the same time as trying to prevent the boat from sinking.

The loaner pump didn't work well though because it needed more power than the electricity that the Viking Dock could provide. It wasn't before long that it popped the circuit breakers. By then the passengers were clued in and started jumping off the boat; nonetheless, they still managed to rescue their fish and get them on the dock!

I went over to the pay phone at the Viking Grill (now called "Dave's Grill") and called the Coast Guard for help. I didn't want anyone to hear about this on the VHF so that's why I used a pay phone. The Coast Guard quickly kicked into gear and brought their 44-footer over and tied up alongside of us and immediately put their huge pump into gear. The fares were still in the process of disembarking but even with all the confusion everyone still managed to work together.

Thanks to all of the things that I managed to do, and because of the assistance provided by Captain Darenberg and then the Coast Guard, everything worked out fine. When I found out exactly what was wrong we got some new bolts and a new gasket made up and put the stuffing box together and, all fixed up, off we went out to sea the following morning, to go catch some more fish, none the worse for it!

1960s — Part Three

Captain Fred E. Bird

Captain Fred E. Bird began his fishing career on one of the *Viking* boats by working as a deckhand alongside of me many years ago. He currently owns the *Flying Cloud* and docks his boat at the Viking Dock so you know that his

Here's my good old friend, Captain Fred E. Bird.

history with the Forsberg family is both long and well remembered. He had lived in New York City and went out to Montauk each weekend to work with the fleet before making the permanent move to Montauk.

As we were working together on this book, Manny called and spoke to Fred E. who recalled with pleasure how wonderful his relationship was with both me and my dad. He told Manny that my Father treated him as if he was his own child and that one day, Dad told Fred E. that he knew that he wasn't his own son but that at times, he was every bit as close to him as he was to his own kids.

Captain Bird first worked with the family back in 1949 and after a stint in Korea, he came back and commuted from Queens, N. Y. to work on the *Viking Star* every weekend with me until he finally moved to Montauk. Captain Bird got his own license and then ran the *Viking Star* II on her ferry trips from Montauk to Block Island and back.

In 1961 he got his own party boat, originally built in 1901, which was probably the oldest head boat afloat at the time and moved it from Sheepshead Bay, Brooklyn to Montauk. He has owned two other boats since. With a very capable second captain, Captain Fred E. Bird hopes to take people out fishing for lots more days to come.

Manny told me that he could feel the love and respect that Fred E. has for the Viking Family as they spoke together and, of course, we feel the same way about Captain Bird!

An unfortunate update: I just found out my old friend Captain Fred E. Bird passed away in his sleep on Tuesday, August 6th, 2013 after having fished all day on Monday.

Built-In Radar

One day, dad gave me the wheel and he took a break on the way in, lying down in the wheelhouse, as Fred stayed on deck cleaning the catch of the day. A heavy fog came rolling in and it was impossible to see much at all. I blew the horn to let others know we were nearby because there was no radar at the time to "see" with. So with window open and ears at the ready plus using a horn to scare others away, I used the compass to find my way to the dock.

But my father, lying down, somehow got a sense that something was wrong. He had lifted his hat up from time to time to look at the Bendix and after a while he told me, "Son, hold her down about ten degrees to the south. You're just a little bit too far north. You're just north of the green buoy midway." Okay, it was pea soup fog and dad wasn't even looking out the window, but still, he told me I was too far north and sure enough, he was right.

Dad told me to look at the recorder. We could see what looked like shark's teeth at the bottom bouncing up and down from below as if it really was a series of shark's teeth down there. He told me that this was the only area around that produced a bottom reading like that, meaning that I was off course and sure enough, he was right.

I corrected the course and my father lay back down and pulled his hat over his eyes. Quickly, the boat came out of the fog and on my left side, just where it belonged, was Montauk Point. The rest of the trip in was easy.

Dad was a living legend and, being the best of the best at the time, he taught me to become his equal. He had been taught a lot by the Merritt Brothers earlier on in Freeport and he taught Captain Al Lindroth much of what he knew and, of course, Al was another of the skippers who improved my knowledge still later.

Another Nice Guy — Captain George Thompson

Throughout this book, we discuss many of the wonderful folks my family has been involved with on the water. Yet one more was Captain George

Thompson, owner of the Point Judith, R. I. party boat *Sea Squirrel*. Earlier, I talked about Al Jarmon who ran the *Sea Squirrel's* replacement, the *Super Squirrel*, and how Jarmon was so proud of the fact that he stole my secret "Old Faithful" spot. As for Thompson though, I have only the finest of words about him. He owned a former Coast Guard boat that he renamed *Sea Squirrel*. She was an 83-footer with four Gray marine engines on two shafts. He fished the east end of Cox's as opposed to the west end which was closer to his dock, but because he had more speed, he generally fished away from the other boats.

The two of us would communicate often with our CB radios, sharing information and never trying to squeeze each other out of our spot. One day, as we were both heading out I noticed a vibration in my boat (The *Starlite*). It was kind of sloppy out too, but we had a full boat of customers, maybe 70 in all, so I had my mate set the anchors and we began fishing. Fishing was phenomenal with loads of cod coming over the rail.

I was up top, counting heads. The custom then was to collect the money at sea, something not normally done now. I checked the rails and then the cabin and lastly the "head's" to be sure I got money from everyone. As I was doing that, Thompson called me on my CB and asked if I was all right. I told him that I was okay but George said I had better get down below and check things out, further telling me that the boat doesn't look right; "your deck is about a foot off the water in the stern."

I replied that we had a full boat and that might be why we were so low in the water but Thompson said "you don't have that many on the boat!" So I went down below deck and lifted up the hatch to go into the engine room. The floor boards were floating all around! Upside down oil cans were bobbing in the water. I looked around and saw that water was coming in from the stern around the shafts via the back bulkhead. We had three-way valves on the engines as a safety precaution. I flipped the three-way over and the water began pumping out through the engine. Instead of using water from outside the boat I pumped bilge water through to cool the engine. I then headed back up topside.

I called George on the CB and told him that he sure was right. We had a belly full of water in the stern and while I had noticed a vibration earlier I thought we might have simply picked up a piece of rope that caused it.

Asking George to keep an eye on me, I tried to find the cause of the water. The *Sea Squirrel* anchored close by watching out for me. The Viking's customers had no idea that we had a problem; they were too busy catching fish! Two mates were busy gaffing fish and I went back below to look around. I lifted the hatch just outside the back door of the cabin and looked down; what I saw was really bad. The compartment was loaded with water and I could see daylight through the bottom of the boat on her starboard side.

I finally realized that the vibration I had felt was caused by a strut breaking on the starboard shaft and every time the boat rolled on a southwest wave the wheel would come up, causing the tip of the propeller to hit the bottom of the boat, eventually cutting a grove in the bottom. I saw a four-inch long slot by ½ inch wide and again, I could see right through the opening. Depending on how the boat rolled, I saw daylight first and then water.

I removed my shirt and got some screwdrivers and called Jimmy Malenze, a regular customer, to come over and guard the hatch so that no one could fall down below. I went down into the water below with just my underwear on and stuffed the hole by forcing my shirt into the slot with a screwdriver. This slowed the water coming in and we began to gain on the intake. By then, the customers had found out but, hey, the fish were biting and they were catching fish. They paid little attention!

We got the water down low enough to take a two foot long by foot and a half wide length of plywood and went about the business of making emergency repairs. Dad and I were capable of taking care of just about every need that could pop-up on the water but this was a very unusual problem.

I took a hammer and some nails and nailed the board right in, over my shirt, into the surrounding wood, and the leak slowed down enough so that the bilge pump could handle the rest of the incoming water with ease. Believe it or not, the repair held so well that we finished the rest of the trip without incident and headed back in.

All this time, Thompson was standing by and I was constantly in touch, letting him know what was going on. The weather improved and then it became a matter of trying to figure out what to do next. The two of us spoke on the radio and I asked George if he knew of a place that we could get the boat hauled out for repair. There was no boatyard available at Montauk and the only place we had used before was in Greenport and they were backed up by a month; I couldn't wait that long for repairs.

George told me about a place in Point Judith that was run by a man named Ken Gallup. He called Ken and asked him if he could accommodate the *Viking* and help me out. Gallup had hauled out many of the other Point Judith boats and was well-known to be a nice guy who ran a good yard. Thompson added that he had noticed that there hadn't been a boat on the Gallup railway in the past few days which meant that, just maybe, this could be the answer. Sure enough, Gallup told Thompson that I could haul the *Starlite* out the very next day. Bright and early, I pulled in and they hauled me out and sure enough a strut had broken. They cut a bad piece of plank out, replaced it with a new one, welded the strut back together and put some braces on it and the repair still is there today. None of this would have been possible if not for the wonderful help given to us by the *Sea Squirrel* skipper.

The "Strain" to Get the Steel *Viking Star* Built

Strain was, in fact, a major understatement! The *Starlite* was catching so many codfish that I filled the boat with fares daily by midnight even though my advertised sailing time was 4:00 a. m. There were a few other boats that did well too like the *Helen II*, the *Marlin*, and the *Peconic Queen* but clearly

the *Viking* fleet needed to expand to handle the crowds. That's how the 104'
Viking Star came to be. It was 1968. I signed a contract to have her built with
Blount Marine in Warren, Rhode Island. I went there with my dad and talked
to the architects before completing the paper work. The cost for the boat was
$125,000 and that was lots of money back in those days. And that price didn't
even include the engines. I got the engines for $10,000 each and bought a
couple of surplus generators and that came close to cleaning us out of money.
By the way, this didn't even include the basic stuff like the wood for the cabin.
Captain Al Lindroth advised me to go get a bank loan from an officer at the
Bank of Babylon by the name of Stanton but the amount I obtained wasn't
nearly enough for the whole deal.

In 1968 we had a trip scheduled for just before Labor Day. Wouldn't you
know the super charger of the starboard Cummins engine in the *Viking Starlite*
broke? My wife Mu and I drove to the Bronx and picked up a new one.

Arriving back to Montauk at about midnight we found there were already
passengers aboard. I quickly installed the super charger. Boy, it was heavy. I
straightened up and felt a sharp jab of pain but didn't really think too much
about it. I sailed through the weekend and later found out that I had strained
myself and got a double hernia. I was operated on and had doctor's orders to
do no driving, take no steps for eight weeks, no going to sea for ten weeks.
That resulted in a one year delay in building the *Viking Star*.

Construction moved on in 1969 though and with the boat itself built we
then had to prepare to make it a usable vessel. Remember now, this is a bare
boat. There was no wood in it. It was like a gutted house, like a shell. The
engines were installed so that we could run the boat home. The generators
were sitting on the bed but there was no electric to them, no exhaust to them,
no water to them, and they were not even connected. Thinking about the trip
itself, at the last minute I pushed Blount into at least giving us a compass and
they did so. I installed it in front of the wheel but we were still far from ready
to go.

I built all of the furniture in my two-car garage in Montauk during the night while still operating the *Starlite* by day. I had a table saw set up and built the dinette seating and the reclining chairs as well as the galley counter top. My father-in-law, George McTurck, built the wooden doors and together we also built life jacket boxes but by then, I was cleaned out of money.

That's What Friends are for!

Out of cash, I still didn't have a new boat that was ready to go catch fish. One night, my friend Eddie Watrel, a commercial fisherman, a dragging man, was at my home with his wife and my wife Muriel ("Mu") and I told them that I was out of money. A day or two later, Eddie's wife called and invited me to come to their home for coffee. I did, and Eddie said, "I understand you need some money" and I said that I did. Watrel asked me how short I was and I replied that I needed about $20,000, which was a lot of money at the time. I told Eddie that I had no idea how to finish the boat what with all of the payments we had to make to simply keep up with our current debts.

Eddie told me that he had $5,000 in cash and wanted to loan it to me and that he wanted me to pay it back in cash later on. He said that he didn't want any interest or anything because he considered me a good friend. All he wanted in return was a signed IOU in case anything happened to him; he at least wanted his wife to know that I owed her some money. I really was shocked at the wonderful offer, as I recall, "Floored." Watrel continued. "Now drink your coffee and go see how many friends you have in town." He knew that we still needed another $15,000.

Lifted by Watrel's wonderful offer, I spent the next two nights with "Mu," going to see some of our friends. We picked up $2,000 here, $3,000 there, and $4,000 elsewhere and in two nights, we had gathered the rest of the money needed and all based on the great terms set by Eddie, "pay it back as soon as you can," and a handshake.

On Easter Sunday Weekend, after the boat was christened and everyone enjoyed a fine lunch, off we sailed. With me were my dad, two sons, and a mate named Charlie Harned.

We had no anchor line though and made a stop to see my friend George Thompson, who we talked about earlier as the owner of the *Sea Squirrel*. He had a wholesale marine business in Point Judith and gave me the line. I attached it to an anchor and then we started the ride out of Point Judith back to Montauk.

A heavy snowstorm was falling with northeast winds cranking at about 40 miles an hour. I had the compass that Blount gave me but it was never calibrated so we didn't know if it provided true readings. Fortunately, dad was in the pilothouse with me and his uncanny feeling about the water was about to be tested. We couldn't see past the bow and there was no radar at the time, no electronics at all, and a monstrous sea from the northeast was pushing us.

The boat would take a sea under her stern and she'd take off. I was a bit concerned and asked dad if we might be too far south and miss the Montauk Light. But my dad had been watching the water and pointed out some rips he saw that told him that we were still on the right course and far enough north.

I worried that the compass might not be accurate enough but dad assured me that we were on course. And sure enough the snow backed down and we got better visibility and right in front of us, appeared Montauk Harbor!

Still more friends appeared later to help me get the *Star* operating. Captain Brad Glas did the wiring for the electric power which needed hooking up to the 100-volt generators and Capt. Wally Drobecker did the plumbing for me.

We had to get a skipper to run the *Viking Starlite* for us as I was putting the *Star* together and I hired Frank Bachnik to do so. My family worked together and did what was needed to get her ready. Dad helped put the paneling up and my sons Paul and Steven took every minute they could when not in school to do everything possible to finish it off.

Money remained very tight and the *Star* still didn't have safety equipment, any life jackets, life rafts, or fire extinguishers, clearly she wasn't ready to take passengers fishing.

Captain Paul holding what was the biggest cod ever caught at the time, 71 lbs., on the *Viking Starlite*.

Captain Frank Mundus had recommended a place called Shane's Marine in Island Park to me some time back and said that they were good people to get along with.

I was out of money but I called Bob Shane up and explained our situation and asked him if he could help me out. Shane asked me what I needed and I gave him a list and Bob said that he had just about all of the equipment necessary in stock. He told me to get my truck to his store and pick it all up and after a few trips I had everything we needed. Bob told me that he trusted me and that all he wanted in return was some sort of payment from time to time after I was up and running. He added that he would like to see a payment arrive in the mail every month and instead of needing large sums, all he expected was a payment of any size and that would let him know that I did not forget him. Shane added that I should take my time and be comfortable and to pay the obligation as I could.

It took two years to finish paying the debt but I remember that I sent a payment each and every month, regardless of its size, and I recall too that Shane didn't charge any interest either, the same terms as my Montauk buddies gave me earlier on. Those were the good old days!

From then on, I bought just about all of the equipment we needed for my boats from Shane for years afterwards until Bob sold the business to West Marine Stores.

A Great Guy — Commander Wolfe, U. S. C. G.

Al Lindroth was so close to my family that one day, he started bragging about the *Viking Star* on the radio to his friend Captain Mike Scarpetti. Mike owned the *Ranger* out of Sheepshead Bay. Scarpetti wanted to see the boat for himself so one day he drove out with his two sons and told them that it was a pretty boat but "He's not going to get that boat running until Labor Day!"

Al made a bet with him that we would take passengers out by Memorial Day Weekend, adding that if he was wrong, he would buy dinner for Mike but if correct, Scarpetti would have to pay the bill. The fact of the bet was discussed over the radio which meant that I was facing a serious task, not wanting to let my friend Capt. Al down.

Mike had no idea though that I had already finished building the furniture nor that I was working day and night to get it all done. All we needed to do was shove the stuff into the cabin, scribe it off with a pencil, cut it off, bolt it in and fasten it all down and attach Formica to the walls.

Sure, the boat didn't even have a ceiling but that wasn't a big deal. I installed the ceiling the following winter between codfish trips. Remember, my goal was to start the operation on Memorial Day weekend and we figured that it wouldn't be cold then anyway so the heat a ceiling would provide wasn't important.

The boat left Point Judith on Easter Sunday with, to say the least, lots of work still needed. A few months later we took the boat out of the harbor on Memorial Day weekend, right on schedule, even though some doubted that we could pull it off. I remember fishing Southwest Ledge off of Block Island that day with 84 passengers aboard. I can recall it all clear as a bell!

The trip would not have taken place that weekend though without the wonderful cooperation of the man whose name is found at the top of this chapter, Commander Wolfe. Wolfe was the top guy in the Coast Guard in New York and he came to Montauk to check the boat out himself.

When the boat left Blount Marine in Rhode Island, she didn't have all the equipment that a lesser Coast Guard officer wanted installed. Not yet being a passenger-carrying vessel the boat was legally allowed to leave but the lower ranked Coast Guard man wasn't happy about it and made some bad comments to his Commanding Officer, Commander Wolfe.

Wolfe came out with an assistant to check the boat out at Montauk. This was most unusual for so high-ranking a person but he wanted see it for himself. They walked through the boat with a big long check list and started marking things off. He told me things like "That doesn't fit here, that's ridiculous, we don't need that," and he cleared just about everything off the check list other than a couple of little items.

He told me that he was there to help me and that he would do everything he could to assist. I asked him about the lights that I was required to have on the boat. It being over 65 feet in length, I was supposed to have Coast Guard approved lights with a Coast Guard "approved" sticker on them. But I showed Wolfe a manual that offered the same light without a decal at $22 less per light. Commander Wolfe told me to buy the cheaper lights and even sent me a letter stating that it was okay with him. He told me to keep it in my files and to this day I can still walk to the file cabinet and show you his letter.

Wolfe arranged to have his inspector at the dock that Friday night and told the inspector that he was to do everything he could to assist us in getting the boat approved for that weekend. He told him that he was to stay there until the inspection was completed. The inspector asked me if we really planned to fish the following morning and I replied that I was indeed ready to go.

We had to remove the table saw off the boat and sweep the sawdust off the deck and take all the tools out but with Viking determination, that was the plan. The inspector stayed with us, even helping sweep up and eventually, he handed me a "passed" certificate of inspection, saying that he had been ordered by Commander Wolfe to make sure it happened. And, as hoped, the boat sailed early the next day. But I don't know if Al ever got his dinner from Mike or not.

1960s — Part Four

Chumming the Sea Gulls

When the first *Viking Star* was built at Price's shipyards, her pilothouse was right on deck, just ahead of the main cabin. Her low profile was typical of the day and some boats are still built that way because they have to pass under bridges while going in and out of inlets. But this caused a problem for us one day.

Dad didn't like talking on the radio much and worse, he didn't like to listen to all the chatter either. Before VHF came into play, the old radios were in constant use and you could hear guys talking from Cape May, New Jersey to the south all the way up the coast. Once VHF was put into use things improved but for this discussion, it was in the time that we only had an AM radio.

The FCC came out to monitor radio use every couple of years. We were required to stand by on 21.82. One day dad was heading in after a good day's fishing and he was doing what he loved to do, "chumming for sea gulls." In order to attract attention to his boat on the way into port, he always had the crew throw the fish racks overboard to the huge number of sea gulls who always knew the *Viking Star* was bringing a fine meal to them. Folks waiting at the dock could see the gulls and that told them that the *Viking* was heading in with a big catch.

The FCC guy was standing up in the bow of a 44-foot Coast Guard boat as it approached the *Star* from the rear, preparing to board. He was wearing a typical New York style suit, complete with a fedora on his head. But because dad didn't have the radio on; and because he couldn't see behind him due to the placement of the pilothouse, he had no idea that anyone was trying to board.

Picture this, okay? Sea gulls flying over the stern. Birds yelling and screaming for a meal, the birds doing what birds do so often, "relieving themselves," splashing poop down wherever it may fall, and some landed on the guys fedora and clothing. And some of the chum didn't hit the water either, instead it landed on the bow of the Coast Guard cutter and some hit the poor FCC guy. His pretty Manhattan suit and hat got all dosed with gull poop and fish guts.

However, he was hell bent to board and as the cutter got up close to our stern he jumped on the back of the *Star* and hit the deck, real hard, as his feet skidded on the guts and slid on his back across the stern like he was on oil.

Remember, Dad couldn't see him because of the low profile of the pilothouse and he didn't have his radio on so he couldn't hear the cutter trying to reach him.

The fedora man jumped up, yelling at everyone near (and none listened), "You are all going to be my witnesses; I want all of your names and addresses!"

The cutter had put on its lights (dad couldn't see them) and started blowing their horn but with the boat in high gear, he couldn't hear that either so dad was oblivious to what was going on until one of the crew told him.

The FCC guy stood up and must have been one helluva sight. He held up his badge but all the 40+ passengers could see was seagull crap all over him and fish slime all over his backside. He went to the pilothouse and told dad that he had been calling him on the radio but dad told him he didn't have the radio on. Maybe it wasn't a good idea but at the time, it became a funny thing to dad and he said something like, "My God, look at you, you are a mess! You ought to be ashamed of yourself. You're a government employee and look at this stuff all over you," and he actually reached over and began cleaning some of the junk off his clothes.

Meanwhile, I had docked my boat a little earlier and was standing at the dock looking at all of that, shaking my head and worrying to myself that dad was going to jail! But the bottom line of it all wound up being that dad got two warnings and had to pay a modest fine for not having his radio on. The story went around the waterfront quickly though, everyone thinking that dad might have been taken away in handcuffs, but it really didn't happen and just made a great story.

Later on, we put a new pilothouse on the second deck on top of the roof so that visibility could be improved to the stern.

The *Andrea Doria*

According to an account found on Wikipedia, the *SS Andrea Doria*, an Italian Line ship that was home ported in Genoa, Italy, was offshore of Nantucket, Massachusetts, en route to New York City when she was struck on the side by an approaching vessel, the *MS Stockholm*, a smaller ship that had been built in Sweden. It was not certain, but some said that 1,660 passengers and crew were saved and 46 died in the collision.

This was on July 25, 1956, and while most of the people on board survived, it still was the largest number of people to die at sea in quite some time.

The *Andrea Doria* was so badly damaged in the accident, being struck in the side, that she quickly listed to the starboard, making all of her lifeboats unusable on that side. Fortunately, her radio crew stayed on watch and was able to reach many nearby vessels who all came quickly to the scene to aide in the rescue efforts.

Some said that defective radar on board the Swedish ship may have been the cause of that ship moving into the path of the *Andrea Doria* while others felt that the initial fault lay with the Italian vessel. Fog played a part in the tragedy and at the time of actual contact the fog was very thick. Finally the fog lifted and the day cleared up beautifully which certainly helped those who participated in the rescue efforts later on.

The *Andrea Doria* had been considered the largest, fastest, and safest of all of Italy's ships; 697 feet in length and 90 feet wide, she seemed virtually unsinkable. But it was discovered earlier that when she was hit by large waves she would list to one side. In fact, during her maiden voyage she was hit by such a huge wave that she listed 28 degrees. However, she had already made approximately 100 voyages by the time the accident took place.

Whatever the cause, and whichever ship was at fault, it was very fortunate that so many ships responded and were able to rescue nearly all on board. Of interest though, with Coast Guard, Navy, Air Force, and many other vessels responding, none of them took the actual and exact readings that would allow for the wreckage to later be found. That's where the *Viking* guys came in!

So one day, 10 years after the *Andrea Doria* slid to her watery grave the morning after being struck, I made plans to go find her! I knew the approximate area to search, finding the writings on a chart, but clearly, there were no exact markings other than she was in a five-mile area or so.

At the time, I was operating the *Viking Starlite* and we made three separate overnight trips with only a mate and a friend on board to find the vessel, many fathoms beneath the surface. We burned loads of fuel in the effort. I worked with charts, systematically marking out areas we covered in small circles. We had Loran, and a side-scanner that I had recently installed in the *Viking Starlite*, an ELAC LAZ 17 model. This side-scanner played a huge part in my efforts to find the wreck because it could read the

Diver Steve Gatto holds the Andrea Doria's Steering Helm, July 1987.
Photo by Bill Nagle.
Photo courtesy Steve Gatto/Museum of New Jersey Maritime History.

bottom over a vast area. I credit my side-scanner with helping me find many other wrecks as well.

On my third trip, I found the wreck! We had taken time off from carrying passengers for hire (this is a key point, remember it) to locate the wreck and on the third trip, we found the darn thing. Boy, was she loaded with fish. I never saw anything like that in my life. The wreck, what a monstrous wreck. It stood 90-feet high. It was just piled with fish, loads of cod and pollock.

The school of pollock was so thick, sitting above the wreck as they generally do; that in order to reach the cod beneath them, we took paper bags and put baited hooks and the line's sinker into the bag and twisted it closed. The bag would sink and when it all hit bottom; we could jerk on the line and break the bag, revealing the baited hooks to the waiting cod. That's how thick the pollock were there.

Evelyn Bartram Dudas took this underwater shot at the Andrea Doria. Check out the big pollock!

When I got back to Montauk I put out a press release that said that I found the *Andrea Doria*! Wow, the phone jumped off the wall. People were calling day and night wanting to know when we were going to make fishing trips to the wreck. A group of divers called and wanted to dive the wreck to prove that we in fact did find the *Andrea Doria*.

A couple of weeks later eight divers and four in crew and I loaded the *Viking Starlite* up with diving gear, food, a kayak for a rescue boat, etc, all supplied by the divers. With full fuel tanks, we were off for a three-day trip.

When we arrived at the wreck there were seven giant foreign factory trawlers dragging their nets nearby and the closest was only about three miles away.

The divers went down in shifts, four at a time. When they returned they were very excited and said, "Yes" it was the *Andrea Doria*. The divers complained that there were so many pollock and codfish that they had a hard time seeing the wreck. One diver swore that he saw the biggest codfish he ever saw in his life and estimated it to be at least 100 pounds. (We never did catch that monster).

[Left] Diver Bart Malone has this water bottle removed from the Andrea Doria. [Right] He also has this Acorn light taken off the Andrea Doria. Both are sitting in his living room!

The tide runs quite hard at times in that area and it also changes direction often. I have seen it change 360 degrees in a matter of hours. That first night we remained anchored and swung off to the side of the wreck.

At 2:00 a.m. The crew on watch woke me up and informed me that there was a big ship getting close to us. It was a giant Russian trawler with hammer and sickle on the stack, going by on our starboard side. They were so close that you could see the lookouts on the bridge looking at us.

All of a sudden noises started coming from the giant trawler — a loud screaming of the brakes slipping on the giant winches. The engines were changing rpm and going astern, the lookouts were now running to the stern. Eventually, the giant trawler slowly moved ahead going to the southwest. I told all aboard that it sounded like the trawlers net had hit the *Andrea Doria*.

The next day the first divers to come up told me that a gigantic net, doors and all, was draped over the wreck. They could see the parted tow cables.

Andrea Doria Officer's china.
Photo courtesy Steve Gatto/Museum of New Jersey Maritime History.

They said the huge net was loaded with fish and I asked if they could cut a couple of bars on the net so the fish could get out. The answer was, "No way, it is a no-no to get that close to a net!" The diving tanks, etc., could get tangled and if so, you're dead!

I could only hope that at least some of the fish found a way out. When that trawler came so close to us my guess was that they probably never saw a party boat before and were curious to see what we were doing.

Our divers retrieved the binnacle (compass) along with silverware, plates, and cups, etc., from the wreckage. I understand that these items remain in a diving museum in New Jersey.

That was the first and last trip I took divers to the Andria Dorea wreck. My stomach was in knots the whole time they were down. 300 feet is a deep dive and some divers came up with blood in their masks from nosebleeds, a very scary sight!

Unfortunately, some boats will still venture to the wreckage with divers because it is so interesting a dive. However, it also is a very dangerous dive and four to five people lose their lives yearly due to the pressure they experience.

The tide can start running very hard in a matter of minutes. In the summer there are many sharks in the area. The lost nets are a hazard to divers.

Diver Evelyn Dudas underwater.

In those days there were many foreign trawlers fishing off our coast; Russian, East German, Spanish, Polish, and others. I don't believe they talked to each other for the simple reason that they kept taking turns slamming their gigantic nets into the wreck! If they communicated this most certainly would have stopped. At one point there were so many lost nets on the wreck that it was unfishable.

This all changed when the Two-Hundred-Mile-Law went into effect. Little by little, through the years, a good number of the nets rotted away or drifted off the wreck.

The *Andrea Doria* still produces some cod and pollock, but nowhere near what it used to. I believe the reason is that the foreign trawlers devastated that area with their huge nets tearing up the bottom, killing the food chain that supports the cod and pollock. Hopefully, one day, the food chain will reconnect and giant cod and pollock will return in the big numbers that once were found.

Elsewhere, we discuss the far-too technical methods that had been and are currently used to allow a passenger-carrying vessel to range far from her port. Remember, the *Starlite* was not operating as a passenger-carrying vessel (meaning that the divers did not pay for the trip!)

I wound up getting lots of very positive publicity out of this effort, of course.

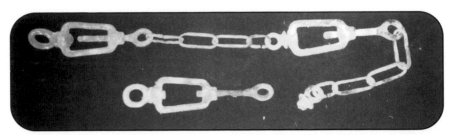

This flower pot tie down is in a cabinet in Diver Bart Malone's home.

All of the dive magazines had feature articles about it, but had we not found the *Andrea Doria*, all that would have resulted was a large expenditure of time, effort and fuel. Sure, we made headlines in many a publication but again, because we were successful. Had I struck out, it all would have been just a waste of time and money.

Okay, at the time, I was licensed to carry passengers up to 50 miles from land. The wreck turned out to be more than 50 miles from shore and because of that, the Coast Guard threatened to revoke my license, and that sure was a very serious matter. But what really was involved was that I wasn't actually carrying "paying passengers," the divers were not charged so technically, I didn't break any laws at all. I hired John Sardin, President of the National Party Boat Owners Alliance, to help me out. Sardin was not a practicing attorney but still he was helpful in the negotiations.

The two of us went to New York to meet with the Coast Guard who really seemed more anxious to get the exact bearings of the wreck than to revoke my license, but I balked because I knew that no other fishing vessel would have the "numbers" that we now had and that the monstrous wreck was mine and mine alone to fish on until someone else with a large boat and a large amount of guts would find it.

But with the passage of time, it came to be that an arrangement took place that took some of the sting out of me because the final decision was to give me the 100 mile "ticket" that I deserved anyway in exchange for me giving the Coast Guard the numbers and coordinates. They simply led me downstairs

First Class dishes from the Andrea Doria.
Photo courtesy Steve Gatto/Museum of New Jersey Maritime History.

and without a test or anything, the commanding officer had his guys give me the 100 mile license right on the spot. In exchange, the location of the *Andrea Doria* became public, ouch!

My boat was only a 65-footer and that was when we made plans to build our first 100-footer. My only competition was Les Behan's 83-foot *Peconic Queen*, but she was a converted wooden Coast Guard boat and not really the right one for such a trip.

When we finally got the new *Viking Star* built and made our first fishing trip to the *Andrea Doria* we blew a piston in her brand new starboard engine and had to bring all 50 passengers in and give them their money back! We had to go to Blount Marine on Rhode Island and get a brand new engine from Detroit installed.

The deal we made for extended mileage distance in exchange for providing details for the location to the Coast Guard took place and we still managed to make lots of trips to the wreck with full boatloads of passengers on board. We clobbered cod and pollock, the wreck was so loaded. Soon, Les Behan bought a converted "crew boat" from the Gulf and he joined me on the wreck. We actually grew quite civil towards each other. He fished it one day and we fished it another, passing each heading back and forth.

Divers John and Evelyn Dudas with lots of gear off the Andrea Doria.

Competition

Way back when, before there was fancy equipment to help find fishing locations, we had to rely on memory, ranges, compass, and at times, luck also. But once any of the more experienced skippers had discovered a good new location, several things took place. For one thing, we wrote as much down as we could, especially about ranges.

If we found a site, we tried to keep it a secret from everyone. For example, Captain Al Lindroth had eleven private spots that he knew contained wrecks that no one else knew about. So whenever he went out, he would only go to one of his wrecks if no other boat was anywhere near him. If he was heading out of Freeport, he was very good about being sure that neither of his biggest competitors were around, like Jay Porter of the *Jess Lu* and Richie Kessinger of the *Starstream*.

It was always that way among the top dogs on the water. Elsewhere, I tell you about the spot that I called "old faithful" and how I kept details about it to myself.

Boats out of Sheepshead Bay, the Atlantic Highlands, etc., were like that and, for that matter, wherever more than two or three boats could be found competing with each other, rivalries were the order of the day.

More About the *Suffolk*

I guess it was around 1965 or so that I put a Loran and side scan sonar system on the *Viking Starlite*. Fishing had slowed down and I decided to go exploring. In fact, I did this often when dad was out fishing and I didn't have enough passengers to make a

Pollock and cod like these are often at the Suffolk.

trip. It's a great feeling to discover a virgin wreck.

Discussed very briefly earlier in this chapter, *The Suffolk Wreck,* I found the *Suffolk,* a place that I don't think had ever been fished before, and it was loaded with huge white hake plus big fat cod and pollock, many between 25 and 45 pounds and some even bigger.

Sunk by a German torpedo in World War II, after locating it, I started making a trip to it once a week. Our regular fare for nearby Cox's Ledge was $12, but for that special trip we charged $20 and instead of sailing at 4:00 a.m., we left two hours earlier. The trips became so popular that I was forced to start making them twice a week.

You only had to be on the wreck for a couple of hours to get all the fish you wanted, it really was unbelievable.

Back in those days our state-of-the-art electronics was a World War II surplus Loran, which was not very accurate. It would get you, in the best-case scenario, within a mile or so of your desired position and that was if the conditions were right and you were really good at using this equipment. It had 50-odd tubes in the set, which were made for aircraft and not for boats as they didn't hold up to the dampness and the saltwater very well, understandably so. You had to stick your head in there to turn the Loran on. It had a big dynamotor that converted the electricity from 12 volts to 110 and of course the lights would go dim on the boat whenever you turned the Loran on. In order to take a reading you had to stick your head tight up to the screen to get away from the light behind you. Then you had a number of procedures to go through. You had to put those "telephone poles" as we called them on the two boxes.

In the next step you had to bring your boxes over and then you had two hills. You had to line up the two hills and then count the different poles that were sticking up and sticking down. The accuracy depended on the user of the machine. When you lifted your head you were basically blind in the sunlight for a while because you had been in this dark machine looking into this tube.

As soon as your eyes cleared up you said to yourself, "Well, now I'm this far and that far and I've gotta' get on this line and then run down the other line." That was the state of the art electronics and you would time yourself until you thought you were getting near the line and then take another bearing. You saved your bearings as much as possible because they drew about 50 amps of current and the 12-volt generators we had on the boat at the time only made 17 amps so you had to be very careful and not take any more bearings than you absolutely needed.

At that time I wound up installing what was considered the best generator.

It came out of an airplane, a twenty-eight volt generator to make 32 volts.

The sonar scanners were state of the art. They were ELAC machines built in Germany and weighed about 250 pounds. They were paper machines that put a pulse out left to right instead of straight down and you could hear a wreck and it sounded the same as in World War II submarine movies. Once you got used to the bonging you could distinguish whether it was a pile of baitfish or dogfish you were looking at. If it was dogfish it would be a harder echo.

A steel wreck had a kind of ring to it and a wood wreck had more of a thud to it. That's the equipment we had and it was considered state-of-the-art at the time. Now of course we have GPS that you leave on all the time. They have accuracy within a couple of feet!

Then, when you got into your area you used sonar to find your wreck. Even if you were there the day before you had to re-find that wreck. Sometimes you could do it within a few minutes and sometimes it took an hour or even more depending on how competent you were with the equipment.

Since I was only in my early twenties I was younger than everyone else. George Glas, Lester Behan and my father were all much senior to me. As the fishing started to slow down at Cox's Ledge I used to take off without passengers on board and go out looking for wrecks, as noted earlier.

I found many of the wrecks that were around by myself and wanted to keep them to myself so that I could control the amount of fish coming off the wrecks and make them live as long as possible. If you take a few fish and leave a few you'll always have fish there but once more boats know the position of a wreck that would be the end of that, one is gonna' outfish the other and that is what eventually happened on the Suffolk wreck.

It was not unusual for me to be chased by other boats wanting to know the location of this wreck and there were a number of ways to protect myself. One of them was if you saw a boat coming you would get off the wreck fast and head right for them putting your sonar right on their sonar thereby knocking out both sonars so that all you could hear was each other. You could not hear the underwater wreck. What you heard was bong, bong, bong, back and forth between the boats.

Some boats had a jamming device that was used in the old AM Radios. It was a Great Lakes Crystal that was inside the radio and if you transmitted on that channel and whistled into the microphone of the radio, no one, yes, no one, could take a Loran reading within about three miles of you. This method was used among some of the hi-line boats up and down the east coast in those days. Anyway, we'd go round and round until the other boat would get tired and leave and go someplace else where he knew he could catch fish and then we would go back to the wreck again. This lasted for a while.

One particular day I saw a boat coming. There was no time to pull the anchor up so I yelled to the mate, "Cut the anchor, cut the anchor off right now." We always had a Dexter knife handy near the anchor line for just such a purpose. The line was cut and we ran at each other and circled each other and he was really close to me, boy, was he close. I thought he "had" the wreck.

I went home that night and called Frank Keating to give him my fishing report. Frank was the writer who wrote the fishing and sport columns for the *Long Island Press*. I told him we cut our anchor line to save the location of my wreck. Then I called my buddy Al Lindroth and told him, "Damn it Al, he was so close; I think he has the wreck." Al commenced to yell in the phone, "Paul," he said, "Let me tell you something. You know a person has your wreck when you see him anchored up on it." Well, to make a long story short, Frank Keating put in the newspaper, "*Viking* Cuts Anchor Line To Save Location Of Secret Wreck." Up until that time I had been sailing special trips to the wreck only once a week and was going to Cox's Ledge the other six days but now I had more people than ever wanting to fish the wreck so I wound up sailing two special trips a week at twenty dollars a head on the *Viking Starlite* at 2:00 a.m. I just couldn't put anymore people on the boat. I was leaving almost as many people standing at the dock as we were carrying.

In those days, we didn't take reservations. That went on for about five weeks. Man, we were really doing it; the fishing was fantastic. Every time I went to the wreck I was being chased down by another boat and I'd have to carry another Captain to cover me because I would be held out over 12 hours and you have to have two Captains aboard if you are out over 12 hours. We'd get back in late. We'd sail at 2:00 a.m., and sometimes we wouldn't get back in until 6:00 p.m. at night but every time we came in we had a big load of large cod and pollock.

"The Hatfield's & The McCoy's"

Other boats were really keen to know where that wreck was, and one day two boats came at me at the same time. I couldn't protect the wreck from two boats at the same time so I went off with one boat but as I did, the other one found the wreck. In the end, all three boats wound up anchoring on the wreck that day. In that particular instance, it was the *Peconic Queen*, the *Helen II*, and the *Viking Starlite*. The *Helen II* was the boat that found the wreck and we got right alongside of her, anchored up and fished the hell out of the wreck that day.

The next day, the three of us went out and fished it again. The day after we did the same thing and the fishing dropped off considerably. Before you knew it, it wasn't worth the effort going out there fishing. The fishing was better at Cox's Ledge. It was over. And that's what happened to the Suffolk wreck between the Hatfield's and the McCoy's. The folks in Montauk referred to the Behan, Glas and Forsberg families as the "Hatfield's and the "McCoy's".

At one point Brad Glas and I wound up rolling around on the ground in the parking lot one morning at sailing time and one other time Jim Behan and I did the same thing in Crisman's Saloon. So that's the story of the Hatfield's and the McCoy's — that's the way it was in those days. You had to protect your fishing grounds and sometimes you couldn't. So the Suffolk and other wrecks that were secret to me for a number of years are all known; they are all public knowledge now. You can buy a chart, you can buy numbers anyplace you want and you can get the exact locations of these fishing areas.

Of course they don't produce the fish that they used to for a number of reasons. The amount of fish that were there in those days are not there at the present time, because of all of the boats that fish these sites just about every day there's good weather.

You have to go out there when you know there hasn't been anyone around for a while and then you might get a mess of fish if you're lucky.

About a year after I cut my anchor line to save the Suffolk wreck the *Peconic Queen* caught it in his anchor line when he was fishing there. He came into port blowing his horn loud and clear with the anchor attached to the anchor line hanging on the bridge on the starboard side of his boat and it hung there for months as a friendly reminder.

Brad Glas of the *Helen II* and I actually became good friends later on and he even helped me by doing some of the wiring for the *Viking Star* when we got her.

At that time, I was quite proud of the equipment I had but soon the *Joseph* Fleet of Captree also put the same kind of scanner we had in, the Laz 17 ELAC side scan sonar — made in Germany of all places. Richie Kessinger and *Captain Al* in Freeport, plus the *Peconic Queen* and *Helen II* in Montauk, did so as well.

Ring Around the *Viking*

When Les first got his super fast and brand new *Peconic Queen*, and because we competed so hard with each other, he set out to show everyone what he had and, of course I was the target. By dumb luck alone, Manny Luftglass was a passenger on the day in question, fortunately, and when I started to tell him the story, he actually made me stop and kept on describing what took place! Briefly, here are the details.

I was underway to Cox's Ledge when the new boat did a complete circle around me from my starboard side so that my passengers could see two things

— a) the new boat sure was pretty and — b) it sure was fast. The "Queen" really was flying.

Captain Behan and I were fierce competitors but that kind of rivalry really doesn't exist much more, simply because of the excellent electronics that are on the market today which let anyone find what formerly were; "military secrets" at one time. I talk highly about Les often and as you may remember, earlier we discussed the heroic rescue effort he did when he pulled fifteen survivors out of the water when the "*Pelican*" turned over out in Montauk.

Before Les got his Newer Boat

The first boat Lester took to Cox's Ledge was the *Joshua B*, which was a converted "A. S. R." (Air-Sea-Rescue) boat and she was a little faster than we were. One day I was with dad and Lester started in ahead of us like he normally did. He got a few miles ahead and suddenly stopped. As we were coming up his mate was on the roof waving a jacket back and forth to attract attention. My father pulled up alongside and asked what was wrong and he was told that the boat had lost steering. Both engines were running fine but the *Joshua B* had no steering. They asked us to get a line on them and steer him back. Since he was fast we wouldn't take much power because he could stay right up with us with us to act as his steering.

My father yelled back, "No problem, get a line ready." As we maneuvered closer to retrieve the towline, Dad forgot about our port engine not having a back-out pin in the propeller shaft and as he put that engine in reverse, bang!, the shaft came out of the coupling and both shaft and propeller hit the rudder. Dad yelled over to Lester, "Be right back, my shaft came out of its coupling." With that said, we went backwards around the *Joshua B*. In a big circle with our other two engines. Once we got to 4-5 knots with water flying over the stern you heard another big bang! Dad stopped the boat and I went into the engine room with a hammer and drove the key back in the coupling and shaft. I will never forget the bewildered look on Captain

Lester's face as we circled around him backwards. When we took the towline and began steering the *Joshua B* back to Montauk, dad made it very clear to me that it is a big ocean, son, so competitors or not, when someone needs your help you give it to them! You never know when you may need their help.

A few months later I was running the *Viking IV* and I got a call from the captain of the *Skipjack* from New London, Connecticut He was fishing in sight of dad that day and asked me, "Why was the *Viking Star* going backwards in a big circle?" He said that he had never seen that boat go that fast going ahead, never mind backwards.

I told him that the shaft came out of the port coupling. He asked, "Why isn't there a pin in the coupling?" Uhh, long story Captain, we'll get to it someday.

And why wasn't there a pin in the coupling? A few weeks before steering the *Joshua B* to Montauk we hit something and broke the propeller shaft. A quick trip to the railway in Greenport to get hauled out and a new shaft did not happen as quickly as expected. Late that Friday night the new shaft arrived and in it went with no time to drill a ½ inch hole for the pin in the shaft. This was in the 1950s and the ½ drills in those days were big and heavy and required more electric power than we had at the Viking Dock in Montauk.

Being in the height of the season, sailing every day, it was over a month before we got a day at the dock to have Cullom from East Hampton come to the boat with his big generator and ½ drill and drill the shaft.

Protecting Your Secrets

This was quite common. Manny told me that one day, his dad was a passenger on the *Rocket* out of Sheepshead Bay and Captain Laddie Martin had taken his passengers to his own private chunk of bottom off of Elberon, N. J. The guys were clobbering porgies but when Laddie saw another boat approaching on the horizon, he ordered all the passengers to not reel any fish in until he said it was okay. Further, he told his customers that if anyone did lift a fish into the boat he was making them stop fishing for the rest of the day.

Now I personally knew Laddie and I sailed with him and he was a great fisherman who went out of his way to be sure to give his customers his very best effort to produce good catches but again, I understand what he did that day.

There are lots of guys who I put into his category. There was Howard Bogan out of Brielle, Al Shinn from Belmar, and John Larson in Barnegat Light, all N. J. Add in Jay Porter, Al Lindroth and Richie Kessinger in Freeport (and me in Montauk).

We were guys who gave it the extra effort and went out on our own time, burning fuel while searching for different wrecks. When we found them, in most cases, they were spots that had never been fished on before. A good amount of them were sunk during World War II such as the Suffolk.

Once you found a virgin wreck, you might fish it but never stay so long that you would pick it clean. If you cleaned it out it might take years for it to get repopulated so the expression I use for this is, "Take a few, leave a few."

Just picture this for yourself. Here's a wreck in the middle of nowhere, lying on mud or sand. It sticks up with all kinds of growth on it, with crabs, mussels and all types of marine growth. It holds lobsters, small and big fish, and when passing fish see such a sight, they will stop and check it out.

If they see the wildlife just discussed, that might be their home for quite a while. Seeing lots of fish will mean that they have arrived in a fish oasis in a desert filled with water. But if the object is void of life, that could mean that something is up and it's time to move on. The spot might hold nothing but trouble for them, trouble in the name of sharks and such. So leaving a few means that newcomers will stop and stick around.

Bottom fishing is far different from surface fishing. Protecting your structure discoveries is self-explanatory, but when fishing for tuna, bluefish and the like, these are fish that are always on the move and there's no harm calling a few friendly competitors on the radio and giving them details about where you are and what you're catching.

The heavyweights are still known for never coming in on time. If you asked someone when guys like Al Lindroth or my dad were coming in the answer would go like this, "You know Al (or Carl); he comes in when he gets in, sometimes before dark and sometimes after dark." If fishing was bad and started to improve, the fishing time was always extended to allow for everyone to bring some fish home. To this day, all of the captain's of *Viking* boats are trained to do this.

Chapter Twelve

1970s

The First Heated Handrail!

Way back in the early 50s, my father was getting on board the boat one morning. I remember it was bitter cold. We were going cod fishing. He grabbed hold of a steel pipe fishing rail on the *Viking V* as he was getting aboard, and his hands kind of like stuck to it. He didn't have gloves on or anything. It was so cold. He looked at that rail. "Dammit," he said, "I sure wish there was some way we could heat that. Wouldn't that be something? By golly, that would be great. If we could heat that pipe rail, you know, that would really be something for winter cod-fishing." Oh, I remembered that and it stuck with me, but it was very far-fetched at the time, as you could imagine. In the 50s, we had a potbelly stove for heat down below in the cabin of the boat, and that's all you had. You put coal in the potbelly stove and you banked it over night in the hope that it would stay going so that you could soak up it's warmth in the morning. If not, you had to build another fire, and that was it. There was one engine in the boat, a World War II surplus 671 Gray Marine, and this we called "modern."

When the *Viking Star* was built in the early 50s, she came to Montauk; 1953 or 1954 I guess it was. We had a potbelly stove on deck in the main cabin. You didn't have to go down below. Well, that also was "modern" technology back then. My father made the rail out of wood when he had the boat built so it wouldn't be so cold in the winter. It was a wooden rail. There were no pipe rails like most of the other boats had.

So, in 1970 when I contracted to build the *Viking Star* I said, "Damm it, we got to have a heated rail somehow, we have to heat that rail." I mentioned it to Blount Marine, the architects up stairs, and they kind of looked at me you know, with a funny look on all their faces. "You know Paul, by the time the water gets around that 100-foot long boat wrapping around the stern and back to the other end, it will have traveled 225 feet or so. That water is going to be hot on one end and cold on the other."

Well, I had a good friend I grew up with whose name was Wally Drobecker. I got to know Wally when I first moved to Montauk. We grew up and went to school together. We hunted together and so forth. We raised our kids a couple of block apart from each other. His wife and mine were good friends and we always went out as a group. He used to have a charter boat when I had the *Viking IV*, but he switched his profession and went into the plumbing business with a friend of his who became his partner. Well, Wally and I remained very good friends all our lives. So when the four of us went out to dinner one night, the same subject came up. "How the hell am I going to heat this rail, Wally?" And he'd get so mad at me. "You know," he said, "I haven't been able to sleep lately. You've got me going with this damn heated rail, Paul. How the hell are we going to do this?" So we kept working on it mentally, and talking about it, and he kept asking questions.

Finally, we spoke to the architects at Blount Marine where they were building the boat. When it came time to put the handrail on the boat, we got them to run it down into the deck of the engine room floor opening so that we could split the water. Instead of going all the way around the boat, we could go half way around the boat; half way around the stern and up to amidships, back down to the engine room, half way around the bow and back down amidships, and back into the engine room. We put the furnace in the engine room and hooked it up with hot water. We had hot water heat throughout the boat, which was very modern at the time, and we had our heated fishing rail. Well, we had a few things to do with the rail to get it straightened out. Number one, we couldn't have it the same temperature as in the cabin where you're using it to heat the air in the cabin, because it would have been too hot. In cold weather you're hands would stick to that rail and pull the skin off, so we had to have a flow valve in there and adjust the temperature so we could get it down to about 110 degrees, which was just about right. When we put the heated rail in, of course, we advertised it and that was big news.

After I built the *Viking Star*, some other guys were starting to have boats built out of aluminum down at Gulfcraft in Louisiana by Scott Tibbs, a real nice guy. I never did build a boat with him. I did convert a boat with him later on, but he came out to see me one day. He asked me if he could go down in the engine room and see how Wally hooked up this heated rail. He was building a boat for New Jersey, the *Miss Belmar* for Captain Al Shinn, and he wanted to install a heated rail. It was very new and he was eager to have one.

Everybody was talking about the heated rail on the *Viking Star*, how great it was. So he came down and he saw the system, and he put one in Al Shinn's boat. Quite a few boats along the coast also had them installed, and that was the beginning of the heated rail. It was invented on the *Viking Star* in 1970. I'm sorry to say that my good friend Captain Wally Drobecker passed away on September 9, 2012.

C. I. A.

One day, in the mid-70's, Captain Frank Mundus found a spot that held loads of codfish and since sharks were what he mainly fished for, he wasn't concerned about sharing details of this spot.

Frank was drifting for shark bait that day, using jigs to catch ling and whiting for live bait. But a few of his customers started coming up with big codfish! He came to the dock with these cod and told me and later, a few other people about it. He gave me the general directions and probably gave the other fellows the same details. He didn't have any accurate numbers on the spot; he just knew approximately where it was.

I was fishing at Cox's Ledge every day that summer as were several other boats. It was mid-season and we were too busy to go searching for Mundus' spot. Sometimes that fall a few other boats went out and looked for the spot that Mundus had told us about. I went out one night with just a mate and we zigzagged back and forth with my sonar scanner on and we found a chunk of hard bottom.

We stopped and lost a couple of rigs in it so we knew we had hard bottom while drifting so I figured that I had found the site. I thought it was just one little spot but later learned that the area around it was a mile or so in diameter of good bottom. It was broken up hard bottom, not all good, productive stuff, but still, a good place to remember and I recorded its site for the future.

One Saturday I was offshore with the *Viking Star* with a good crowd of customers and we were fishing a wreck called the *Ranger*. I guess I had fished it pretty hard that season because there weren't many fish on it. My customers managed a modest catch of pollock and cod, and a few hake as well.

The day was very foggy and was coming to an end but I really wanted to put my customers into some better action. On the way back to Montauk, I decided to stop on the new location and try a drift or two.

I noticed a couple of boat targets on my radar in the fog and didn't pay too much attention to them, but I didn't want to hit them either. I thought that one may have been a lobster boat and maybe the other a dragger, but didn't think that another fishing boat could be on the spot that I thought was mine alone.

I stopped on the spot I was looking for, maybe three quarters of a mile from one of the other boats, and went outside. "Let the lines go, guys," I said. I didn't blow the horn or anything, thinking it best to be quiet. The other boat out there may have recognized the sound of my horn and he might rat me out to my competitors. I wanted to keep this spot secret.

We were in black, drippy fog. You couldn't see fifty feet in front of you but we started catching codfish pretty good. "Wow," I said, "If we stay here and the fish keep biting we could probably make it into a good trip and bail out of this disastrous day we've got going."

Well, lo and behold the fog cleared up and nearby, there was the *Marlin V* with Captain Richard Rade on board as well as Willie Butler on the *Lazy Bones*!

The three of us were looking at each other when all of a sudden Willie starts laughing on the radio. He's laughing so hard you had the feeling that he was rolling around on the wheelhouse floor. He couldn't say anything for a while and finally he got up and said, "You know what? This top-secret spot, nobody knows the other guys have — the fog clears up and the three of us are here, looking at each other. This is some secret place alright!"

He managed to stop laughing long enough to say that there was only one name appropriate for that place; that "top secret" place that we all thought no one knew about, and he called it the C. I. A. Grounds!

The C. I. A. Grounds are west of "Cartwright" and south by southwest of Montauk.

Tile Fishing

One day Captain John Larson got blown in on the *Miss Barnegat Light* (changed later to *Captain John.*) He had been tile fishing down in the Hudson Canyon, and then he went up to the Fishtail, also known as Block Canyon.

The *Miss Barnegat Light* at sea.

He caught some tilefish there but then got caught in a storm and was blown into Montauk. So he tied up at my dock and walked into my office. We had a cup of coffee together. Sitting there I said to him, "Boy, I don't know what the heck I'm going to do, John. This cod fishing business really stinks. There are not many cod fish around. Business is bad. I'm twelve thousand dollars in the hole." Man, that was an awful lot of money at that time, a lot of money. I said, "I don't know how the hell I'm going to pay my bills." He said, "Hey, go tile fishing."

My Start With Tile Fishing

Party boat fishing really fell off, especially cod fishing. Big giant monster foreign trawlers from just about every country were raping our shores, everywhere from twelve miles out, depleting our cod fish stocks. That made things tough for us in the wintertime, because we weren't doing much business since there were very few fish. And no fish *equals* no people! At best, we might produce 25 to 35 fish a day on the boats on weekend days. During the week it was hard to even get enough customers to sail with. Captain Chuck Willer ran the *Viking Star* for cod.

Taking John's advice, I soon converted the *Viking Starlite* over to use for tilefish.

"Hell, I said, I don't know where I'm going to get gear to go tile fishing. I don't know anything about it. I've got to rig up and I don't want to take the *Viking Star* out of the passenger business. Business is slow but there is some

Here's a fine tilefish caught on hook and line.

on the weekends. I'd have to take the *Starlite*." Well, the *Starlite* was 65-foot long, the same as the *Captain John* but the *Captain John* was steel and the *Viking Starlite* was wood, although probably the best built wooden party fishing boat on the coast. She was a good sea boat, very heavy and strong but not very fast. Well anyway, we rigged her up with some kind of a hydraulic rig that didn't work very well as a hauler. We bought some gear, got it rigged and went out tile fishing. It was tub trawling then before long lining was invented.

We coiled the line and hooks up in tubs, the same ones that were used with a washboard for laundry. They were about three feet in diameter and a foot high. It was a half-mile of line (actually Venetian blind cord) to a tub, a hook every 12 feet. We baited each of 250 hooks and coiled it into a tub and placed as many as ninety tubs of gear into a big walk-in freezer. Circle hooks hadn't been invented yet so we used standard "J" hooks.

Baiting the hooks became a separate issue though as more and more boats got into tile fishing. I tell you lots more about this when I talk about the Saint Patty's Day Fiasco elsewhere. We had these tubs tied together, one behind the other and set them out with an anchor on one end and an anchor on the other end with a buoy. We had three to four tubs of gear spread out over a space of a mile and a half to two miles with a buoy anchored in the middle. That way if one end or the other parted off, we could get to the middle buoy and retrieve our gear. This happened quite a bit because the line that we were using was rejected Venetian blind cord all just thrown into a box. We'd buy it in monstrous 4-foot by 4-foot boxes. It was just as it came off the machine but they'd get a strand here and there out of the machine that they couldn't use for Venetian blinds and we would buy it cheap and rig it up and use it as the backbone for the tilefish gear. The only problem was that the backbone wasn't that strong since it was rejected string so we had to be careful. In rough weather you parted off a lot and there'd go the buoy, and it was a real pain in the neck. As a matter of fact, if you had too many big tilefish on it, you were parted off pulling it up. Tilefish big? There weren't any little ones. They were monsters and there were plenty of them. The *Viking Starlite* was the first boat to be tub trawling tilefish from out of Montauk; no one out of there had done this before.

Everybody fished around the Hudson. The furthest east they went once in a while was to Block Canyon.

We could put out as many as thirty tubs a day and stayed out for three days, meaning that we would wind up using ninety tubs on a trip. On a good outing, we could produce as many as eighteen to twenty thousand pounds of tilefish. But it sure was hard work. Hydraulics in those days wasn't what it is now. We would have to manually help pull the gear up in the worst of weather and both boat and crew weren't designed for that amount of work. Hauling off the bow was tough going. We pushed the fish down the deck of the boat past the side doors of the cabins. We filled shopping carts to move some of the fish and dumped all of them into a pile on deck in the stern and cover them with canvas. It was so cold that the fish would stay there just fine.

The gear would come up and there'd be 10 to 15 fish floating in front of the boat that came off of the hooks as the lines were being pulled up. We'd be gaffing them while hauling the gear. With a small amount of gear we were putting 5000-6000 pounds a day onto the *Viking Starlite*.

We couldn't come into Montauk because there wasn't any place to pack up the fish in the middle of the winter. All the commercial boats in Montauk were draggers for yellow tail flounder and they were going to New Bedford; they weren't shipping any fish to New York. The places that packed out fish in Montauk were closed for the winter. So, I had to go to Newport, Rhode Island.

I went to the Paris Condoles Dock. They were nice people and treated me well. My good friend Phil Rule Sr. of the *Audrey Lynn*, one of the top swordfish men on the coast, recommended them to me. "They'll take good care of you" he said, and he was right. After unloading, we'd get some guys to bait our tubs up once more and wait out the weather so that we could go out and do it all over again!

A Key Change of Bait

While I was in Newport, Rhode Island we used to use skimmer clams as bait for tilefish. The problem with that was you had to open the damn clams before you cut them up to use them for bait.

There were a lot of boats in Newport, Rhode Island that were dragging blue back herring.

They put them in barrels and shipped them to the market at a very low price. So I bought a barrel of herring and tried baiting up the gear with it, and boy, it worked beautifully, wow, that was great. That caught them better than the clams and we didn't have to open them. We just had to cut them and put them on a hook. We'd get two or three baits out of each herring.

One of Many Bad Days at Sea

So, off we went and one day we were way off shore down around Vetches Canyon with a good load of fish on. We'd been fishing hard two days and we headed back in. The weather reports in those days weren't as good as they are now, and we didn't know it, but boy up came a Northwester and it blew 50. We were in 75-85 fathoms of the water, and I want to tell you something, it gets rough out there in that depth of water, especially for a 65-foot boat that was not built to have 10,000 pounds of tilefish on the deck. We never even iced them; we just packed them on the freezing cold deck. The spray and the cold air temperature kept the fish chilled down. Once in awhile, if it was a sunny day we would throw a tarp over them otherwise we just left them in the cold, open air.

We were planning on coming into Newport, and, boy, we got into some rough weather. It was rough as the daylights, really rough, and I said to myself, "Boy, this is no place for this boat, not with this load on deck." I looked down at my son, Steven. He was lying on the floor of the wheelhouse trying to sleep, sliding back and forth on the floor. I said to myself, "I hope that the last thing I see isn't my son drowning alongside of me. This is really nasty." We took on a couple of heavy seas. I was afraid to go down below to see if there was any damage to the cabin. I wasn't worried about the hull but I was concerned about the cabin of the boat. We had water flying all over. I couldn't let the wheel go. I had to steer. It was the first time I felt comfortable about seeing foreign trawlers because once we got into the 45 curve outside Cox's' Ledge, there they were — most of them Russian, East German, and Polish. There was a gang of them fishing and dragging. "Gee, now I feel better." I said to myself, "I got other boats around." Of course, I was small enough to be their dory, for crying out loud, but at least I felt comfortable that there were other boats there too.

We made it into Newport, packed out our fish and headed back to Montauk baiting the gear on the way back. We figured out a way to keep the baited gear useable if we had to wait a few days for weather. We would put it in the freezer; freeze it right in there with the tubs. We used round, galvanized washtubs, and they held a half mile of gear perfectly.

I came in one day from Newport and there was the *Captain John* tied up at the Viking Dock. I was totally surprised but there he was. John Larson was aboard the boat and I go up and say, "Hey John, what are you doing here? The weather's fine." And he says, "You've been catching some fish, right?" I said, "Nah, we've only been catching a few tile. We're not doing that good John." He said, "Baloney." He says, "I know what goes into New York and they're coming out of Newport, Rhode Island, and you're the only one packing tilefish there." "Paul," he said, "This is a small industry. You're not going to get away with anything. You've been catching a helluva load of fish, and now you've got company. I'm here to help you." Well, I couldn't get away with catching all those fish because now I know the rest of the fleet was going to start coming up too, and they soon did.

After a while, so many other boats got into commercial tile fishing, reducing the stocks and making the "baiters" even more independent, that I decided to let Chuck Willer stay up north with the *Viking Star* for cod and my sons Paul, Steven, and I took the *Viking Starship* down to Key West for several years to fish the Tortugas Banks. At the end of the third year "long-line" tile fishing was invented. This was altogether a different style than we had used before. Instead of nylon line in washtubs, it was cable on a hydraulic driven drum. The drum held twenty miles of cable. There was a snap at on the other end of each hook (circle hooks by then) and after you baited the hook you snapped it onto the cable as you were setting it all out. When you hauled it back in you unsnapped the hook and if there was a fish on, you threw it to a mate; if it was a bare hook you just put it into a basket in front of you. We moved the captain's steering and control station down on deck so that the captain could run the boat up on the gear and unsnap the gear at the same time. This made us lots more efficient and we could bait the hooks at sea. We had one person baiting the hooks all day long, allowing us to make up two sets a day with thirty-five to forty miles of gear out, depending on the weather. That was quite different from setting fifteen miles of fixed gear. We were more than doubling a set and with circle hooks, it was more efficient a system, they caught better than the J hooks did.

This system worked so well, and so many other boats were doing the same thing, that we started cleaning the fisheries out and using our big, two engine boat was too expensive what with how much fuel we burned on these very long outings that I finally decided to stop it altogether. It would take a week of steam-cleaning to just take the stink out of the boat and to use the boats for both headboat and tile fishing was impossible because to passenger-fish, we had to put all of the seating back into the boat each time.

R. I. P. Captain John Larson, My Good Friend

John Larson and I remained good friends right up until his death. He had a heart problem with three bad valves in his heart. The prognosis wasn't good but his only alternative was to have an operation. We had a good, long talk two days before his surgery. We had a great visit on our cell phones talking about the good old days, the old times when we tile fished together and so forth until the battery in my cell phone went dead. I'm so glad I had a chance to talk to him because he didn't make it. He was a good friend and I miss him.

One of the things we talked about was when he was in Montauk during the winter in February or March, and Montauk Lake was partially frozen. And we're going out and it was blowing northwest. We always left on the backside of a Northwester. We let her blow Northwest for a day or two and just as soon as the clouds started to thin out a little bit, that meant it was time to leave, take the Northwester out, keep it on your hiney, right on your stern to help push you out there. By the time you got there the next morning, theoretically it would be nice and calm, and ready to fish, but at least it was fishable. Well, I was going out and John yells at me; he calls me on the radio and he says, "I've got a little problem."

"What's the matter John?"

Towed Out to Sea

He said, "I won't be able to go. My keel coolers are frozen. We forgot to put antifreeze in the engines and the keel coolers on the bottom of my boat are frozen. I don't know what the hell I'm going to do but I can't get circulation. The engines are overheating." "Damm it John," I said, "You're going to be here for a month if you stay in. (The water temperature was 26-27 degrees, cold enough to freeze the salt water.) You're frozen solid. You're lucky you didn't already break them. You can't stay here. Get a line ready, I'll pull you out to the gas buoy outside Montauk. The water temperature there is always above 35 degrees and what the hell, the further you get off shore the better off you'll be. Before you know it we'll be in 40 degree water and they'll thaw right out."

He agreed to it and we put a line on him. I got him out the inlet and boy, the Northwest was blowing a bloody gale; and we're crashing and slamming, and the rope he had wasn't that good. It was only a half- inch anchor line that he hadn't used in a long time and it was coming apart. If it snapped, we'd have to go back and grab him quick before he wound up crashing on the beach or on the jetties. All we had to do was get past Shagwam and then the wind would be broad side. Once we turned to the lighthouse it would be just aft the beam and once we passed the lighthouse it would be right on our stern and we would coast right out. But if I lost him before that and he didn't have any power, he would drift right up onto the beach.

I finally got my own anchor line out and grabbed hold of him. About the fourth round of this line-breaking we got him going and were moving along. We got to the lighthouse and we were just making the turn and the wind was on the stern. John called me on the radio and says, "Hey Paul, there's something wrong with this." I said, "Now what the hell is wrong?" I was quite nervous. Since it was my idea it would be my responsibility if we wound up on the beach. I also didn't want to see him lose the boat because of me. "Well," he says, "You know, I often heard of boats being towed in from the fishing grounds, but this is the first time I've heard of a boat being towed out to the fishing grounds." I said to him, "Don't you forget it. I'll never let you forget it, that's for sure." And I know he didn't. To make a long story short, as soon as he got to warmer water, his keel coolers cleared up and he was off and I was off and we went fishing. We kept in contact on the radio and we caught about the same. We both had good trips, we loaded up.

There were a lot of tile fishing boats then, about eight or nine or so. One was John's partner, Captain Lou Puskas, who was the inventor of tub trawling tile fishing. And then I came along and a bunch of other boats got in on it too. My boat was the furthest east out of Montauk. Everybody else was in New Jersey. But for years afterward, anytime I bumped into anybody and John Larson's name came up, I'd say, "Hey, next time you see John tell him you met the guy that towed him out to the fishing grounds. Not in, we towed him out." John always got a kick out of it because different salesmen and various people in the business would always run into him and say; "Hey, there's this guy out there from Montauk who says he towed you out to the fishing grounds." He immediately knew who they were talking about and would always come back with the remark, "How's Paul doing?"

Moving the *Miss Barnegat Light*

John Larson and I remained real good friends. When he built the *Miss Barnegat Light*, his aluminum catamaran, I also became very interested in catamarans. I went down to Louisiana with John and helped him bring the boat up to Barnegat, New Jersey. I wanted to ride on the boat to see how it was. She was built by Breaux, who had become the Cadillac builder of the south, as far as I am concerned. The boat was just beautiful. In fact, they had to put a third coat of varnish on the trim in the cabin, and they were a day late in doing it. We wanted to leave but they wouldn't let us leave until they finished that third coat of varnish. That's how particular that yard was. They were an expensive yard, but gee, they had good workmanship on their boats.

Well, *Miss Barnegat Light* wasn't as fast as she should have been. She had two 500 horsepower Caterpillars, and they turned out to probably be the worst engines Caterpillar ever built. They just weren't good engines. They made a V8 and V12 series and there was a lot of trouble with both of them. They stopped making them right after that. They didn't deliver enough horsepower and she couldn't get up to get away from herself. If a catamaran can't get up on plane it's no good in any kind of a sea because the tunnel between the hulls fills up with water, and the slamming on the bottom of the tunnel from the water hitting the bottom of the deck makes it very uncomfortable. Besides, you're dragging all that water with you and because you're not going very fast the fuel efficiency is terrible. You have to have enough horsepower to get that boat up and away from herself. Drop the water out of the tunnel and then it's great.

The catamaran is a boat that is square with big deck space, a lot of room, ideal for a party boat. You can get a lot of people on it for fishing, but you have to get her up and get her to go fast. It's a stable boat also, nice big cabin, but not excellent in a head sea. John had an old saying, if an architect ever tells you the tunnel is high enough in a catamaran, fire him and get a different architect, because the tunnel is never high enough. John was well experienced and he should know.

But anyway, I rode up on the boat with John. He was very nervous. He had no money and was over-budget. What else is new when you're building a boat? John said something like, "We can't make a mistake. I don't have any money. I can't bend up propellers. I can't bend up shafts or anything. We can't make an error. I'm broke. I'll be lucky to get this boat to New Jersey." We had to be extra careful, double-think the other guy all the way up. Our crew was made up of John, a few mates, plus me and one of John's sons. We took turns operating the boat. We didn't have the modern technology we have now; we didn't have GPS or anything. We had the old Loran and it wasn't that accurate. We had one line that was good, but we just had to use common sense. We had water come up the exhaust to one engine and fill the engine up. John wouldn't let me use the hacksaw blade trick on it for fear of losing his warrantee.

We were going into Clearwater Beach, Florida to pick up John's wife and younger children who were going to meet us and then take the ride through Lake Okeechobee and on up to New Jersey. Marion, his wife, a lovely woman, was there with the kids. As we were coming in, we had to go through this very narrow old bridge (now it's a new higher bridge, very wide). So there we were with a brand new catamaran with one working engine and one engine dead, dragging a propeller on the broken-down starboard engine. She wouldn't steer very well. The side that the dead engine was on wouldn't turn so this meant that the boat would barely turn to port. Well, we had to get that boat perfectly lined up in front of that bridge. I had to stand out on the bridge telling John how much room we had on each side. I stood on the port side because he could hardly turn to port and I wanted him as close to the bridge as he could get to that side. He could turn to starboard and if he got too close I could just motion to him to move a bit more to starboard. That was the narrowest bridge I've ever seen for a boat with one engine. I didn't have two feet along my side of the boat but we came through without touching the bridge. I couldn't believe it. When we got to the dock John looked at me, I looked at him. We tied up that night and he said, "I need a drink," and pulled out the bottle of Scotch, (that's what he drank at the time). Boy, he needed that for sure.

We had Caterpillar people come down and get the water out of the engine. We had water up the exhaust because the exhaust came through the inside of the hulls in between the hulls under the deck. It sounded like a good idea to have the exhaust come between the two hulls and it would be a good idea if the boat could get up and get away from itself but when the boat was down in the water and that tunnel filled up with water, nosirree! If I remember right I think we shut down one engine because it had a plugged up fuel filter and that's why the water went right up into the engine. He has since redirected the exhaust out the stern. Anyway, later on John got Mercedes Benz 331 engines installed and then *Miss Barnegat Light* became a real good boat for a while. She got up and flew at 23-24 knots. In my opinion those 331 M. T. U. engines were to become the worst engines ever built in the world, unfortunately we didn't know it at the time.

Chapter Thirteen

1970s

The Mid 1970s

Viking Starship **and Engine Problems**

In 1976, I decided to build the *Viking Starship*. We launched her in 1977 right after Labor Day. I wanted to put the big Cummins KA2300 in the *Starship* and I was all lined up to do it because I liked the engine better. John had just installed brand new MTU's in his boat and was already bragging about how fast the *Miss Barnegat Light* could go, and how nicely the engines were performing. Of course, he didn't yet have any hours on the engines. I wasn't comfortable with the MTU's and didn't care for displacement for the horsepower. But dammit, Cummins wouldn't back me up. We were building a new boat. We ran short of money and the engines were $150,000 for the pair. I had $75,000 I said, "You know, can you work with me, hold a mortgage for that other engine for a year, that's all. Let me get going and I can pay you off." But they wouldn't do any financing. They just said, "No, we feel if you don't have enough money to pay for the engines up front, we don't want to do business with you." At that time Cummins didn't offer any financing. They all do it now. Caterpillar has a program, Cummins, Detroit, they all have financing now.

Engine Nightmares Continue

I had a partially finished boat with no engines. Money ran out. The bank didn't have all the money they promised to give us and here we were. But MTU was there and they gave me an offer. "We'll help you out Paul. You buy your engines from us and we'll hold the $75,000. Don't worry about it." So I wound up with new MTU's on the boat. Well, they got me out of a dilemma, but what a horrible, horrible engine. These engines were designed to be in tanks converted for the marine market. They were brought to America and a lot of them were taken to the Gulf for the oil industry to be used as fast crew boats running guys out to the oil wells. When they first brought them in they were the lightest engines for the horsepower in the world. Wow, everyone thought that was wonderful. A lot of horsepower, not much weight. But once you got over 1,000 hours or so on those engines, things started to happen and boy, did they happen. It was constant, constant. Parts were very dear. One starter was $5,000, one manifold $5,000. If you slowed the engine down too fast, you cracked the manifold. It was nothing but problems over and over and over again. The engines leaked oil and did they smoke! When you started them up they smoked so bad you could gag a maggot! Oh boy, they were terrible. What a mess, a slimy mess in the engine room, you just couldn't keep up with them. If something happened to one engine within a few hours the same thing would happen to the other one. It was just amazing. If the water pump seal started to leak in one engine, sure enough, within a day or two the other one would start leaking. It was a nightmare with those engines. I sure didn't get much sleep with them.

Finally, for no reason at all, a little hole blew in a piston. Luckily, it was during the winter. And of course there wasn't any money. I sat down with a young man who had grown up with my son Steven in Montauk. His name was Andy. Andy was our mechanic at the time. I said, "Okay Andy, let's see what the parts are going to cost. You tell me how long it's going to take you and me in this engine room to rebuild these two engines, because I know if we just blew one piston, we're going to blow one in the other engine real soon. We have to rebuild both engines." He came back a couple days later and we sat down together. He showed me the parts list and all, and then he said, "You know, this is going to cost a lot of money. It is going to take us two months to rebuild these engines. They're like watches, everything is so intricate; everything's tough to get at. You know Paul; you ought to consider putting other engines in the boat. You never were happy with these engines, and you're most certainly not going to be happy even after we rebuild them."

At the time, M. T. U. Engines smoked so bad when they were cold that the Montauk yacht club wouldn't allow a boat that had an MTU 331 engine in it to dock there because of the awful smoke they would throw while being started in the cold. The engines were lighter than normal and that made them attractive to boat owners but no one really expected the maggot-gagging smoke that the engines would throw. Once then warmed up, they weren't so bad but the morning cold start-up? Bad-real bad!

Fixing the Engine Problems

So with that I talked to John Larson. He decided he had to have them because that was the only engine that would make his catamaran go. The Becker boys sold their boat, "*Tampa*" which had MTU's on it. In fact, most of the boats down in Louisiana were having trouble with those particular engines. They were pulling them out. John's boat was also having a lot of breakdowns. It wound up that he owed MTU quite a bit of money for parts. Warrantees ran out on the engines so I decided to have a talk with John. "You know," I said, "I'm looking at that 3412 Caterpillar. It's only 600 horsepower but that's all I need on *Viking Starship*. We don't go fast anymore anyway; we can't afford it with the high price of fuel. My competition, the fast *Peconic Queen*, isn't in business anymore so I don't have to worry about him running past me. I'm going to see if I can get these Caterpillars in the boat but I don't have any money." Well, after talking on the phone for a few nights John and I put things together. Finally he talked with his Caterpillar people in Philadelphia where he bought his engines for his commercial boats, and we put a deal together with them. I had almost enough money for one engine but I needed a pair. John said that he would pay "x" amount of dollars to Caterpillar at the end of the season as payment for my MTU's, and that was enough money to cover my second Caterpillar engine. In the meantime the MTU's would be stored in a tractor-trailer in a trailer park at Caterpillar so he could run there and get parts whenever he needed them during the season. Boy, I couldn't believe we put this thing together. Here we had two brand new Caterpillars being delivered with very little money. I forget the exact amount, but it was less than it cost for one engine, and John had his parts. For an example, he owed MTU a crankshaft, and a crankshaft was $25,000. Well, I would have loved to have seen MTU's face when he handed them a crankshaft instead of $25,000. Cylinder heads cost $2,000 apiece. There were twelve of them on each engine, one per cylinder, and they cracked quite a bit for no apparent reason, just cracked. Anyway, another guy and I tore the MTU's out of the boat in Montauk, cut a hole in the deck, got a crane and loaded them onto a truck. I got my two sons, Steven and Paul, to tow me over to Thames Shipyard in New London, Connecticut where I planned to install the engines. I called them ahead of time, told them what I was doing, and they said "Fine Paul, you bring the boat over here." We did business with them all the time. I brought the boat over and the owner of the shipyard, John **Wronowski** walked on board and looked around. "Well, you know what," he said. "You broke a record. This is the first time I've ever had a boat come in here with no engines. I've had them come in here with broken engines, or two engines and one not running, but this boat has no engines, just a big hole here." I said, "Yeah, I left them in Montauk." I told him what we did and he shook his head and said, "Unbelievable."

That's when a friend of mine, John Wadsworth, the owner of the *Sunbeam* fleet, stepped in to help me. I had known him for a lot of years. He is a fisherman out of Waterford, Connecticut, the town next to New London. I stayed at his house and it was great. I had a free bed and thought I'd be there for maybe a couple of weeks but I was there for two months. The engines were delivered onto the *Starship's* stern and I took my time, sliding them in the back door.

My sons were tile fishing with the *Star* and the *Starlite*, and I started working alone. I got the engines down, got them on the bed and hooked them up to the transmissions. I was working every night until about 9:00 or so. One night around 9:00, I hear this BOOM, this banging on the deck. I look up and here comes John Wronowski, the owner of the yard. "Well," he said "We just got the fittings for the exhaust, Paul. We got the L's and the elbows and stuff here." Then he drops a 12-pack of beer. "I'm willing to bet you that we can have these pieces all tacked together on these engines for the welders in the morning before you and I have that 12-pack of beer gone. What do you think?" "Alright with me John," I replied. Well, we worked until midnight. The 12-pack of beer was long gone and we were still putting the damn exhaust together. But we got it done well past midnight and the next morning the welders came down, welded it up into place and it is there today.

New Caterpillars and then the Long Ride

I had to make an offshore trip to George's Banks two days from then and I needed the money real bad. The Coast Guard came down and took a ride with me on the boat up and down the Thames River to make sure everything was okay. The inspector said, "You really going all the way to George's Banks with this boat tomorrow?" "Yeah, I sure am," I replied, "I've got a crew coming across on the ferry." Three or four Irish exchange students that work for us every year were there with scrub brushes, mops, and detergent. There was a mess inside from changing the engines, and they were scrubbing the boat down. I had all the extra left over stuff that I had to bring back to Montauk up in the bow of the boat.

The girls did their job well and I left for Montauk with the Coast Guard inspector shaking my hand, saying "Well, good luck to you. That's a helluva way to break in new engines, 100 miles each way." "Well, they've got to be broken in sooner or later," I said, "And that's the way to do it, I guess." When we got to Montauk and there was a crowd of anglers already standing on the dock, waiting to put their gear on the boat. The girls got off as the fuel man came to fuel us up. A couple of the crew members walked aboard getting ready to put the bait on. One of the regular customers yelled over, "Hey Captain, when can we get on the boat?" "Just as soon as we get all that stuff off the bow of the boat," I said. "That big pile of steel, exhaust fittings and so forth. We gotta' make room for everybody up there." "Well, we can help you with that," he said. So, by golly, three or four of our customers formed an assembly line and pulled that stuff off the boat real quick. I hugged my wife, went home, got out of my filthy, greasy clothes and took a shower. I was worn out but after I got cleaned up, I went back and finished getting the boat ready. We sailed a few hours later. We went to George's Banks, with two brand new Caterpillar engines in the *Viking Starship*, and those 3412s remain in that boat today. They're the best engines we've ever owned. I don't know how many times we've overhauled them, but I know the first overhaul was 30,000 hours and the most we got out of the MTU's were 10,000 with a lot of troubles in between. But we did 30,000 on those Cats and we've been in the 20s ever since, every time we have to overhaul. They've been really fine engines. And that's how John Larson and I got through the engine dilemma with MTU and Caterpillar. John changed over later on, when Caterpillar came out with a 3412 that pushed up to 1400 horsepower with major changes. Basically the same block that's in the *Viking Starship* is in the *Miss Barnegat* today. Before John passed away he told me he was very happy with them and the boat was performing well. That was the end of the MTU's for him — he got rid of them. There are very few of those engines left in America and the poor people that have them wish they didn't, I guarantee you that.

Well, now I had the *Viking Starship* and a big mortgage. I got the boat after Labor Day, of course, after the season was over. That put us behind the eight ball, and the boat wasn't quite finished. We didn't even have heat in it. I had to put that in during the winter, the first winter between tile fishing. I wound up converting the 100 foot steel *Viking Star* to tile fishing. Now I had a real good boat on demand.

We used to stack the fish on deck with her too. She held 20,000 pounds from the side door to the back of the cabin on each side, 10,000 a side, that's what she held. We were tub trawling. Captain Chuck Willer was running the *Viking Starship* for me, cod fishing, and we were tile fishing with the *Viking Star*. When I was ashore I was working on the *Starship* still finishing the boat.

You Do What You Gotta' Do

We fished. The bigger the boat, of course, the worse the weather you could fish in and we definitely went out in all the worst kinds of weather. The bigger the mortgage, the worse the weather seemed. One day we were in a blazing snowstorm along on the backside of a Northwester. We're setting gear and I didn't think anybody else was out. I had the radio on but I didn't hear anybody and couldn't see anything on the radar through the snow. You couldn't see any distance even if there was anybody there. I didn't pay any attention to radar anyway; it was just about useless. I was more or less paying careful attention to where I was putting the gear, working this edge, when all of a sudden I look up and there's the *Vivian*. Donny Meyers on the *Vivian* was directly ahead of me and he must have looked up and saw me at the same time as I saw him. Luckily he turned right and I turned right, and we just missed each other. To this day I don't know how we did it but we got clear. We never even got the gear tangled, believe it or not. He was setting gear toward me; and I was setting gear going towards him. I thought for sure we were going to get tangled, so did he, but we never did. I was so thankful we missed each other I wouldn't have cared if the gear got tangled or not. Anyway, he called me on the radio and said, "Dammit Paul, what the hell are you doing here? I thought I was all alone." "Don," I said, "I thought I was all alone. What are you doing here?"

He says, "I've got a mortgage payment. I've got to make some money."

I answered, "Well, so do I. Now I guess we both know why we're here." Well, we were the only two boats there and making jokes about almost hitting each other. We caught the hell out of the tilefish. Donny was a good fisherman too, a hard fisherman. He put a lot of time in and got the hang of it real good. People always ask me what's the roughest you've ever had, the worst weather? It's hard to say what the roughest was, but like most fishermen; I've been in some really horrific weather.

Worst Weather Ever

We were coming in from tile fishing on the one particular trip. We had a good load of fish on, too. We had three days of fishing in and we were pushing 25,000, almost 30,000 pounds on the *Viking Star*, and it was really blowing, a snowstorm was blowing northeast and it got worse and worse and worse. We were making ice pretty good. All of a sudden I heard "BANG." The mate hollered through the hole in the floor of the wheelhouse (that was my coffee hole; the one used to pass up my coffee) "We just blew a window in on the starboard side. Everything is floating in the cabin here, water all over the place." "Dammit," I thought as I slowed her down. I turned her around putting the starboard side to the leeward and thinking, "What am I going to use to plug up that broken window?"

I let the boat drift and I went down below. The whole cabin was filled up with tubs of gear. Well, when we fish three days we average 30 tubs a day, so we had 90 washtubs of gear in the cabin of the *Viking Star*. We took all the seating out so we could have more room. We just left the galley clear. When we ate we used the gear as seats. 90 tubs of gear were hard to walk around. Well, all this stuff was a mess in the cabin. Everything was wet and soggy. The wind was blowing and it was snowing. I took a mattress off one of the bunks down below and stuck it in the window behind the handrail. Then I tried to figure out how we could tie the mattress in, to keep as much water out as possible. Hell, we were still way offshore, in deep water, and it was rough; man, there was some helluva sea on. George Block, one of the deckhands, was alongside of me helping me tie the mattress in the window when all of a sudden, BOOM, the boat went over on its side and kept going down, and down, and down. "Oh crap," I said, "This is it; we're going to roll right over." The *Viking Star* went down until the deck was deep in the water. The water was running down into the bunkroom. I'm looking right through the broken window, holding onto the handrail, up to my waist in water. I looked over George's shoulder and I see all those tilefish floating off the side of the boat. Come to think of it, that might have helped save the boat. She went down, and down, and down, and stopped. Why that boat didn't turn upside down I'll never know, but all of a sudden she lifted back up.

We lost quite a bit of tilefish off the one side, but I could care less about that now. The *Viking Star* came back up and I said the hell with this. I ran up the back steps, got inside the wheelhouse, put her in gear and headed her down sea to the west.

Water was over the bottom bunks in the bunkroom; the mattresses down there were floating around. I yelled, "Turn the damn bilge pumps on, you jackasses." "Oh, okay," they said, and got 'em going. "Where we going?" "I'm going down sea." I yelled back, "I don't care where, New York, New Jersey, some place, any place, I'm going down sea. That was too close for comfort. We can't make Montauk, that's for sure." And I'm looking. "Maybe I can make the Verrazano Bridge and swing up; then I'll go up to Long Island Sound and then to Montauk. I'll at least get out of the weather." Couldn't go into Shinnecock Inlet, that would be too dangerous and as for Jones' Inlet, I wouldn't have anything to do with that, so it looked like maybe Jersey or New York.

Well, to make a long story short, we edged her up to the Northwest and we got her in a little closer to Long Island. We got inside 40 fathoms and the weather got better and better even though it was still snowing heavy. I held her in and went towards land. I got to within a mile of shore and started going east along the beach in the lee. We came up that way around to the lighthouse and into Montauk. With that, the guys got us pumped out.

On that trip the *Viking Star* had cable steering; now she has hydraulics. Hauling tilefish gear with that steering meant you had to keep the boat right on the gear, so it was normal just before a trip to send somebody down with a grease gun and grease all the fittings and the pulleys for the cable steering and also stuff some in the quadrants, etc. And they did, but they didn't dog the hatch down. Consequently the hatch blew off and a load of water went down there. It's just lucky we didn't lose our boat. After they pumped her out one of the mates passed me up a cup of coffee. The guy's got a big smile on his face. "Hey Paul," he said, "We didn't lose as many tile fish as you think." "No?" I said, "What's up?" "We must have 1,000 pounds or so of fish in the lazarette," he said; "They went down there with the water when the hatch blew off." They started gaffing the tilefish up out of the lazarette and packing them on the deck of the boat. That was a close call and I really started being more careful with the weather after that.

One More Bad Time at Sea

As careful as I had become we had another bad experience once when we were way off shore tile fishing. Capt. Chuck Willer was with me and the *Mi-Joy 747* was there also tile fishing with us. The party boat business had dropped off and Captain Willer had a mortgage and he was doing the same thing we all were doing, whatever we had to do to make it.

It blew out of the northwest real hard. We managed to get our gear back but *Mi-Joy* had six tubs of gear left, 3 miles of gear still left in the water. He couldn't get it back. It was blowing too hard and he couldn't hold the boat in place where the gear was. He gave me the exact location numbers and asked me to haul it in for him and that was that. We got blown off, we couldn't run, we couldn't do anything. The two of us were there with one other boat, the *Gra-Cee*, run by Lou Puskas. We could do nothing but drift off to the southeast. We were off the 1,000-fathom curve and the seas got monstrous. They got bigger and bigger. We couldn't run into the sea and we couldn't run with it. We couldn't run broadside to it. All we could do was knock her out of gear and let the engine idle while we drifted. Every once in awhile, sea would hit the side of the *Viking Star* and come right over the top of the cabin roof. Water would squirt in under the back pilothouse door. Nowadays we have a real nice, watertight door, but at that time it was wooden.

As I said earlier, Chuck Willer was with me. He was assistant captain and also a good friend. I was in the bunk and dry but he was on the pilothouse floor and getting water sprayed on him. "Damn it Paul," he said with his usual stutter, "H-h-how much can she t-t-take?" I answered, "Damned if I know but I think we're going to find out because this is the worst I've ever seen this ocean. This is ferocious. And luckily, it's snowing so heavy we can't even see that well." Well, we lost contact with the *Mi-Joy*, lost contact with the *Gra-Cee*. There was high squealing on the radio but with a snowstorm that was normal. We didn't know where they were. They knew they were drifting with us. Two days later the wind dropped out and we had a day's work to get back to where we wanted to be. We headed back and after a day and a night made it back to the gear. We hauled the *Mi-Joy*'s gear, made one set that day and finished up our trip. Then we headed home. A couple weeks later *Mi-Joy* came to Montauk and picked up his gear on his way in. We kept the fish; there weren't that many anyway but at least we got his gear for him.

Yet Another Bad-Weather Trip — Ice!

Another time we were going tile fishing and Chuck was with me. We were leaving Montauk in heavy ice, lots of ice. We were about three hours just trying to get from Gosman's out past the jetties. The ice was about 4-5 inches thick and piled up. We'd go just a little bit and a chunk of ice would get between the propeller and the bottom of the boat. It was just the right thickness to jam up against the bottom of the boat and stop those 1271's dead — both engines. Of course, we were only idling; we didn't dare go any faster than that. After about three or four times of that I said to Chuck, I said, "You know, we could break a crankshaft doing this. That's a helluva shock on those engines, you know? When in hell is that tide going to change anyway?"

He says, "I don't know. I guess we're going to find out because we can't back up. We can't go ahead. We can't turn around. I'm getting the feeling we shouldn't be here in the first place." I said to him, "Yeah, nice to think of it now. We only got a little tiny distance to get back to the Viking dock, but we can't get back there so I guess we're going to find out when that tide is going to ebb and then drift out with the ice." And that's how we got out of that trouble.

We got out and we went fishing. When we came in, the ice was packed up again. A couple of kids jumped off at Gosman's Dock and ran across the ice to the east side and back, waving in front of us. I looked at Chuck and asked, "Well, what do you say? Do we try it or not? There is open water inside. I can see the open water up inside by the Coast Guard Station and the town dock. It's only jammed in the jetties here and up to Gosman's and then it starts to open up." He said, "Yeah, what the hell; give it a go. Let's try it." So I pushed her up. We had a good load of tilefish and it kept the stern on the *Viking Star* down deep and the bow was up pretty high and she climbed up on top of that ice and just kept cutting through it just like an Ice Breaker. We just kept going and we were doing about 3½-4 knots going through that ice, ice flying all over the place. We got right into that town dock. I couldn't believe it. Of course, when you're in ice you can't turn. You have to go straight because your boat won't turn in that stuff. We had to get lined up just right, and once we got into the partially open water we were able to turn around to the town dock and got to Duryea's dock where we were packing our tile fish that year.

Later on, with the number of boats coming from Jersey and all, and because they stayed open for the winter packing tilefish, Montauk became a very important tilefish port. The boats from Jersey would come in, make a trip or two out of Montauk and then go back to New Jersey. They would fish up our way because there were too many boats now in the Hudson Canyon and we were all looking for the primo fish. The more fish you could catch in one day, naturally the more money you made.

More About Tile Fishing

A couple of additional things come to mind about tile fishing. One particular time we were off shore and there were only a few boats out. It was pretty nasty weather. It was just nasty enough to keep a lot of guys in, but it wasn't too bad for the boats who financially couldn't afford to stay in, and we were one of them. I was fishing not too far away from Lou Puskas on the *Gra-Cee*. He was one of the original guys to start tile fishing (in fact, he was the first one to do it.) He was John Larson's partner; a real nice guy, a real rough and tough guy all his life, really rugged. We were down on oil on the starboard engine of the *Viking Star*. That engine was really burning a lot of oil. She was tired and we just had to make some money before we could afford to tear the engine down and overhaul her. We thought we had more oil aboard than what we did, and suddenly found out we were short. Louie and I were about eight, or nine miles apart and since we were the two boats closest together we were kinda' keeping track of how each of us was doing. *Gra-Cee* was a good little boat, but only a 65- footer; the *Viking Star* was a 100-footer. "Gee, Louie, "I said, it looks like I gotta' quit. I fished all day today and it's my second day, but it looks like I have to go. I'm out of oil on the starboard engine. I can't keep this boat on my gear with one engine very well in this kind of weather. I don't know what the hell I'm going to do. You wouldn't happen to have an extra can of oil with you?" (Our oil came in 5-gallon cans). "Yeah," he says, "Come on over here. I got it for you. Don't worry about it." It was dark, about 10 or 11:00 at night. When we got done hauling and got our gear in, I slammed and crashed over to him. When I got along side of him, around 600-700 feet away, I saw this flashing, arcing going on towards the back end of the boat. "What the hell is going on here, I thought. It looks like he's got some wire shorting or something." Finally, it stopped. Louie calls me. "I've got your oil here Paul. Get a little closer, I want to make sure you get it in the dark." He said he'd throw it overboard with a polly ball tied to it so we could gaff up the rope.

Then he said, "The damn knife in the hauler came out, so I fixed the sucker. (This is a special knife used to kick the rope backbone out of the hauler). It's not going to fall out again," he says, "Crap always happens in nasty weather." Here the guy was, with his boots and oilskins on, with the sea breaking over the side of the boat. The bottom half of his body is in the water more than out of the water, and he's welding a knife into the hauler. I couldn't get over that. Luckily he didn't get electrocuted. I couldn't believe it. We got our oil and, come to think of it, I don't think I ever returned it. Dammit, I don't remember replacing the oil.

Baiting for Tilefish

"Long-lining" hadn't been invented yet so the only type of tile fishing I could do that last year before heading to Key West was tub-trawling. To go tub-trawling, you had to bait the tubs up, and that of course put you at the mercy of the people baiting the tubs. We had walk-in freezers and we would bait the tubs up and then put them in the freezers. We had another freezer not turned on that we heated and set tables up in. We got up to six people lined up in there and they would be the baiters. We paid the baiters eight dollars a tub, eight dollars a half-mile to bait the hooks and coil the line in the tub. There was a hook every twelve feet, between 200-250 hooks per tub. Most of the baiters lived from tub to tub and they wanted to get paid right then and there.

They would do one job and then wanted to get some dough so they could run to the local bar. We had a set of standards that they had to do at least two tubs before we'd write out a check. We also hired a guy as a bait-master. His job was to stand and watch them baiting gear and keep track of who baited which gear, what tub. When they were done he made them put a cardboard tag in each tub with their name on it. That way, if it didn't go out of the tub correctly and wasn't done right, we knew who messed it up. The bait-master's job was to keep track of everything. He got two dollars a tub to do that. That amounted to ten dollars every half-mile. We were at the mercy of the baiters. When too many boats came into Montauk everyone was stealing each other's baiters. In a way, it was funny.

Christman's Saloon used to be open then, right alongside the Viking Dock. Harry Christman said to me one night, "You know Paul, everybody always says money is green but your checks are yellow and as far as I'm concerned, money is yellow because all I do is cash your paychecks and the baiters stay here and drink their money up." Then he said, "They run over and bait a couple more tubs of yours, then come running back over here and drink some more. I'm doing a helluva business here, because of this tile fishing in the winter. I never thought things would be so good." Well, the place isn't there anymore. Mr. Christman passed away and the place closed up. Anyway, that was the problem with baiting the tubs.

The St. Patty's Day Work Stoppage

We were still getting ready for this particular trip and only had forty-seven tubs of gear in the freezer. Then the baiters decided to go on strike. It was five days before St. Patrick's Day. To bring in St. Patty's Day properly they thought it was time for them to all go and get drunk, stay drunk the week before St. Patty's Day, and still be drunk a few days after St. Patty's Day. By then all their money would be gone and they'd have to go back to work. So, no one would bait any gear and there we were. All the boats were stuck in the harbor and none had baited tubs of gear. Well, at least I had my 47 tubs of gear. We were getting into spring, and this was to be our last trip of the season before we had to go in with a steam jetty and steam the cabin out. We had to blast her out all good and clean and put the furniture back before we could go back to party boat fishing. It always took a week to clean the boat up to carry passengers for hire or it would smell like the rotten herring we used for bait.

On top of that, I didn't have any crew. My crew decided to go with the baiters. Nope, this is a special holiday, St. Patrick's Day, and it's a big drunk time. So, Chuck Willer and I sat down and I said, "Dammit, Chuck, I gotta' get the rest of the gear baited up and get out of this. This is it. I'm really discouraged with this mess. I think it'll be the last year I'm tile fishing. I'm really thinking about going to Key West to try and find a dock."

I decided to go out anyway with just the forty-seven tubs. Chuck stayed and ran the *Starship* that weekend. He took his son out of school and I took both of my sons out of school and the three boys and I took the *Viking Star* offshore tile fishing. With forty-seven tubs of gear I made a quickie, two days, we usually fished sixty tubs in two days so we were a little short, but we did it. We had 8,500 pounds, which amounted to a pretty decent trip for two days considering everything. We came in and the price was sky high because all the boats were still tied up because of the strike. No one else was fishing. I had the whole fishing grounds to myself. I had the only tilefish in the market. Of course, a lot of people in town were very mad at us, namely the baiters, and they were going to do everything, oh boy, they were going to light the boat on fire; they were threatening all kinds of things. They were so mad because we went fishing but luckily nothing happened; nothing developed. We got paid for the fish and that was our last trip. We pulled the gear off the boat. I sold it real cheap to John Nolan on the *Rainbow Chaser*. He was learning. He was offshore lobstering at the time and he hadn't done too well with it and wanted to go into tile fishing. I said, "I'm out of it John. I'm going to try to get into Key West next year." I had a wife who was hollering because she thought tile fishing was too dangerous. Anyway, he went out with us on a couple of trips to learn the ropes and now he's one of the top tile fishermen in Montauk with a nice, big beautiful steel boat; he's very successful. When long lining was invented, that ended the baiter problem. In long lining you bait the hooks on the boat and snap the baited hooks on the backbone as you set the gear. There are currently four boats tile fishing out of Montauk.

Chapter Fourteen

1970s-80s

The Late 1970s to the Early 1980s

Fishing Florida Waters

Anyway, that was the tilefish days. Finally I decided to go to Key West, Florida with the *Viking Starship*. I fished in The Tortugas. I remember my second wife Betty saying, "Anything but tile fishing, Paul, anything but tilefish. I'm ready to take the chance. Just stop tile fishing. It's too dangerous." She sat and worried too much. "Everybody is worried about tile fishing and the weather you guys fish in." So, Key West, here we come.

The Start in Florida

We went down to Florida for four winter seasons with the *Viking Starship*, fishing out of Key West to the Dry Tortugas. It was very interesting and a lot of fun. We sailed overnight fishing trips on the *Viking Starship* out of Oceanside Marina in Stock Island in Key West, fishing the Tortugas, and we did very well. Fishing was very good. We built a good clientele right away. Docks were always a problem. It was kinda' tight in the Oceanside Marina for the big *Viking Starship*. Tex Schram owned that marina. He also owned the Dallas Cowboys and the golf course there in Key West. He kinda' looked down at us as a party fishing boat at his marina. He didn't like it but his manager liked it because we burned a lot of fuel. We bought the bait there. We brought business to the marina from our passengers. The stores did well, including the tackle shop. Once the manager left after the third year, Tex Schram hired another manager and that manager didn't like us at all, so we were out. That's the end of that.

So we went down to the city in Key West and we sailed out of there. The last year was a nightmare. The parking was an issue. Everything was lock and key. The people in the city were hard to get along with. The corruption was terrible. Everybody had their hands out and it got to a point where I would get very discouraged. However, for a time we did very well. We bought a condo down there and Betty and I lived there. The fishing was fun and interesting; it was new fishing. It wound up that my wife was answering the phone and booking trips. It was a problem because she had four kids, all younger than mine, and two of them were still in school and the schools down there were different than in East Hampton, Long Island. The kids were unhappy about going to school in Key West. Key West schools were far behind the northern schools and that was a problem when we returned to Montauk the following season. Anyway, I got so discouraged with the docking situation I finally said, "Well, that's enough. This is the last year we're going to do this. We're done." Steven and Paul were up in Montauk, running the business while I was in Key West and they were making pretty good money. For sure, I didn't want to disrupt their families and ask them to join me in Florida. So we went back to Montauk and we never went back.

But before we headed back, I got myself into quite a mess, as you will now read!

overtime, and it's going to cost everybody $20 to change their documentation over." I said, "That's fine with me." We stood there, pulled the $20 out and paid, fortunately, because about 15 minutes after that, they closed.

We got our documentation changed and off we went. We were loading the groceries on. We went to get 20 people, and I charged them $20,000 for the trip, and I hired two boats to go with us and paid them $1,500 dollars apiece. I towed them down to Cuba. Once we got there they went into Cuba. Beautiful weather, slick, calm weather. We were going out at night and with the lights on all the other boats you didn't have to know where Cuba was — you just had to get in line and follow the line. Everybody was going in one direction. I stayed outside the 12-mile limit and sent the 2 boats in. A little later I got a guy on the radio. The two guys that had the boats spoke perfect English. They were American Caucasians, but the guy that came on the radio had quite a Spanish accent and he was in uniform. He said, "Look, we feel it's too dangerous for these little boats to bring these people out 12 miles. We can get your people ready in no time. You come in here and just come to the sea buoy outside the break waters." I said, "Well, I'm uncomfortable."

"No, no," he said, "It's okay, it's okay. It's safety. We have to be careful of safety. This is a safety-first issue. We don't want anybody to lose their lives."

Well, he talked me into it and that was my mistake. I went into the sea buoy at the entrance of Mariel Harbor, and what's out there? Here comes a gunboat, pulls up alongside, and a bunch of soldiers jump on board my boat, dressed in fatigues with automatic weapons, etc. I knew I'd been had, so into Mariel Harbor we go, and the guy is telling me to make a right turn. There's a gunboat there on my left side. For some reason he wanted me to not get too close to the gunboat. I don't know why, a big gunboat, and he kept telling me, "Turn right, turn right." Well, I had my Polaroid sunglasses on and I could see there was no water there. He was trying to get me to go aground hard to the right, so I turned to the right, but I made it a very gradual turn. I didn't know how to tell this guy there was no water there, and we gradually made the turn and

Cuban gunboat, with armed soldiers on the bow, approaches the STARSHIP in Mariel Harbor, Cuba.

missed the reef that was there, not by very much, but we missed it. That was the important part. And we got in, and they told us we're to anchor up. They told us we were to have <u>no</u> radio contact at all. <u>No</u> radio contact with America with the big radio, the whole works. And, no swimming! They were worried about some people trying to run out of Cuba, by swimming out to us and climbing aboard the boat as stowaways. They were worried about us, and I found out later on that they couldn't figure out who was who in the water.

Man, it was hot, I'm telling you, early that spring. And the boats kept coming, and they kept coming. Day 1 went by. Day 2 passed by. Day 3 had gone by. And every day I'm calling the Cubans, asking them where our people were. When are we going to get ready? Finally a Major came out. He said, "Look." He says, "You've got a nice big boat here," (he spoke very good English) he said, "You help us and I'll get your people. You help us transport people back and forth to the dock. People want to come in and visit Havana, see beautiful Cuba, and we don't have enough boats to ferry them back and forth from all these boats. We never thought we'd have so many people come from America."

What a line of crap. So, I said, "Okay, if you promise to get us our people, I'll be glad to help you out." Well, we started going from boat-to-boat, picking people up and going into the dock. Mariel Harbor was broken up into two harbors more or less, and you could see from one harbor to the other, but there was a piece of land dividing most of it. Some of the boats were getting up and going. They were supposedly loading people but they went by a dock and they went up into the other harbor and the Cubans had just moved boats from harbor to harbor and people thought those boats went in and got their passengers and left and went to America. But they didn't. They just got transferred from harbor to harbor to show that there was some activity going on. But you had to be really careful to see what was happening. I was up on the roof of the pilothouse of the *Viking Starship* and I could see with my binoculars how this was working, and I said, "You know, nobody is leaving the damn harbor. They're just going from one place to another, but nobody is going out to the channel." So, I said, "We'll help them out."

We went to the dock and everybody was screaming, "There goes the *Viking Starship* to get their people," and so on. We made a trip for the Major. We got to the dock and we dropped off a group of people. The Major says, "Oh great. Give me six of your people and I want them to make a phone call to their relatives and tell them to get ready because we're going to come and pick them up. Tell them to pack their clothes and so forth." So, six of my people jumped off the boat, off they go, following the Major and they got in a bus with the Major, and he drops them off. He says, "Go down the street, make a right here and turn there on the corner, and there's a telephone there, and you can call your relatives." It was a public telephone booth. Well, when they turned the corner the line to the telephone booth was over a block long, and everybody was falling into the same trap, trying to call their relatives. The phone system wasn't that good at that time in Cuba. I don't know how it is now, but a lot of people didn't have a phone from what I understood, and a neighbor would have it, and they would run and get the person if they had a phone call, and get them to come over. It all took time. All these people were standing in line and my people came back after about 6-8 hours of it and they were just totally discouraged. They were very disappointed and they really, really thought that this was just a big game to the officials. A lot of them were nervous. Some of them escaped Cuba and they were back there illegally, and they really didn't want them to know just who they were. They left there illegally. They were afraid they might go to jail.

Proud to be an American

Tensions were getting tight. I had one man in our charter who wanted to trade himself for his son. Somehow or other his son got caught trying to escape Cuba and he was in prison, and he was doing a life sentence, supposedly. This guy was 55 years old. He had been in America a number of years. He had his wife and his daughter with him, and he wanted his son. They escaped from Cuba one way or another, but his son was in prison and he wanted to trade himself for his son, and he said, "I had a good life. I lived my life. I'm 55." He said, "I live a good life. I want my son, my son, he come to America, beautiful America, enjoy America. I trade. I do his time." And he was really serious. He really tried to do that, but of course, that never happened.

We had one guy that was there who was a professional Jai Alai player, and he wanted to get his mother-in-law. We found out later on when we got back to America, that his wife had a baby while he was on our boat. Most of the people that chartered my boat owned restaurants or shoe stores. Most of them spoke quite good English and they were very successful in America. They thought a lot of America. They were very proud to be Americans and live in the U. S., and they wanted to get their relatives out of Cuba to enjoy the great

A view of Mariel Harbor filled with American ships.

life of America. Actually, I can't blame them. Bill Grimm, my Assistant Captain, has nicer handwriting than I do, and once we were in the harbor and we knew the jig was up. I told Bill, "Listen Bill, you fill the log out. Keep the log on this trip. Who knows how long we're going to be here? We were supposed to be here overnight and we're on day three already. Now we're operating as a ferry. But you keep a log on what's going on." And we stayed tied to that dock and different officials would come up to us and tell us to move. Well, the dock was such a size that when we were there, no one else could tie up. We took up the whole dock, and other boats wanted to come in and get water (there was a fresh water hose there). We grabbed the water hose and refilled our tank. We held 600 gallons, and we were using buckets of salt water to take showers and then we would just rinse off with the fresh water shower on the *Viking Starship*, to save water. We made a couple trips as a ferry and we held up the dock about 6 hours.

Major so and so told us, "Okay, okay." He said, "Stay here, stay here." Yeah, okay. We thought we were going to get our people right quick like. Well, when our people who had left the boat came back, they were very discouraged. Castro put up a bunch of buildings right there. He had a bunch of tin buildings put up at the dock where they opened up a load of shops. They were selling all kinds of trinkets, cigarettes, and watermelons. Oh, by the way, a nice watermelon, one watermelon, cost $25 at the time. A carton of cigarettes out of a store cost $25 at the time. They were selling canned food and stuff, and the cans were rusty. I didn't know how long the food was in them, and some of the guys bought some stuff, like stale bread and so on. We started to run low on food. You know, when you're hungry, any food starts to look pretty good, but the prices were inflated and Cuba was making a lot of money on them. So, we get back to our mooring where we had to be anchored up. We were done with the ferry for a while and we never heard any more from the Major. Every once in awhile I would send one of our Spanish-speaking passengers in, and they would go to the office, and tell them that the Captain was getting very upset, that he had to get back. Well, we never got too far with that.

And then Came the Storm

Then one afternoon we got a hell of a storm. It blew over 70 miles per hour. Man, was it blowing. And these boats are still coming into the harbor in all shapes and sizes. It was pouring rain. You couldn't see anything and our anchor had dragged. We couldn't hold anchor. There was a steel mooring right in the middle of the harbor, an old rusty government mooring. I got up along side of that and I yelled at our crew, "See if you can get a line on that mooring — lasso it. I can't see." Boats are flying by us here, dragging, going up on the beach behind us. I didn't want to be one of them, but if I get somebody's anchor line in my wheels, I'm not going to have any power and then we'll be one of them. This guy, Julio, the professional Jai Alai player couldn't get the rope on the mooring. He took the rope and jumped overboard with it, and wrapped it around the mooring. Now we had to get him up on the boat. We had a rope ladder that we launched, lowered down, and we got him up our rescue ladder. Now we were tied down to the mooring and it was really blowing. Man, it was cranking, raining hard, and we didn't know what to think. Other boats were drifting down by us and a couple of commercial fishing boats — crab boats — threw some lines to us and tied up on the side of our boat, put some balls between us, the big orange floats that fishermen use for bumpers. They tied up alongside of us because they couldn't hold anchor. They didn't want to go on the beach. We had two on one side and one on the other. As a matter of fact, I was told that one guy got his hands crushed between the two boats. He was all bandaged up the next day. They said he lost a finger. I don't know if it was true or not.

The next day, shrimp boats were coming in and bringing in boats that they found floating upside down. One of them said that he found a beautiful boat out there, with nobody in it, floating upside down with a really nice outboard engine on it. He picked it up and put it on his deck. He said, "We got a nice boat out of the deal anyway."

No one knew how many people lost their lives going to Cuba during the Mariel boat lift with that storm. I believe quite a few people died, drowning in that storm. There were a number of little boats the shrimpers had found, with nobody in them. Who knows who and how many were lost!

Communications

Anyway, the storm passed finally and we still weren't allowed to use our radios. I had one boat in Key West calling us on the big radio. I could have the radio on but I couldn't answer him. I wouldn't dare take the chance. I'm the biggest boat in the harbor. I was told definitely no long-range radio. You could only use your local radio on low-power with safety circ., boat-to-boat. No calling America, not to the states, and if I answered, it would be an excuse for them to seize my boat. So, I didn't want to take any chances at all.

I was called by George Sieman from the *Mitchell III*. I heard him call me over and over again, and I said, "Damm it, I just can't answer him." There was a commercial fishing boat about two boats over that had just come in. For some reason they never told him not to use his big radio, or else he didn't hear it, or whatever. I heard him on the radio talking, calling Marathon, Florida, where he was from, and telling his base, his company, that everything was fine and he was in Mariel Harbor, and he expected to get his people pretty soon.

That evening I saw a guy with a little boat who was going by in the harbor, and I flagged him down. I said, "Get me over to that boat, will ya?" He brought me over there and I told the Captain the story. They didn't shut your radio off, but they will, and they made it very loud and clear. That's why the air is so clear, there is nobody talking on the big radios from Cuba. I suggest you talk to your office there, change the name of your boat, you know. So he said, "Wow, I didn't know that," and I gave him my phone number in Key West and I said, "Do me a favor — have your office call this number and tell them everything is still A-OK, but that we are still stuck here. We didn't get our people yet, and we are in the harbor. Give us messages back and forth." So, he was fine. The name of the boat was *Mary* Something. I think it was *Mary L.*, but he changed the name to *Stardust* for the call. He called Marathon base and they answered, and he answered back with, "This is the boat *Stardust*," and they recognized his voice. They knew who he was. He said, "I have a message from the *Mary L.* This is *Stardust*. And I also have a message from the *Viking Starship*," and he would give the phone numbers and the messages. His office picked up what was going on right away and they knew it was the *Mary L.* talking to them. So, that's how we got messages back and forth to America. Each day we got a message in.

I had a man on the boat named Joe Alexander and he was my galley man. He passed away recently. He did the cooking for us. His wife was a woman who was very excitable. She was getting very nervous that we were gone three days and she didn't hear from her husband, but now the message came back that everything's okay, we're still in the harbor, but that we didn't get our people yet. She started calling everybody. She was calling the radio stations.

**An industrial part of the Cuban Harbor, photographed by
Steven Forsberg on the *Viking Starship*.**

She was calling the TV channels. She was calling everyone. She got the phone number of the people at Marathon and was calling them quite often. "I want to know this, I want to know that," and, of course, half of the messages they didn't send to us, and some they did. But there wasn't any way we could answer. We were stuck there. Well, it turned out to be a good thing because being that she got the press on it and everything, we were being brought up on radio, and we were being brought up on television. "*Viking Starship* is still in Cuba and no one knows what's going on." Now the press started to use us to get a lot of people to listen to them or something. It was something to talk about I guess. We were the biggest boat there. We were 140-foot long. There we were, and they can't get through to us, and they're not allowed to use their radios and I think the pressure got to the Cubans. Finally, we were there, day-in and day-out and I was yelling at them and I think they heard what was going on with the TV and everything, that the *Viking Starship* was on TV everyday, and there is still no word from the *Viking Starship* and so on.

Getting Passengers on the Boat!

Finally on day seven they gave us the word, come in to get your people. We came to the dock and, once again, we took up the whole dock. There were busloads of people there, hot in the buses, with no air-conditioning of course, and there were a bunch of Americans stranded. There were a lot of people there a lot of days by then, out of money, hot, wanting to go home, their boat's broken down or whatever, and no one's leaving, but suddenly we're loading up our people so they're screaming, "Take us, bring us home. Paul, help us out." Somebody from Key West knew my name and then everybody knew me as Paul and they kept calling me Captain Paul through the fence. I didn't know the people. There were a couple hundred people there and I had no control over it. Anyway, all of a sudden the soldiers were all around us and they started to load Cuban people from the Embassy on the boat.

Now this is the way the people got on board the boat. The men had on T-shirts and a pair of shorts, and no shoes. Nothing in their pockets. They were searched as they were getting on the boat. The women, the same thing; T-shirt, shorts, and a pair of shoes, nothing in their pockets. That's how they were leaving that country, with nothing but the clothes on their back, carrying nothing, no baggage, nothing at all. They really must have wanted to get out of Cuba and I was really taken aback by what I saw.

How to Get Water (with Wrigley's!)

When they started putting the people on I grabbed a hold of the one guy in charge, I guess a soldier, and I said, "Hey, how many are you putting on here? Look, Coast Guard license, 149 — 149. Coast Guard license. I only carry 149."

"No, no," he says, "Too big a boat, 149. We put more than 149 on. You be okay. It's okay. It's okay, Captain, it's okay."

Well, they were putting these people on one at a time. I had quit smoking but when I was in Cuba I was back smoking again. When I quit smoking I chewed gum instead and always had chewing gum in the wheelhouse. All of a sudden Joe Alexander said, "You got any Wrigley's or any kind of chewing gum left over?"

"Yeah, I got some Wrigley's Spearmint here. Why, what's the matter?" He said, "I need it down in the galley." "Okay." I gave him a big package of 4 packs, wrapped up, and then he took it down below. The guy who was putting the water in the boat was only going to give us 100 gallons. We held 600 but our tank was empty. With all these people getting on board the boat, 100 weren't nearly enough. We needed more water. The fill was right there in the galley of the *Starship* and the guy who was putting water in was about to shut the water hose off. Joe would reach down when no one was looking and would hand him a pack of Wrigley's Spearmint chewing gum and he'd turn the valve right back on again and keep putting water in. This continued until we got our 600 gallons of water. More Wrigley's gum *equals* more water. We were only supposed to have 100 gallons. I'm amazed at what a package of gum was worth.

Continuing to Load the Boat

Anyway, they kept loading these people on and while they were loading them a friend of mine named Ray on the party boat *Calusa* came over. He sailed out of Islamorada, Florida. He comes over and said, "You're going Paul. I got to get my son back, take my son." And he passes him up to me. I think his boy was about 11 years old or so. And he said, "His mother's worried, I know, and we can't contact her or anything, but when you get back please call her and she'll come to Key West and pick my boy up. I don't know how long I'm going to be. Just tell her I love her and I don't know how long I'm going to be here but we're okay."

His was a boat they got to go aground on the reef and he was still stuck on the reef. After the Cubans put him on the reef they wanted a lot of money to tow him off. Finally he negotiated and they were running around trying to borrow money from people to get towed off and somebody, somewhere, a

Cuban, came along and towed him. He didn't charge him I understand.

So, he was on the other side of the dock. He passed up his son to me and I told the boy, "Go up the front steps of the pilothouse and go in the back, and you sit on the floor. I don't want them to see you. You're not supposed to be on this boat and I don't want to have any problems." I was getting very nervous. I'd never seen so many guns and people in fatigues in all my life. I most certainly just wanted to get the hell out of there. We were loading on our people and the boy sat there, very quiet. He kept his head down. I said, "Don't let them see you. I don't know what they're going to do." The father waved and off he went. We finally got all our people loaded and then they brought in a commercial fishing boat along side of us, a lobster boat, and they put about 60 people in that boat which was only about 45 feet long. The deck was underwater and the guys were plugging up the scuppers on the deck because of the water coming in. Then I said, "Man, look at this." We had orders to start pulling away from the dock. I didn't know how many people we had on board the boat as we headed out.

We Got the Americans Too!

Before we left the dock, one soldier came to me and said, "How many of them you want?" and he pointed over to the Americans at the fence. I saw one guy with a bandage on his leg, with blood stains on his leg and he was on crutches. I didn't know if the leg was broken or what, but there was blood leaking through the bandages. It must have happened during a storm or something. So I said, "Listen, how many people do we have on the boat?"

"I don't know, I don't know," he said, "But how many of them do you want?" So I said, "Look, let me have the people that need medical attention." At that, this guy went ballistic. I'm telling you, I stepped back when he screamed and hollered at me about how good the hospitals and medical help is in Cuba. "We have the best in the world — who do you think you are to even suggest such a thing?" he said.

But their ambulance, of course, was a 1939 Chevrolet. This guy's got blood coming out of his bandages — I thought real quickly and luckily answered, "Oh my goodness, everybody knows Cuba has the best hospitals in the world. That's known all over. I was taught that in school, absolutely, but I just figured that there were so many people here I might be able to help out. You'll be overloaded. Your hospitals, you know, would be overloaded with all the Americans coming here, and some of them being hurt and injured." That cooled him down somewhat, although I didn't get any of the Americans that had a bandage on them anyway. I put 80 Americans on the boat. Finally I said, "We got no place to stand here. I don't know how many people I've got on board this damn boat but I never had anything like this before in my life. That's enough, I can't take any more." It was a hard thing to do because the people were screaming from behind the fence, "Hey Paul, come on. I got the liquor store. I got the jewelry store in downtown Key West. You know me; I've talked to you before. Let me get on." How can you put him on and not somebody else?

Finally, Time to Go (Or Maybe Not Yet?)

I had to go up in the wheelhouse to get away from it and finally I got orders to pull away from the dock. They told me to stay close to that lobster boat. The one guy who spoke pretty good English said to me, "You stay with him." I answered, "Yeah, I'll be staying with him. He's got himself a load of people on that boat." We started to leave the harbor and when we were right in the middle up comes a little gunboat with a couple of soldiers in it and two Americans also. They hollered up. We stopped. They yelled up, "We're reporters from the *New York Times*. We want to get aboard. We've got to get back to America. We've had enough of this. We've got to get out of here. We know Paul Putecalie, the writer from the *New York Post,* the sports writer, we're friends with him," and this and that and so forth. "Let us get on." I said, "Alright, if it's alright with those guys with the guns." And yeah, yeah.

When we pulled up alongside, the guys with the guns wanted money or they weren't going to let them get off. And these guys didn't have any money on them. They were broke. So one of our Cuban-Americans passed a $100 bill down. Well, they never saw a $100 bill. They didn't know what to think of it. So they chit-chatted back and forth to themselves and the Cuban-American was explaining to them what it was. Finally they let these two guys aboard. I've got to say one thing about these people who chartered my boat — when we were getting ready to load the people on board the boat, they went up and bought loaves of bread, because that's all they could buy were loaves of bread. And they got back on with arms full of loaves for the people. Now, they didn't know these people that Castro put on our boat. They went to get their relatives but they didn't get a single one. There wasn't one relative on the boat. I give them credit. They still were very happy they were doing what they were doing. They were bringing a bunch of people to freedom from their country even though they weren't relatives, but they had hopes their relatives would be on another boat coming. Whether their relatives ever got to America or not, I do not know. I assume so. I hope so for their sake because these were nice people.

Reaching the 12-Mile Limit

And off we go. We get outside the inlet in the harbor. Boy, I could feel the weight on the boat. I never had this much of a load on a boat before but it was so calm, not a bit of wind, beautiful weather. I had this lobster boat running with us, a commercial guy, a Cuban-American, but he didn't speak any English at all. Luckily two of the guys I had as interpreters were on our boat and they told him to stay close to us. We headed for Key West, Florida and for safety's sake we ran slowly with them. We were only making about 6-7 knots. As soon as we get outside the inlet the people start coming up and asking when are we going to be outside of the 12-mile limit. Everybody in the boat was nervous, including me. When we first arrived in Cuba Bill Grimm and I had hidden the 0.38 pistol down under the floor boards of the engine room. Once we got out of the inlet we took that out and kept it in the wheelhouse between the two of us because we didn't know what to expect. We had a security issue with all these people on the boat, wondering what's going to happen. We had the gun with us anyway and it was loaded. We weren't allowed to have it in Cuba but we had it anyway. I said, "Well, you see those gray boats up there? They're the Cuban gunboats and they're on the 12-mile line." I can see them on the radar and I could see them visually. "They're 12 miles from land," I said, "And those white boats off in the distance a couple miles on the other side of them, well, that's the American Coast Guard, so that must be International Waters. Once we pass those gray boats we'll be in freedom."

Well, that message went around the boat real fast. Folks went all around telling everybody what was going on. Well, we got to those gray boats and passed those gunboats, and once those gunboats were just behind us, the screaming brought tears to my eyes. The people were singing, clapping, jumping up and down. I don't know what the songs were, it was all in Spanish, but there were smiles on their faces. It was just like they found a new life. It was amazing. I felt so good. I remember my eyes tearing up. I couldn't believe it. I said, "Wow, something good is coming out of this after all." So we went along a little ways more and the Coast Guard calls me on the radio, a Cutter, and said, "I see you're coming out of Cuba. Can you tell me how many people you have aboard?" "I have no idea." I said, "I can only give you an estimate." And he answered, "Well, what do you estimate?"

"Well, I have between 450 and 550 people aboard, POB. And the gray boat along side of me, the commercial fishing boat, I estimate between 50 and 60. His deck is below the waterline. They have plugs on the deck and we're moving slowly so he can keep close to us and keep up with us for safety's sake," I answered. So, the Coast Guard vessel comes back and now we have a senior voice on the radio. The first voice had been a young guy, now I have a senior. He called me back. *"Viking Starship's* Captain, will you repeat the amount of people on board, POB?" I answered, "Yeah, I'm carrying between 450 and 550, the nearest I can estimate. I never had this amount of people on a boat before." I said, "We're a U. S. Coast Guard inspected vessel. We are licensed to carry 149 passengers on board. We have life jackets for 170. However, I was ordered at gun point to put these people aboard and I had no control over it, and we are bound for Key West." He said, "Well, have a good trip Skipper. Safe sailing to you and all those people on your boat." Most of the boats that came out of Cuba were severely overloaded.

I had been forced to take whatever people on board that the soldiers told me to take and quite a few of them had been prisoners that Castro simply cleared out of his jails. But I am happy to say that I did manage to take a very large group of people that had been in our American Embassy.

Some Boats Never Made It

There were boats broken down all over the place, mostly small boats. The Coast Guard had a bunch of them tied up to their sides with ropes hanging off the Cutters, and they didn't know what to do with them. They wanted to go to Cuba but they were broken down and the Coast Guard couldn't tow them into Cuba. They were very close to Cuba, but right outside of the 12-mile limit. The Coast Guard had their hands full. There were boats all over the place. There must have been 20 broken down boats that I could see that were tied up to the Coast Guard boats, due to problems of one type or another. The Coast Guard asked me, "That boat over there up ahead of you, just up near you, could you find out what's wrong with him?" I said, "I'll alter course and get over there and yell down to him." And we did, and he answered back in Spanish that he was broken down but he still wanted to go to Cuba. He didn't want any help from us. We were going the wrong way. He wanted to go to Cuba. So I told the Coast Guard guy that and he said, "Do you think you can get a line on him and get him over here and tie him on to us with all the boats that we have here?" And I said, "No sir, I got my hands full. I've got a lot of lives at stake here and there are two guys in that boat. They're going to have to fend for themselves or somebody else is going to have to get 'em to you. They're okay. Their engine's broken down. They're floating. They're not sinking. I'm bound for Key West. I'm severely overloaded and I've got to keep going." So he said, "Okay skipper," and he signed off.

A little later on, we finally were about half way across to Key West, I still didn't want to let anybody know where I was, what my position was. Just about that time I get a call from the U. S. Coast Guard at Key West. They had heard I was on my way and they wanted to know my position, but I wouldn't give it to them. I gave my estimated time of arrival — 11:00 p.m. I was pretty scared and concerned about some nut job coming up alongside of us with a real fast boat and a gun of any type or any kind pointed at us and pulling the trigger. Even one bullet will kill three or four people. People are lined up four or five thick on the deck and we also have them down below, oh, all over. I wouldn't let them on the roof of the top deck, but I let the crew up there. I didn't know about the weight. I didn't know how the boat would handle the weight with a lot of people up there but we were certainly full down below. I was very concerned about that so I wouldn't give my position.

All of a sudden this helicopter comes up alongside of us and I go uh-oh. There were no markers on it. It didn't say who it was. It was not Coast Guard. All of a sudden a guy opens up the door and he holds this big camera, this projector outside. He was taking pictures of us with this big projector as we were going along. So it was a press camera. I later found out it was a *Miami Herald* man holding the camera. Well, that could have just as well and easy been somebody with a gun. Finally they left and we were the centerfold of the *Miami Herald* the next day with all these people on the boat coming home to Key West. It was a big, beautiful color photo.

So anyway, later on I'm passing boats still going to Cuba. And they called me on the radio and wanted to know how it is in Cuba. And I told them the truth. I said I'd been there seven days. I don't have one relative aboard that we came for, and I got somewhere around 500 people on the boat, so if I knew what I know now, I would turn around. But nobody turned around — everybody kept going.

Getting to the Head of the Line

A little later on I turned on the marine operator channel with the VHF. I figured I'd call my wife and let her know we're coming, that we're on our way. To make a long story short, 27 boats were waiting for a clear line for the marine operator, boats that were on their way to Key West and the marine operators were totally jammed solid. I heard the operator say to the private boat in front of me (I could tell by the way they talk on the radio, different than the boats that are on the radio all the time like a work boat, a party boat, or a commercial boat), "You're number 27 on the list." So I said I might as well get on the list, and I called the marine operator.

"This is the *Viking Starship*," I said. The marine operator came back to me right away and said, "*Viking Starship*, we've been looking for you. Come in with the number that you're calling." So she put me ahead of everybody, right then and there. I don't know what those people must have thought. I gave her the number of the office and there wasn't any answer. My wife wasn't in. I found out later on she was down the docks most of the time looking for me to come in, watching for the boat. So we called Barbara, Joe the galley guy's wife. She jumped up and down on the phone screaming, "Oh, gee, great, lovely; wonderful." She is a very, very excitable woman. Everybody was very happy and I gave her an ETA and so forth. She said, "Well, I'll go get Betty. I'll tell Betty. She's down at the docks now. They have a telephone booth there (we didn't have cell phones then), and she uses the pay phone and she calls me every few hours, to find out if I heard anything. So when she calls me I'll tell her you're on your way." I appreciated that and we signed off. As we were coming into Key West we got into number 1, the sea buoy just outside the 6-

mile reef, and boy, I hit a boat flotilla. There were a bunch of them, around 5 or 6 Customs, Police boats, Coast Guard boats, who all circled us and gave us an escort in. We pulled into the dock in the City of Key West, the old Navy dock. (It's not there anymore.) We tied up at the dock broadside as instructed. The TV cameras were going and the press was all over the place. A guy in uniform got on board the boat and said to me, "Don't talk to the press. Follow me. Keep your head down, walk to that building directly ahead of the boat. Don't talk to anybody."

The Real Truth

I'm a little ahead of my story. I had some decent, good people on the boat. They caught me in the wheelhouse and they wanted to know how they could inform the authorities that we had people from prisons and institutions; rapists, murderers, and so forth on the boat. I just told them well; when we get to Key West tell anybody that is in uniform, anybody who looks official. You know, that's the way it is. Say, "Yes, we have them on board the boat. I appreciate you knowing it." And these good Cubans knew pretty much who was who and they were very concerned because they were afraid it was interfering with them coming to America and being free.

The Lost Kid

Below is a brief account of one of the tragedies that occurred during this time of turmoil.

A small boy came up to the wheelhouse with the interpreter and he wanted to know which boat his mother would be on. "I don't know," I said, "She'll probably be on a boat behind us." And okay, fine. So the boy left and the interpreter came back up. "What was that all about?" I asked. "Well, his mother's not coming." He said. The boy was about eleven years old and though I have no way of verifying if this story is true or not, the interpreter told me that the boy and the mother were trying to get over the fence into the American

Embassy. (Some of the people we had on board the *Viking Starship* were from the American Embassy.) We were the first boat to bring Embassy people back to America. They put them on our boat first and the boy was one of them. Anyway, the way it went was he said the mother was behind the boy, helping the boy climb up over the fence, pushing the boy over the fence, and the dogs attacked the mother, and the mother was not coming. End of story.

The people in the Embassy grabbed the boy and dragged him into the crowd so he couldn't see the dogs attacking his mother. So, he didn't know his mother was gone. I'm told that he didn't have any relatives on the boat and there were no relatives that he knew of in America and that he could not speak a word of English. "Boy," I said, "What the hell is going to happen to this kid now? You know, coming to a strange country, can't speak the language and so forth. No mother, no father, no relatives." My guy replied "Oh, don't worry about it. We have ways of taking care of that. If we can't find his relatives, somebody will take him in, but we do this internally." The interpreter continued, "We take care of each other. Cuban people are proud people. We take care of each other." And that's how that story went.

And then I Got Grilled

So now when I got off the boat I've got these guards around me, custom people. They were in blue uniforms. One guy was in front of me, one behind me, one on each side of me, and there we go and the press is hollering, yelling all kinds of questions. I was given strict orders to not answer anything. Keep moving. Keep walking. Keep going. Keep your head down. We got into the building and we sat down inside, and now I'm in interrogation.

This guy behind the desk, he's got me sitting there, and I want to tell you something. Man, I was a very tired person, with the stress that I'd been through for seven days. I had been in a communist country where I didn't belong; I wasn't supposed to be. That meant my boat was not insured. I had a big mortgage on it. I'm not supposed to be in a communist country with the boat.

The bank could foreclose on the mortgage if they wanted to over that. It meant I had no insurance on the boat. And if Castro ever found out that I had MTU Mercedes-Benz engines in my boat, I may not have gotten out of there because he had the same engines in his gunboats. Of course they had the most horsepower; and were the lightest engine in the world at that time. The parts were hard for me to get and they were probably harder for the Cubans to get. Well anyway, to make a long story short, I'm worn out. I'm really exhausted. It was a very tiring trip across and my fuse was very, very short to put it mildly.

They started interrogating me and going with these questions, and I blew. I stood up and I almost hit the guy behind the desk. I went *berserko*. I screamed bloody murder. I said, "You bastard." I went crazy. I called him every name in the book. I said, "You're asking me these questions here, you don't even know how many boats are in Cuba. I listen to the radio and the news channels, and they'd say there's 1,500-1,600 boats in there. No, there were over 3,000 boats. If there's one, there's over 3,000. You guys have no idea of what's going on." I said, "I got bad people on my boat. I've got murderers. I've got rapists. I've got some very bad people on my boat that came out of the prisons." And I said, "I've got some very good people on the boat too, people from the American Embassy, and you don't even know that. You don't know anything."

And the guy got me to sit down and settle down. He gave me a cup of coffee. He says, "Settle down, slow down." Two guards are in the room, one on each side of me. They got me to sit down with them, cool down, and the guy said, "Look, we know you've got people from the Embassy and the prisons, on your boat." I said, "Well, how do you know that?" He said, "Central Intelligence told us. You're the first boat to bring them in and that's why the big hullabaloo here. We're very concerned about it. All the people are being taken care of. They're going on buses now to Miami and they're going to be filtered out." I said, "Great, now I feel better about the whole damn thing." I go, "Man, I'm so tired I can hardly see straight. I've been through a war zone here. I'm really exhausted. I have some stress on me and I'm burned."

So he says, "Well, Cap, we've got a couple more questions." And this and that. He asked me a couple more and he said, "Go in the back room and lay down. We have some mattresses back there, lie down and take a nap. We have to do the paperwork now and we have to get some Visas for these people that you brought in. It's going to take some time getting all this done, you know." I said, "Okay."

"We might have some more questions later on," he said, "But go take a nap. Your boat's okay. They're unloading your boat. You got any messages?" I said, "Yeah, ask my assistant, Bill Grimm, to come in." He came in and I told him "Bill, when everybody's off the boat, take the boat back to the Oceanside Marina Dock. It's no problem. They want me to stay here. I'll see you tomorrow, whenever." And he says, "Fine." And that's what he did.

Seniorita *Viking Starship*

I'm in a back room lying down. My wife Betty was a very beautiful woman of Irish-descent and she had jet-black hair at the time and spoke a little Spanish. She most certainly could pass for being part Spanish for sure. She was down at the dock all the time, on and off, and she got to know the other Spanish women that were there waiting for their relatives and their husbands to come home. They thought she was Spanish and immediately started speaking Spanish to her. She spoke enough to get by and then they realized she was the Senorita of the *Viking Starship* — well, that put her on a pedestal after that. This is Senorita *Viking Starship* because; number 1, the *Viking Starship* was a good boat. It was around already that they didn't gouge the people to go to Cuba. We only charged $20,000. Some boats were charging $80,000, $90,000, $100,000 dollars, all kinds of telephone numbers.

We were one of the good ones and they were very proud of us. So they took good care of my wife. Every time she came, they'd shake their heads, "No, the boats not here," and so forth. When the boat came in they grabbed her right away, "Oh Senorita *Viking Starship*, the boat is here, the boat is here."

They had the fence cut so that a person could sneak in the fence and they brought my wife to it and showed her how to go through it and which building I was in. She went through the fence and got right in there. Some security! All of a sudden she was tapping me on the shoulder and woke me up when I was laying on the mattress. She gave me a big hug and all. She liked me then. Unfortunately, we got divorced a few years later, and that was that.

Unsaid Words

A couple of things went on in Cuba that I didn't talk about at the time. Number one, two or three days after we arrived in Cuba, our lovely President Carter (I really love this guy) made a change in policy. Before we went to Cuba he said on the radio and in the press that we had to be nice to our Cuban friends, what with the "Open Arms" policy and so forth. He said that this is a great opportunity for some of the Cuban people to come to America. Families are split up and so on. He even made it possible and easy for us to change our Federal Documentation to be legal so that we could go to Cuba in the first place. Now, a couple of days after we arrived in Cuba he reversed the story, which he was known to do on other issues while he was President. "I didn't say what I said, I didn't do what I said, but that isn't what I meant, what I said. I didn't say that," were some of his stories. In other words, he backed down and all of a sudden all of these boats were breaking the law by being in Cuba. I'm already there and I can't get out. Not only can I not get out, but I can't leave without taking a load of refuges with me! Believe me, if I could have gotten out then and there, without taking on passengers, I would have, but they wouldn't let me. They had their gunboats at the entrance of the harbor. That's the one thing that really, really upset me a lot.

Another tragedy that occurred while we were in Cuba was when our helicopters crashed in Iran trying to rescue the hostages. Every day this little Cuban boat came around and charged us 25 cents for the Cuban newspaper. It was in Spanish and the American-Cubans bought two-three papers and passed them around the boat throughout the day. Well, the day after the helicopters crashed in Iran and rescuing the hostages was a flop, that day, newspapers were given away free. They didn't have to pay the 25 cents. On the front page was a full-length cartoon of President Carter standing there, pointing up at the sky, and those mangled up helicopters on the ground, and he's yelling in Spanish, "Fly, fly, fly." Boy, was that insulting. I tell you, that was insulting, but that's the way it is; that's the way it was.

Welcome to Miami

Once we were back in Key West, Florida, as Captain of the vessel, I had the responsibility of taking the Visas up to Miami. They let me go home later that night with the promise that I would come back early the next afternoon; by then they'd have the Visas ready. Well, they didn't have them ready until about 3 o'clock. We packed them in two plastic milk crates and put them in a carry-all and prepared to take them to a specified location in Miami. I'm still very tired; exhausted in fact, but luckily my wife was able to do most of the driving. I was so exhausted I kept falling asleep in the car.

We got to the specified location; a warehouse converted to a receiving station for the refugees, and went inside. My wife carried one box, I carried the other; thankfully they didn't weigh much. We walked in the door. "Where do we go from here?" we asked. The clerk asked, "What vessel?" "The *Viking Starship*," I answered. Immediately the woman went screaming through the place, "*Viking Starship, Viking Starship*." People started applauding. I couldn't believe it. They were applauding. Now I just left from being heavily questioned by Customs Officials and these people are clapping and coming over to me and thanking me, and so forth. They were so happy. I was like a hero to them. Boy, I sure felt better after that. We gave them the Visas and left and went home.

The next day I went down to the boat. All our business was gone. The press had the roads from Miami to Key West all jammed up with people trying to get to Cuba. The few people we had who booked trips on our last fishing trip canceled, and we lost the other two trips before that because we were stuck in Cuba, so I lost a good amount of money by going to Cuba.

It wound up that we got the boat all loaded up and we left. There were all kinds of talk about boats being arrested so I figured the faster I got out of Key West and went north, the better for me, and that's what we did. We went back up to Montauk.

The Rumor Mill

We were coming into Montauk and I was talking to the *Viking Star* on the big radio. I was someplace just below the Hudson Canyon and John Larson heard me. He was out fishing and he called me, "How'd Cuba go, Paul?" I says, "Oh man, John, I'm just kicking money all over the pilothouse here. This was great. I got a big suitcase full of money here. I don't know what to do." And he said, "Boy, I've been calling and calling. I told your wife that I had the fuel tanks full, ready to go." He was fishing out of Fort Meyers Beach that winter. "I just got back to New Jersey," he said," But I filled the tanks up. Hell, I do 20 odd knots; I can get to Cuba quick from New Jersey. I could have come down there." He says, gloomily, "I thought you were a friend of mine." He was so damn agitated that I didn't call and get him in on a little of the money that I made. I also heard rumors where I had the boat paid off and I was making three trips a day getting $100,000 for each trip. Oh, the rumors were unbelievable, especially in a small town like Montauk, but the truth came out later on.

Anyway, we got back and my insurance man called. It was Chris Mahlstadt, of Island Wide Insurance. He's still my insurance man. He was very thankful that I got back. He told me about insurance companies calling him and saying, "Is that our boat in the centerfold of the *Miami Herald?* Is that our boat?" And then they'd call and ask, "Is that our boat on the front page of the *New York Times?* Is that our boat?" Oh boy.

Anyway, we got back and started our usual fishing. And that's basically the Cuban story. George Block was one of the crew on the boat. He's since passed away. Bill Grimm was my Assistant Captain. He filled out the ship's log, and his log was quoted, I think, in the *New York Times* or the *Miami Herald,* one of those newspapers. And Eddie, who still lives in Montauk, was on the trip, too. He was just a kid then, mating on a boat. My son, Steven, was with us on the boat. For a long time it seemed that every time I would get in trouble and was some place I didn't want to be, my son seemed to be there with me. Joe Alexander, the galley guy passed away recently with cancer. Chuck Willer also passed away with cancer. The two of them died about ten days apart. I can't recall everybody who was with us at the time but there are others like Patty, the only girl aboard. It was very, very, stressful, I guess is the best way to put it, and very emotional too.

Seeing those people and hearing them sing and cheer when we got to International Waters, and watching them board my boat with nothing but shorts and a T-shirt makes one realize how badly they must have wanted freedom. It made me feel good about America and what a great country America is. Seeing people coming like that, by golly, it most certainly is a good feeling.

Chapter Fifteen

1980s

The *Viking Freedom* —
A Steel Commercial Fishing Sailboat

fter Cuba, I spent one more winter in Key West, but I had always had a dream of building a sailboat. I had worked side-by-side with the builders building the *Viking Starship*. My sons Paul and Steven, plus my stepson, and some of the crew went up with me to Blount Marine in Warren, Rhode Island and we worked together with a couple of guys from the shipyard. We worked there for about four months, and a month after that we were finishing the *Starship* up. I became very interested in building boats after that.

Just previous to building the *Starship* a local man in Montauk built a couple of steel commercial fishing boats. The first one he built was right near the Viking Dock and next door to a motel. He was right in front of me, right in my face, and he was also my next-door neighbor. Johnny Steck was his name,

The *Viking Freedom* at sea.

and he built a 60-foot boat. So after we stopped going to Key West I decided, "I gotta build myself my boat, I gotta try it."

My sons Steven and Paul were growing up. Both became Captains and were doing very well. I was starting to take a back seat and began building my dream boat, my sail-assisted commercial fishing vessel. In 1983 I read a couple of books to give myself some sort of guideline as to what size steel to use. So I bought a bunch of steel and plans for $1200 from Walter Merritt. He was down in Norfolk, Virginia and he had built a number of sailboats. He designed a sailing tug called *TugAteen* which was featured in several different magazines and that's where I got his name. I called him and I told him what I wanted. I said that I just needed the idea of Scantlings and sizes of steel. I knew that the hull that he had could be modified to do what I wanted with it, but I needed a starting point.

business. I couldn't get it done. I thought it was going to rust away before we finished it up.

A year before that, I met a guy by the name of Junior Duckworth from Tarpon Springs, Florida. He's the top builder of the south with a small but highly efficient boatyard. At the time, my son, Paul, was interested in having a commercial boat built and that's how we became acquainted with Junior. He could only give us about fifteen minutes of his time because he was busy; he had a couple of boats under construction and time was money. So I called him up and I said, "Hey Junior." I told him who I was. He says, "Oh yeah, Paul. I remember you. Did your son ever get a boat built?"

"No," I told him and then I explained what I was doing. "I'm tired of lying in the snow and I'm looking for a place to take the boat where it's going be warmer. I'm taking the winter off from fishing so I can spend most of the season working on her. It will take a year or two before it's finished." He says, "What do you need?" "I need just enough space so I can go to work," I said, "And if I need help, such as a welder, I'd appreciate it if you could loan me one when I need him. I'll do all the fitting work myself." "No problem," he said, "Bring her down here."

So we brought her down on a trailer. It took eleven days for the poor driver to get there. He went through two snowstorms plus he got a flat tire. He finally got to Tarpon Springs on a Friday night. About 4:00 he called the office and said, "I'm 30 miles away, please don't close. I've got to get rid of this damn boat. I can't look at it through the weekend. I can't be stuck in Tarpon Springs. I'll be there in 45 minutes or so." Well, I didn't know at the time, but Junior always stayed until 6 or 8:00 at night. He is a workaholic, a very nice man, and the most honest man I've ever met. I've done quite a bit of business with him since. Anyway, this truck driver comes whipping into Duckworth Steel Boats. It's dark and he's got a flat tire spinning around on the wheel. "I got that a few miles back," he says. "I could care less. I just got to get rid of this boat. I can't hang on to this thing much longer."

The *Viking Freedom* leaving Montauk for Tarpon Springs, Florida.

Well, I had a rental car and was looking for a house to rent. I turned on the lights with the car so he could get the boat blocked up and get the crane going and get her off the trailer. I was happy the boat was there. All of a sudden I look around and we've got about 15 people working, helping out, moving blocking, and so forth. I got Junior on the side and ask, "Hey Junior, you know, who's who here? Who's getting paid? I can't afford this big gang. I'm on a very limited budget, you know." He looked around and he says, "Nobody's getting paid here. All these people are fishermen. Ned here works for the company and this is on his own time. These fishermen here are from the other side of the street and they saw the boat come in. That's the way it is around here when one of us needs a hand everybody helps each other out." Then he said, "Take notice Paul, when they need a hand on the other side of the street, why, we go over there and help them out too." Boy, I said to myself, I think I'm going to like this place. I think I'm going to like Tarpon Springs.

Well, I sure do. I've been here since and gee, I brought the boat down in 1988 and launched it in 1990. I've been here since, with the exception of a 4-year hitch to go to Puerto Rico. We got the boat built little by little in two winters. I went down there for those two winters.

How the Boat was Named

I had first named the boat *Viking Elizabeth* after my wife at the time, even though my daddy had told me to never name a boat after a woman unless it it's your mother. (Early on, I told you about how he got in trouble by naming his first boat after my aunt instead of my mother). Elizabeth's children were also in the business with us. Once the boat was finished I sailed and fished my way up north and we had her there for a summer doing a little tuna fishing. Then with Elizabeth on board we headed south on the Inter-coastal Waterway. She got off at North Carolina for a while and I fished and eventually, I headed to Key West, Florida where Elizabeth joined me and I fished for tuna out of there that winter.

But my marriage began to fall apart and Elizabeth and I got into a very vicious and violent divorce.

I took the boat to Trinidad to get it away from all of it. I was in trouble with the business. We were in a financial mess; my wife and stepchildren were running the business. I had put too much time in building the sailboat and I wasn't around. I thought I was retired. It didn't work out. So I put the boat in Trinidad, hauled it out, put her down there far enough away, hard to get to, and she stayed there two years in a safe yard. I flew back to Montauk and went back to work and got the company going again.

Once the divorce was final, I said goodbye to her kids, all at the same time as my son Paul started to drift away from fishing because he wanted to try real estate. He did very well for a time and still did some fishing but his main interest had become real estate.

Then I went down to Trinidad, got the boat and with two friends, brought her up to Tarpon Springs, Florida. I fished on her out of there and lived on her for awhile — winter seasons — very comfortable. Before leaving Trinidad, I put a circle around the name "Elizabeth" and put a slash through it, the international sign for "no Elizabeth." Then I sailed up and down the coast with her fishing, bouncing back and forth to Montauk every now and then to help Steven run the business.

I met a beautiful lady, Patricia, some time after the divorce. After we did some local sailing she suggested that I change the name of the boat to "*Viking Freedom.*" That's the name of the boat now and she truly is my "*Freedom.*" I really enjoy fishing and sailing with her and have never enjoyed a vessel so much in my life and I love it more as time goes by.

Patricia thought putting "*Freedom*" in the name seemed compatible with having freedom on the seas, plus the added bonus of never having to change the name again and she sure was right!

I put a copper eagle on top of the mast, with a 4-foot wing span, the sign of freedom, and I put the name *Viking Freedom* in gold leaf letters. So be it. The boat fits the name, and the name fits the boat. I hope that I'll be able to take the *Freedom* out to sea for many years, until I no longer have the health to do it anymore.

I've taken her north and, together with Steven, explored offshore and we found some wrecks together. Today, he still fishes some of those way offshore spots with customers, producing some truly wonderful catches for them.

Winning the Lottery!

I brought the *Viking Star* to Duckworth Steel Boats in Tarpon Springs for work. We rewired and repainted her, and basically redid everything. We put in a new generator and replaced the whole interior with all new Formica and a new seating arrangement. Then in 1993, we did just about the same thing with the *Starship.*

We have a wonderful working relationship with Duckworth Steel Boats and work right alongside of their men. I know many of them personally on a first name basis and consider them good friends. Junior himself is a wonderful guy to work with.

A former Duckworth employee named "Lucky" Lee used to come around the boatyard and collect money for the Florida Lotto. He had retired but still came faithfully every week to collect the Lotto pool money from the employees. I was working on the *Starship* in 2003 with Captain Rich Castellano. I had been putting in my $5 every week and Rich asked me what it was all about. Well, I told him and even though he was almost down to his last $5, he put it in with the rest of us. He couldn't let that go by; he'd never forgive himself if we won; hey, this was the Florida Lotto!

Lee was an old man, around eighty, but he still went around to everybody in the yard once a week. I used to give him cash in advance because I never knew week-to-week where I would be. He'd keep track of it for me. Every once in a while he'd tap me on the shoulder and tell me that my money was running out so I'd give him another pile of cash so he could keep me going with $5 weekly.

Well, one day I walked into the workshop and there's Lucky Lee with three or four other guys standing around looking at this piece of paper and talking. I walked up and said, "How you doing today, Lee?" He said, "Hey Paul, we won the Lotto!" I said, "Yeah, and good morning to you too," and walked away. He was yelling after me, "No, I'm not kidding you; we won the lotto." I said, "Yeah, okay Lee, great," and continued walking away. I went around the corner and looked back and watched those guys huddled around talking, still looking at that piece of paper so I went upstairs to see Barbara, the accountant for Duckworth at the time. "Look out the window down there," I said. "See those guys in the shop with Lee? They said we won the Lotto."

She jumped up like a jackrabbit. "What?" She runs down the stairs with me watching her through the window thinking to myself, let's see what happens here. Then I walked downstairs and got behind some machinery where I could hear a little bit, thinking I'm going to watch the joke happen. Suddenly Barbara turns around and runs back upstairs, all excited. I went after her and she's looking on the computer. A little later she says, "Yeah, we won the Lotto, Paul, we did, we won the Lotto."

Damn, I couldn't believe it. I went out and told Rich and he said good morning to you too Paul and just kept working on the boat.

About half an hour later I go back upstairs and asked Barbara if we were still winners and she says, "Yeah, we're still winners." I really got excited then and that's how I used my day up; I was back and forth on a regular basis asking if we were still winners. And each time, they told me, yes, we're still winners!

Meantime, everyone in the yard is talking about it. Rich still couldn't believe it either.

"Hey Lee," I said, "That's a very small ticket stub there; God forbid if you lost that, we'd all lose, you take care of that, will you?" Don't worry Paul," he replied, "I've got the perfect place for it. Junior and I are going to Tallahassee with it tomorrow to get our check. He already talked to a lawyer and he's on the phone now with an accountant to talk about how to pay taxes on it and then we're all going to get our money." "Boy, that's great Lee, don't lose that ticket," I told him.

He repeated that he had the perfect place for it. And the next day, he and Junior went and got our check. Curiosity finally got me to ask where he hid it and he said that he had thought about a hiding place for years in anticipation of winning. His hiding place was in the bottom of his parakeet cage, right under the bird poop lining paper. He knew that no one could ever think of looking in a place like that. I said, "You crafty man, you sure picked a perfect hiding place."

Anyway, after taxes were removed, we each got $184,000 and I knew exactly what I was going to do with my share. I always had a dream of having my sailboat in my backyard. There weren't many places in Tarpon Springs that could fit a sixty-foot boat with a six-foot draft but my dream came true. I

The *Viking Freedom* at our dock in Tarpon Springs, Florida.

had my eye on a house that was up for sale and I used that money as a down payment. I bought the house on the river and I'm in it today. My boat is in my backyard and I'm as happy as a clam at high tide. So, yes, I guess you really can win the Lotto.

Rich also bought a house nearby in Hudson, Florida and he has his own boat in his backyard so we both did very well. That was a great year for both of us and I'm very thankful I put my five dollars in. Lucky Lee passed away a few years ago and now Junior Duckworth's son, Joe, is handling the Lotto money and we're all still putting money in it. Hoping that lightning would strike twice though, we have doubled the amount to $10 weekly. It hasn't happened yet but we have high hopes.

Out of thirty employees at Duckworth's, fourteen were in the lottery and I can't think of a more deserving bunch of people to win that kind of money. Suddenly there were a lot of new pickup trucks in the parking lot and some guys paid off their houses. It was a really nice thing to see happen to a real good bunch of hard working guys.

Chapter Sixteen

1990s

The Viking that Never Was!

Rather than talking about this boat in the list I gave you nice readers way earlier, since this particular boat never operated with the name I had selected for it, I feel that a separate chapter is called for, okay? The boat was to have been called the *Viking Galaxy* and when we launched her on March 3rd, 1999, she wore that name. She was to have been the Montauk Ferry but things got so nuts that we never used her for one day!

We started construction at Duckworth's and at 154 feet in length, she was really a beauty. My plan was to use her as a ferry to run passengers and up to 25 cars back and forth from Montauk to New London, Connecticut. My dad ran the ferry operation from Montauk to Block Island, starting way back in 1951 and I continued it after he stopped. In fact, the 120-foot *Viking Superstar*, discussed in great detail earlier by my friend Chan Stone, is now operating as the ferry, but it isn't allowed to carry vehicles.

It was and remains a hassle trying to get to New London from Montauk by car and the idea I had made sense to everyone, everyone, that is, until some clown started a rumor that I was going to use it to carry gamblers back and forth to the casinos, Mohegan Sun and Foxwoods, and that never was in my plans. The ride by car takes forever and my ferry would have cut the time way, way down but again, a rumor started to brew.

The story said that Perry Duryea, owner of a lobster house in Fort Pond was making the deal but for sure, I never knew anything about it, if in fact such discussions had ever taken place.

So a meeting was called at the East Hampton Town Hall. It was the largest crowd that had ever attended a meeting there. In fact, they could only fit twenty percent of those who showed up; everyone else was outside yelling and screaming so it had to be moved to the VFW building in Amaganset.

We went from everyone loving the idea of a short boat ride, with their car on board, to the opposite, with screams of "stop the ferry." Most everyone liked the old ferry but many felt that the purpose would change, regardless of what I said. Bumper stickers had been printed and worn by owners of the cars who used to love my old ferry! I spent a ton of money fighting the battle in court and because I had a pre-existing ferry operation they had to let me operate this boat, but they denied me the right to carry cars and that killed the whole idea for me. I couldn't make enough money just carrying passengers. Folks still use the *Superstar* to go to Block Island or New London so that they could visit friends and relatives but they can't take their car with them!

While all that was going on, the boat was still under construction at Duckworth's, and the banks were yelling for payment. Duckworth's had plenty of room and we laid the keel and a few frames, starting with internal money from the Viking Company but I had to borrow a bunch as well. On top of all that, marriage #2 started going sour and my wife and I wound up in a very vicious and violent divorce and we had to stop construction on the boat for a few years.

Of course, before my marriage fell apart, I was dealing with the *Viking Galaxy* mess. We finally got the project underway again, all the while knowing that the boat would never be the ferry I had hoped it would become. So there I was, with a partially built 154-foot long steel boat, with three big Caterpillar engines in it. I really had no use for it, it became a dinosaur. So I talked with Duckworth and told Junior to get the torches out, cut it up and I'll scrap the steel and try to pay the bank off.

Junior urged me to stay with the program, saying that there was no rush to make a decision. That he had plenty of room for the boat to sit unfinished.

I fell behind on my bank loan payments and, of course, had no money left from the loan to even finish the boat. The loan officer wasn't even talking to me and that's not a very good sign.

Finally, somehow or another, we got it finished enough to launch and float. And one day, shortly after we put it in the water, a man came up to me and said, "That would make a hell of a casino boat, you know that?" I replied, yeah, I'm interested in doing anything with it I can and he asked me, "What do you want for the boat?" I told him the price and he said, "Alright, what's it going to cost me to hold that boat for a week?" I thought real quick and said, "I need $10,000 a week to hold the boat. So, okay, he writes me a check for $10,000 and says, "I'll see you next week. I've got an idea and I'm going to put a few things together here. I think I can run it as a casino boat right out of Tarpon Springs."

A week went by and he said that he and his brother had built a lot of houses nearby, thousands in fact, and made a lot of money doing so, and he tried to get his brother to partner up with him on the boat since they always did everything as a team. But his brother had recently found out that he had prostate cancer and he himself was in the middle of divorce proceedings so the deal was off!

We wished each other well and buyer #2 appeared from Savannah, Georgia and also said he would like to buy it and use it as a casino boat. He gave me an

$80,000 deposit. I was flabbergasted, feeling that this time, the boat was sold.

I went to Junior and brought myself up to date with him for his work and gave the balance of the $80,000 to the bank to bring me up to date on the interest on the loan. When I told them what the buyer was going to do with the boat they were upset because they said, "We don't finance casino boats!" I told them that, it's that, or they may have to eat the steel because I couldn't use it for the ferry that I had planned for and had no idea if anyone else might want to use it as a ferry somewhere.

This buyer sent an architect back and forth to me, drawing up all kinds of plans, but he didn't pay me any more money. I finally told him that his money was used up two weeks ago. So he comes out and gives me another $20,000!

A few weeks went by. I had collected $100,000 from him and one day, he called and says, "Stick your boat where the sun don't shine; I don't want it." He walked away from his $100,000 and there I was, sitting with my boat again, advertising it through a few agents when up comes another company — ready to deal.

They were on the New York Stock Exchange and had a real good place to put the boat in North Beach, Miami. They had a good idea and a fine location and before you knew it, we made a deal. This was not to be a purchase but instead, a lease with the option-to-buy that should really be very good for me. They planned on putting a ton of money into upgrading the boat.

The deal was signed and they gave me more than enough money to cover my bank payments and they put over $2,000,000 into it to make it a truly first-class casino boat. It had carpet that was loomed in Scotland and the rug alone cost $125,000. The ceiling cost more than another $100,000!

They put bigger generators in and a much larger electrical system to handle the slot machines and so forth. We delivered the boat to Miami and they went into business. But they were not business people and they quickly failed. It only took four months for them to fall behind on their lease payments and one night, I decided that it was time to go get my boat back and in the middle of the night, I stole my boat back and brought it to Tarpon Springs again.

So there I was, with a gorgeous boat with all kinds of slot machines, but the machines were leased and my buyer was behind too in those payments. The lessor told me that I could keep the machines in the boat as I looked for another deal.

Sure enough, a young guy came along and threw $100,000 at me and said that he was going to bring the boat to Fort Lauderdale to use as a casino boat. But he really was a novice. He had the boat docked behind a hotel that didn't even have an adequate dock and this guy was so bad a businessman that he just couldn't do anything right and once again, there I went, stealing my boat back because he was way behind in payments.

Back in Tarpon Springs, with four deals done and undone; some folks from Port Richey, Florida approached me. They were already running a successful small casino boat operation in Florida. They were a family business, mother, father and son, and they really ran a fine operation. Their boat was quite old and tired though and they wanted to upgrade and for sure, the *Galaxy* was quite an upgrade. Their son came and looked at it and fell in love, feeling the boat was perfect for their operation. We quickly put a lease with purchase option together and the boat is currently still running out of Port Richey and they remain current with their payments, thankfully.

The boat is too big to tie up at shore so they anchor it offshore a bit and run small shuttles back and forth from land.

Once a month they bring the boat to the Anclote River in Tarpon Springs to fuel up. I had put real big 20,000-gallon tanks in her. They fast feed the fuel and are out again in a matter of hours. This is required at high tide because the boat rides eight feet deep in the water. The boat actually goes right past my house and I can hear her low rumble when she comes in and goes out and it doesn't matter how early in the morning it is, I get out of bed and run to the window and get on my hands and knees and say a prayer of thanks as I watch that beautiful boat go by.

Here's a picture of the *Galaxy* when it was first called the *Ella Star*.

She is a pretty, pretty boat and I had a lot to do with designing her. The architect and I worked side-by-side. I really am grateful that I finally made a deal that stuck. It probably would have taken the Viking Operation down. Chances were that we might have had to go bankrupt over it if we hadn't found a solution that stuck, but it worked out.

A Stop in Puerto Rico

I decided to go to Trinidad. Before leaving Montauk I spoke to a woman who worked at Dave's Grill on the Viking Dock in Montauk and told her what I was going to do, "Gee, stop by and say hello in Puerto Rico. You have to go right by us to get to Trinidad." So on my way I stopped in at the west end of Puerto Rico. I stayed there about a week or so and had a good time. She and her sister showed me around. I met quite a few people down there who used to work in Montauk. A lot of people from Montauk go down there surfing. It's the surfer's capital of the world, Rincon, Puerto Rico.

Well, on my way to Trinidad my brain started working. There were a lot of whales in the Mona Pass down there; in fact, there were whales all over the place! So the next year we wound up bringing the *Viking Starship* to Puerto Rico. My two sons, Paul and Steven, brought her down and were soon in the whale watching business. We ended up staying in the Mona Passage on the west end of Puerto Rico for four winters.

We put a big diving platform on the stern of the *Starship* ourselves and we had boats pick up people elsewhere and bring them out. They didn't have a dock there so the little boats would bring them out to us, tie up to the platform and put them aboard. Then we'd go out whale watching. We went whale watching out of two ports. We thought we were mainly going to be taking American tourists, but we took mostly native Puerto Ricans. Consequently, we had to put a naturalist on the boat who could speak Spanish and English. We were totally surprised that we were going to be carrying that many local people. We did quite well with it for a while.

We also made some fishing trips to the Dominican Republic Banks and caught a lot of different kinds of grouper and snapper. No other headboat had ever sailed to these waters before, nor carried passengers on whale watching trips.

The grandkids learned diving and surfing and somewhat of a different culture in the four winters we were there and while it was a good educational experience, it started to become a complex family issue. My grandchildren went to school down there and when they went back to Montauk, they were behind in their schooling. Plus moving the families back and forth was a hassle. Both of my sons have three children. There were six kids moved and two families and so finally we said, well, something has to give here, so family first and we gave it up. But we had four interesting years while we were down there. Ultimately though, my marriage to Elizabeth fell apart and after a dreadful battle, we were divorced. At the very least though, I do want to point out that she had been the first woman (to my knowledge) that held a 100-ton Captain's License!

Meeting Judy

After the divorce, I met another nice lady named Judy Koenig, a Special-Ed school teacher. She belonged to a ski club and I give her credit for getting me even closer to my grandchildren and to this day, I head west to the slopes with as many of my grandchildren as can join me. This is a fun part of my life and a great time for them and I credit Judy with getting me into that, she was a really fine person.

More Vacation Stuff

When the grandsons were younger, I took them to the Caribbean for a week on Spring Break and we went from island to island swimming, sailing and fishing together — we really had a great time. As a matter of fact, that's when Steven Jr. learned how to swim without a life jacket.

Chapter Seventeen

2000s

Our Navy Seal

My oldest grandson, Paul Drew Forsberg liked diving so much that right after 9/11 he joined the Navy and became a Navy Seal. He has become a Chief Petty Officer and is the proud father of a baby girl. I'm very proud of him too — by golly, quite an accomplishment. So far he has spent most of his time in the mountains of Afghanistan and Iraq and here the poor guy thought he was going to be in the water swimming and diving a lot. But he enjoys his chosen career, he lives it.

More Grandchildren

Besides Drew and his brother Carl and cousin Steve, key Captains of the Viking fleet, I also have more fine grandkids. They include Samantha who is an assistant occupational therapist as well as the mother of her lovely little daughter, Loia; and Melissa, married and devoted mother to her two little sons

I'm holding our baby seal, with his dad Paul B. on my right
and Uncle Steven on my left.

Here I am with my three grandsons.

and we have Tessie who is finishing up college. Further, my son Steve has Grayson and John Fisher in his second family.

More About and from Our Family

My two grandchildren who are key to the success of our business are Carl and Steven Jr., who still do their surfing, but they are both also great Captains, each running Viking boats as noted earlier. I have my son, Steven, and my grandsons running the business with me. I am very fortunate. I have some great people that have been with me in the company for years, some of them over twenty years. Eleanor has been with me in the 20s, and Captain Dave Marmeno has been with Viking full-time since 1986. Captain Dave, a very great captain. A good man. I've been very fortunate with all the employees who have been part of Viking. They are not just employees, they are like family. If anybody gets in trouble, if anyone has a problem, someone in our "family" will step in to help. Boy, word gets around the company when someone is at the door, "What can we do to help out?" We're just like family and that's the way we are. I'm very lucky. There are no politics in it. We all have a job to do. We love the company and we get along great. In the summertime our staff swells to 55-60 people. In the wintertime, off season, we're down to about 14 with our maintenance and office personnel.

Some Memories from my son Paul B.

When growing up in the Viking household, we learned how to answer the phone by the 3rd ring — regardless of what was going on. It also had to be quiet in the background. I was answering the phone by about age 10.

When in the 6th grade, I was almost left back — not because of grades, but because of missing school. Wednesday was the busiest day of the week. The crew was notorious for not showing up on Wednesdays. So dad would drive home, give me a nudge and say, "Get-up you gotta' go to work."

Of course he would already be a little stressed, because of no help, and we would be late sailing. He would shake me, go to the kitchen and pour himself a drink of OJ and walk to the truck. If, for some reason he had to wait for more than 15 seconds, I got a talking to all the way down to the boat.

Needless to say, I learned how to get up, get dressed, and get in the truck in less than a minute. I packed my work clothes in my bottom dresser drawer in a specific way so as to save seconds in getting dressed. My boots were always at the ready, and in them were my pliers and knives.

The *Viking* fleet is built on customer service (we were, and remain the best in the business) and the Cox's Ledge Codfish Boat had Free Ice for the fish.

We'd take the boat to get fuel one day, and we would go to Gosman's Dock everyday and fill up burlap bags with ice and transport it to the boats via our pick-up.

One day while getting fuel, one of the Gosman's came out to tell dad the price of fuel had gone up from $.09 to $.11. Yep — 9 to 11 cents a gallon. Dad had a fit, threw his hat down on the dock, jumped up and down on it and yelled bloody murder. Then he raised the fare $2. I'll never forget that.

Back then, the mates pay was $12 a day. I was paid $6, however, I was making between $50 and $150 a day in tips. Back in 1972 that was a lot of money!

I used to catch eels and sell them to the charter boats for bass bait. One time I was accused of stealing eels from a guy's cart — which I never did. This guy accused me, yelled like the dickens, and called me all sorts of names. Dad asked if I took them and I did not — (I knew who did though). The guy hauled off and sucker-punched dad and knocked him off his feet.

Dad got up, picked up his hat and walked away — I was shocked at what happened — the guy actually dropped to his knees and began to sulk. Dad said it takes a bigger man to walk away than it does to fight. It left a life-long impression — that's the kind of guy he was and is.

I had my Captain's License before I graduated from High School and was running the *Viking Starlite* before receiving my HS diploma.

Back in about 1977, (I had just graduated HS), during the winter, I was planning on going longlining with the *Viking Starlite* — she was a 65-foot wooden boat built in Deltaville, Virginia.

It was a little early in the year for cod fishing when the boat was ready, so we decided to take her offshore tile fishing. It was my very first trip offshore. On the boat were me, Dad, my brother Steven, and this guy Sammy Sazinski (a/k/a Sambo). Steven is three years younger than I am.

On the way in, somehow Sammy had smuggled a bottle of booze on board, drank it and passed out cold. We got caught in some really bad weather. This was before Weather Faxes and we did not have a single sideband radio. The weather was really bad and dad would not leave the wheel — he couldn't — it was that nasty out.

I kept going down to pump the engine room (wood boats leak) and soon realized as it was getting nastier and nastier we were losing ground and the water was coming in the boat faster than we could pump it out.

My brother and I began looking for the leaks, and found the #2 compartment was leaking like hell — the rough water had ripped the guard rails off the boat and every 12" was a 3/8" hole where a bolt should have been.

The holes got plugged with strips of rags and my T-shirt and we made it into Newport, Rhode Island to offload the fish.

Dad was abnormally quiet the whole time. On the way back to Montauk from Newport, he said to me that would be the last time all three of us would be on a boat together because if something had happened (and it was close) it would have wiped out the family. To the best of my knowledge, the three of us have never been offshore together or on a boat in bad weather ever again.

Some Memories from Paul B's son Carl

This is Paul's grandson, Carl Forsberg. I would be happy to add whatever I can.

I pretty much grew up around the Viking Dock, as my father Paul Jr. worked

Here's my grandson, Carl on the Viking dock.

here. Grandpa, as well as my father and Uncle Steven, would take me and my brother out on multi-day cod trips to Georges Bank when we were very young. I remember catching codfish and everyone on the boat would yell out, "Another double-header for the 6-year old!" Then Grandpa would hand me a scrub brush and tell me to start scrubbing. This lead to a lifetime of two different relationships between me and my grandfather. I still work for the *Viking* fleet, and business is business and personal is personal. These two do not cross paths with my grandfather.

In a working relationship my grandfather is the hardest working man I know, and he expects the same out of all of us. I wish I had half the knowledge he has. He is a great teacher as well. He will work you to the bone, scream at you if you screw up, berate you, etc., but after you got the job done he will explain why things have to be done in a certain way. I just never took anything personal. He knows the boats he built better than anyone and knows how to deal with the Coast Guard when it comes to safety on our boats. He also fights hard again unnecessary fishing regulations. He is totally iconic to me as a boat builder, a fisherman, and a businessman.

In a personal relationship, he is an excellent grandfather. My family lived down the hill from him and we were separated by woods — he had a huge trail bulldozed and cleared for us so that we could have a one minute walk up to his house instead of a ten minute walk.

He has always lead a busy life, but still took time away from work to take all his grandkids (myself, my brother and sister, and my three cousins) skiing in different places around the country as well as Canada. He took us to Canada, Colorado, California, etc. for usually around a week and would rent a condo or something big enough to house all of us and after skiing we would have a family dinner and he would tell us stories about fishing, old Montauk, etc.

He also took me, my brother, and my cousin Steven Jr. for a week-long sailing trip around the Virgin Islands on his custom sailboat.

He would also take us on multi-day commercial tuna trips. I remember as a young 12 year old going out with just him and one other man, Joey "Flapjaws" and landing a number of huge Big-Eye tuna and him teaching me how to dress them out, while emphasizing how to keep the quality of the fish the best for the best price.

There is much more I could muster up, but I hope this helps.

Some Memories from my son Steven D.

I was born and raised in Montauk, New York, fishing capitol of the world! As a small child I grew up fishing with my father from the time I could walk. Fishing is the only job I have ever had. In fact, I could not see myself doing anything else. As a child I started off working deck and as soon as I had earned my Captain's License I began running the Viking boats.

In the 80's my brother Paul B. and I made a living by commercial fishing during the winters. Throughout my career I have had the opportunity of trying several different types of commercial fishing from long lining, dragging, scalloping, gillnetting to pin hooking, but in my heart, recreational fishing is where I love to be.

Captain Steven D. with a big fluke.

I have pioneered offshore party boat tuna fishing and continue to run the offshore Deepwater Challenge trips. Now-a-days a lot of my time is spent in the Viking Office scheduling the trips for boat and crew. My role in the company has evolved into a managerial position, ensuring that every boat sails on time and is running in tip-top shape. I spend long hours sweating it out in the engine rooms of all of our boats. That said, I would rather be at the helm any day of the week than sit behind a desk!

I have a great interest in marine construction and enjoyed designing and building our latest vessel, the *Viking Fivestar* with my father and son.

Some Memories from Steven D's son Steven N.

I was born and raised in Montauk, growing up on the Viking Dock. In fact I sailed on my first two-day Tuna trip at age five. By age eight I was working as a mate on a charter boat and by age 11 or 12, I was a regular mate on the Viking fleet party boats.

At age 18 I earned my Captains License and by age 19 I had upgraded to my 100 Ton License. That fall, I began running the two-day Tuna trips and have never looked back. I love all kinds of fishing but offshore fishing is my passion.

My family has been involved in the Party Boat Fishing Industry for four generations. I currently work in our family business with my Grandfather Paul, my father Steven and my cousin Carl. The industry is changing and we here at the Viking fleet intend to change with it. In fact, we just finished construction of our newest vessel, the *Viking Fivestar* in Alabama. I made several trips to Alabama to help oversee the construction. During my limited time off I enjoy visiting my sisters and my niece in Florida. I am also doing some remodeling at my house in Montauk.

Some Memories from Office Manager Eleanor Donnelly

I have worked for Paul for around 20 years. I met him when he was in the process of his second divorce, a difficult time for him. I was hired by a woman named Linda Shoemaker to work in the office during my summer vacation from college in Ireland. It was a job that I returned to every summer until I graduated from college and moved to the U. S. The office was very low tech back then. We were extremely busy with telephone calls and ticketing as it was a time before computers and the internet. Paul spent every day in the office.

He is the epitome of the patriarchal boss. He treats everyone like they are part of his family. This can be endearing and at the same time, difficult. One of his many skills is his ability to delegate work. He will always give you the latitude to solve a situation and present a solution. He does not like to be bogged down with the details; he has too much going on. He is a broad stroke kind of guy and would rather hear the bottom line of any situation and what you propose to do about an issue.

He has an uncanny knack to bring out the best in his employees. What has made my experience at the Viking fleet so meaningful for me is the sense of belonging he has created for us all. You want to do the best job! His excitement becomes yours and his energy motivates you.

(Some More — A Few Days Later)

His business instincts are very sharp. He is the guy that will always have the feeling in his gut and heart that he is correct. He is sharp, instinctive and confident in his deliberations and interactions with people. Paul relies heavily on his intuition and he is typically right, very, very, very rarely wrong — if ever! He has the knack of reading people and using his insight.

An ex of his once described him to me as a diamond in the rough. This is a good comment. He may not have a formal education in spelling or social etiquette; but that has never ever held him back in any walk of life. He has addressed crowds of people and has the talent of holding a couple or a couple of thousand people rapt when he talks. He is a brilliant story-teller. He is the man that walks into the room and everyone immediately knows who he is and wants to be next to him. He has star quality. He enjoys his social occasions and loves a good laugh.

He has the ability to really command a room. Men and women love him. Men want to be him and women want to be next to him. He treats all the women that cross his path like ladies. Many times I have heard him scold fishermen for cursing, using language or speaking out-of-turn in front of the women that work for him. I think this is a throw back to Paul's own Mother. She really was a classy woman, a true lady. She was dressed and groomed like a model every time you met her. Though she was in her latter years when I met her, she was always impeccably dressed and had perfect manners. She was calm and collected, never reactionary. Actually very much like Patricia, Paul's partner. She is gentle in demeanor yet supportive, strong and very glamorous. A lady!

Paul is also the hardest working guy you will ever meet, first in and last out. Nothing is ever too much of a challenge. He will stay up night after night to get a job done. This must have been instilled in him from many years without sleep at sea. He will outwork the best of men, decades his junior.

Note: publisher Manny here — Paul and I elected to print the above thoughts from his relatives and friends virtually word for word. Chances are that you will recognize some things they said from things you already read earlier as Paul wrote about them.

Editors Note: the following are some thoughts from Orla Reville, another key part of the Viking family. And in this instance, since I knew that Paul has been playing a huge part in helping his industry survive, I solicited details of what he has done. He is not a bragger and clearly, didn't know that this information would become part of his book but if you do read these words; please know that permission had to be pried out of him, okay? Manny

Testimony: By Orla Reville

Paul attends at least two fisheries management meetings per year. He has done so for the past 15 years that I know of, maybe more. At these meetings Paul testifies and addresses the various councils. He is doing so on behalf of the entire fishing community, and not just on behalf of our fleet.

Sadly, and as badly as this reflects on the industry as a whole, Paul Forsberg is the only industry representative present at many of these meetings. There have been many instances where had Paul not been in attendance and campaigning loudly an entire fishery could have been needlessly shut down. The regulations got tougher and tougher over the last decade, putting many boats and entire fleets out of business.

If it was not for Paul, the Viking fleet would not have survived as he came up with innovative ways to survive the crippling closures. The greatest example of this was him joining the Federally run, "Research Set-Aside" program which, in essence, gives you a license to buy "the right to catch fish" during a closed season.

One of many of Paul's public appearances.

Paul came up with the idea and the Viking fleet joined the mainly commercial sector in the program. This allowed us to stay in business for years when all the other boats sat at the dock and laid off their crews.

Among the many states that Paul has traveled to and testified at are: New York, New Jersey, Connecticut, Texas, Delaware, Alabama, Florida, and Louisiana. And chances are that I left one or two off this list!

All of the expenses for these trips were paid for by the Viking fleet. A typical trip includes airfare, lodging and food, not to mention lost work time, costs upwards of $900 each. (Sometimes you are given two days notice to get yourself to the meeting and buying last minute flights blows one budget!)

Please note that Paul is such a respected industry member that he was appointed Scup Fishery Advisor for New York. This position however comes with no compensation to ease the expense. On the conservation end, attending meetings has cost the business (again, besides the cost of losing Paul for days at a time), approximately $27,000.

Paul will never give up and will be at meetings until he is no longer with us, which I pray will be many, many more years. Over the last six years or so, my role at the Viking has grown to attending the meetings with Paul and dealing with the State Representatives from the various states we hold license and permits in. Paul's unsurpassed reputation has opened many doors for me and made my role a lot easier.

I see myself together with Paul's grandson Carl becoming more involved in this as we fight to stay in business. On a side note, the regulations in New York have relaxed greatly over the past several years proving that Paul's work does indeed pay off.

The fight must always continue. The bonds and working relationship that we have between industry and the State Representative's are a direct result of Paul's work. Generations to come will be able to thank him for saving their right to catch fish on a party boat, if there are any left!

Chapter Eighteen

Florida Again

We opened up an operation in Tarpon Springs, Florida again in 2004. We had left Key West as discussed earlier and were doing really well in Tarpon Springs, until the government got in the way. The government's been getting in our way a lot anyway, what with all the fisheries management stuff.

We shut down for a while in 2010. It is a shame. We had a good business going.

The fishing is fantastic in Florida's "Middle Grounds" in the Gulf of Mexico, but then they started with this nonsense with the seasons, closing our seasons off during the main part of the year, the winter season, and that just totally destroyed us.

We had 12 great employees in Florida and we had to lay everybody off, everybody lost their jobs for nonsense. There are plenty of fish but not according to the government.

Patricia and me relaxing in Florida.

In the spring of 2011 we brought our smallest boat, the *Viking Gulfstar* back to Tarpon Springs to try and start up again. And, 2012 was a wonderful year for us. Business was great as was the fishing.

**I will continue to fight for the rights of fishermen
Taken in the spring of 2010 in front of the White House.**

Chapter Nineteen

Various Regulations

et me give you an example of just what kind of things we have to go through to satisfy the government today. For example —

Let's untie the lines of the commercial steel-hulled sailboat I built, the *Viking Freedom*, and head out into the Gulf of Mexico out of Tarpon Springs, Florida. First, any commercial fishing vessel has to have the proper paperwork. If you forget to renew your permit you lose it and can't get it back. Here's what you need if your paperwork is all up to date: you bait up the boat, put on fuel, ice, food and water, etc., and get ready to go fishing.

The Vessel Monitoring System and Observers

The "VMS" is on. (Vessel Monitoring System). This is a piece of spy equipment that all commercial boats must have and we pay monthly fees too, so that the National Marine Fishery Service can see where each boat is, even if it is tied to the dock!

It's something like what convicted felons might wear for a time when they first get out of prison like you see on television, a metal ankle bracelet. Well, this "bracelet" is permanently affixed to the boat and it never goes away. It's there as long as that vessel is a commercial fishing vessel so that the government can spy on her and knows where she is at all times. If the monthly fee is not paid up to date you don't get a renewal for your permit and you can't go fishing.

From time-to-time you also have to take a Government Observer, a human, with you to spy on you directly and watch how you fish and where you fish. He even has the right to write down your exact fishing positions for your favorite spots. This all goes down on record. Now I wonder how far a government employee would get if he went into restaurant kitchens and wrote down all the secret recipes of some of the most famous chefs in the country. Do you think that would be acceptable to restaurants? It's definitely not going over well in the fishing industry; nonetheless, we are saddled with it.

The Observers I've met so far have been very nice people. They've all been trained very well, they've been programmed very well too, and they all believe that they are doing a great job for the fisheries. However, they do not have any control over the information they obtain from us once it leaves their hands and goes to their higher-ups. They have no control over how that information is turned around to fit the agenda of whoever has control of the information.

More About Observers

Since there are fewer commercial fishing vessels every year due to the strenuous regulations we must go through, there may be more Observers than there are vessels to observe! That means that these Observers are often required to go on the same boats over and over, aggravating the fewer boats that remain in the commercial fishing industry.

We are now required, whether we carry an Observer or not, to allow our VMS (Vessel Monitoring System, remember?) — I call it our "tattletale machine" — to let the government know where we are going fishing, and we have to let them know what we expect to catch — what kinds of fish. Once we catch the fish and we're on the way back in, we have to give the government three hours advance notice before getting to our dock, via the VMS, how many fish we caught and what kinds they were. We have to guess their weight within ten percent to avoid a fine. If we give less than three hours advance notice, that's another fine.

When we get to the dock we have to fill out a long form saying where we fished, how we fished, and what kind of fish we caught and how much they weighed and this data must be mailed to the National Marine Fisheries. We also have to send a copy of these papers to the D. E. P. of Florida.

Next, we have to tell the buyer of our catch, what the general area we fished in was so that he could put it on the receipt. Most times, when we hit the dock, a D. E. P. Officer from Florida is standing there waiting for us. We call them the "fish police." The officer is standing there all decked out with a gun and badge and nice uniform watching us as we unload the fish, trying to find us doing something wrong. And if we underestimate the size of a fish or two by a sixteenth of an inch, even if we brought back thousands of pounds of fish, we will probably be hit with a nice fine. While we are unloading the fish he'll watch every move we make.

We'll also have someone, usually a woman, from "weights and measures" who measures and weighs every fish, cutting the ear bone out of each to get scientific data on the age of each fish and here again, we have to tell that person where we were fishing and how much fish we have.

At times an Inspector from the National Marine Fisheries is at the dock with two other Inspectors studiously watching us unload our catch. Then we get a receipt and with it we must then fill out a form notifying the government what fish we had and how much we got paid for them. From time-to-time we also have to report on our expenses and tell them how much profit we made. This occurs randomly.

Paul's friend Harry Klauber is holding a huge grouper.

Catch Shares / Bag Limits

Now let's talk about "catch shares," one of my real pet peeves. Let's go commercial fishing —

I'm going to explain what happens when a boat comes in. I'll give you a specific example of a trip that I made on the *Viking Freedom* on the 20th of October, 2012. We had a total gross sale of $3,330 for grouper, snapper, porgies, etc. We had to pay $1,200 to someone who owned the "catch shares" and rented them to us so that we could go out and catch those fish. That entity made $1,200 for our five-day trip and wasn't even on our boat. We envisioned that person sitting at home in a reclining chair wearing a big smile. Much of the rest of the $3,330 gross income went for fuel, bait, insurance, food, etc. Anything left over was left for us to share. I left something out too. Besides paying someone else for the right to catch their fish we also paid the National Marine Fisheries three percent of what we got for the fish to repay them for being so smart for inventing the "catch shares" program in the first place. You, the consumer, has to pay for all of the above in order to enjoy a fresh fish dinner caught in American waters by Americans.

Party / Charter / Private Boat Fishing

Your free rights to go salt water fishing are being taken away from you. I could write a separate book on this subject alone but thought that if I spent that much time on it, it would make me so nutty that I might not want to get back on the water again. So instead, let me just give you some more simple information on the subject.

Gradually, the environmentalists have been working their way into the National Marine Fisheries. In 2008, when President Barack Obama was elected, he appointed Dr. Jane Lubchenco as Under-Secretary of Commerce for Oceans and Atmosphere and NOAA (National Oceanic and Atmospheric Administration) Administrator. She came from PEW Environmental Foundation. Since then, everything has escalated into the cause of the environmentalists. Dr. Lubchenco brought a number of her constituents, environmental friends, etc., into very important positions in the National Marine Fisheries. Now that body is in full control of the environmentalists. When it comes to the recreational share of the total biomass of fish in the ocean I feel that all the numbers are arbitrary based on faulty or prejudiced science. Dr. Lubchenco left the department at the beginning of 2013, but chances are good that her replacement will follow in her footsteps. Only time can tell.

The Recreational Fisheries are now controlled by bag limits. It's also controlled by pounds — the total poundage of fish we are allowed to catch divided into bag limits equal to the length of the season and the amount of fish each person is allowed to catch. There is a contradiction from the government as to how many fish a person is allowed to catch versus the allowable poundage. For example, if a person is allowed five fish and he catches them, if their weight exceeds a certain weight limit he must pay back those pounds by having the season shortened or by making the bag limit smaller. If the science deems that we caught too many small fish in any given season then we are over-fishing by not allowing the fish to grow big enough. Therefore the season must be shortened, the bag limit lowered and/or have an emergency closure. If we catch too many big fish, then we are catching all the breeders and the same applies. We must then shut the season down or shorten the season or reduce the bag limit. As noted earlier, I feel that this is done with arbitrary numbers and faulty science.

Once the public is totally exhausted and worn out from all the seasonal closures, shortenings, harmful bag and size limit changes, I fear that they will allow catch-shares to apply to the citizens as well. One such change being proposed is that you will go to a store before going fishing and buy a tag for each fish you would like to catch. Then you will be allowed to go catch them. The store owner will get his share of the tag sale, the National Marine Fisheries will get their share, the environmental business community will get their share, and in a dream world maybe, there will be plenty of fish for everyone and a full season as long as you are willing to pay for them. Bingo! Catch-shares implemented in recreational fisheries!

Back to Commercial Fishing — The "I. T. Q."

Let's talk again about catch-shares for the commercial fishing sector —

Catch-shares were implemented over the last few years up and down the coasts of America in different fisheries. Since this so something I know so much about let me again discuss the subject as it applies to catch shares in the Gulf of Mexico for red snapper and all grouper. We have several commercial boats that fish out of Tarpon Springs, Florida and our biggest is the *Viking Freedom*.

When catch-shares began, what with the myriad assortment of dreadful rules that went into play, the government tried to convince us that the right way to go would be via catch-shares. They said that they would like it and that we would like it. It would be nice for everyone. We wouldn't have to worry about a season being open or not and that we could go out and fish at any time we choose and be allowed to catch quite a bit of fish. The government took the last five years of the commercial fishing vessels catch history, then took the best three of those five and averaged them out, and that was the share that the commercial fishermen were supposed to get and be able to catch whenever they decided to go fishing.

However, once the National Marine Fisheries got us to agree, we were double-crossed. This was similar to what took place when the "I. T. Q." system came in. The I. T. Q. system stands for Individual Transferable Quota and this system hurt rather than helped. For example, for grouper fishing, instead of allowing us to keep 100% of the weight that we had caught in the three years referred to above, they cut it down to allowing us to only keep one-half of that volume! Worse, for gag grouper, we could only keep twenty five percent of our average three-year prior tally. The national marine fisheries claimed that there weren't enough fish in the Gulf of Mexico for all the fishermen to get what they had caught in the past, and what they had agreed to be allowed when they went along with the catch-share program. Here again, faulty science. The small guy can't survive with so modest an allowance, so he often winds up selling or renting his allowance to others. (That's the guy I told you about earlier who sits and watches TV). The small guys are eliminated and they wind up selling out with the giants buying their shares and the industry really can get badly hurt!

More About Regulations

I'm sorry if some of these next thoughts repeat themselves elsewhere, but honestly, I'd rather say something to you twice than not at all, especially about how I feel regarding over-regulation. Let's start again with environmental fishery regulations and how they are changing the environment in the oceans.

Turtle Regulations (No, I'm Not Kidding!)

In order to be allowed to be in the long-line fishery for pelagic fish, you must go to turtle school. These schools are offered periodically at different places around the country and hopefully, the course will be given nearby at the time you need to be re-certified. It might be a day away or it may be held at the next-door town. Wherever it is, if your time is up, you have to go there. It takes the better part of an entire day to attend this class. Usually there are two teachers. They show videos and then give a written test.

In fact, there are two tests that consist of pulling hooks out of make-believe turtles in the form of cardboard boxes. Depending on how many students are in the school, a good part of the day is used up for this process alone.

In the school, you learn about the different types of turtles, how to tell one kind from the other. The agency requires long-line fishermen to go back to school every three years to renew their diploma. I guess they figure we have very short memories of how to unhook turtles. Anyway, it isn't all bad. Hey, we get a beautiful diploma; it's about 10½ inches by 8½ inches. The one I was given has a nice picture of a beautiful swordfish on it and a gold seal down on the bottom.

My boat, the *Viking Freedom*, even gets a diploma with the gold seal and the added bonus of a picture of a turtle. We have to have them on board the vessel at all times. I put mine up in the wheelhouse so I can look lovingly at it from time-to-time. But I do have a good feeling about it because if I ever do catch a turtle I'll know that I will be able to unhook him properly and that the turtle will most likely be able to swim happily away. However, since most turtles travel all over the world, if he goes outside of the United States to some of our neighboring countries that harvest turtles, that turtle may be in big trouble. You see, a good-sized turtle normally can feed from eight to twelve people and if the turtle that I release gets to one of those countries, there's a good chance that it could wind up in a pot of boiling water. Oh well, at least I'll know that I fed some hungry people anyway. Poor turtle, he doesn't know where he's swimming but we saved him for a while at least.

Another thing that we must abide by is a rule that says that if we do catch a turtle and release it, you must move your boat to an area that is a minimum of a mile away from where the deed took place. You cannot continue fishing, your Long Lines must be brought in and even if the water is filled with fish beneath you, you must move a minimum of one mile. The turtle wins and the fisherman loses. More — if the turtle cannot be saved; you are required to fill out a death certificate if you pull in a dead turtle. You must notify the authorities. Other than that, it is pretty simple being a long-liner and living with the turtles. We need to recognize though that as time goes by there are less and less long-liners and with all the regulations that protect sea turtles, there are more and more of them and as a result, more encounters will occur between turtles and long-liners. Now this could become a huge problem. With more turtles and less boats there will be even more encounters and eventually, still further restrictions will go into effect against fishermen.

Goliath Grouper

We have a fish in the Gulf of Mexico called Goliath Grouper and they are on the "endangered" list, meaning that no one can keep a single Goliath, regardless of its size. They grow to as big as 1,000 pounds. I've personally caught them up to 425 pounds. They were put on the endangered list some years back and remain on it.

Many of the inshore wrecks in the Gulf are occupied by many Goliaths. They are found in waters as shallow as 30 feet and if you hook a "legal" grouper, snapper, etc., on any of the larger wrecks we have, chances are pretty good that the fish will be eaten by a Goliath before you can bring it to the surface. There goes your dinner as well as your rig because the Goliath will break your line instantly.

So now we have many inshore wrecks overrun with these "endangered" fish and we cannot catch and keep any of the critters and worse, they eat many of the fish we are trying to bring into our boats.

Moving offshore into deeper waters of the Gulf, say to upwards of 200 feet, there are lots of Goliaths out there as well and while seeking legal grouper, snapper, and other bottom dwellers, we often have our fish eaten by one of these "protected" beasts.

We find that customers on board party and charter boats have to throw back more fish then they are allowed to keep. Many grouper are legal but still others are not. Ditto snappers, half of the varieties we catch are either "undersized"

It's not a Goliath.
Here's Paul with a huge legal grouper.

or "out of season." This sure makes people upset, especially when they see with their own eyes that many of these fish are quite plentiful.

Dolphin (Mammal)

On commercial boats, we have what is called "IFQ"s (Individual Fishing Quota's) or "Catch-Shares," discussed elsewhere. Between the regulations that apply to private, party, charter and commercial boats, at times, the gulf (as well as the ocean) gets countless fish put back in. And we have a critter that takes advantage of these rules called "Porpoise" or "Dolphin." Cute to many, these exceptionally smart mammals have become a menace to anglers in lots of places. We have, without intent, trained these beasts to follow our boats to get a free meal. The law says that you cannot feed nor harm them in any way and while "Flipper" in a pool at Disney World may be fun, you cannot imagine how many fish they consume on the fishing grounds.

As smart as they are, they follow our commercial and party boats and often learn that the fish coming up on an angler's line taste just as good as those that they catch by themselves. And that's not even counting those that we are forced to throw back (due to regulations), that float away because of air bladder problems. They eat these floating balloons just like eating candy bars. Worse though, is that they will often grab a fish as an angler is reeling it in and that means that we are "feeding the dolphins" even though we don't want to do it.

Shark Fishing

Commercial shark fishermen have very short seasons in which to legally fish, and as a result there are far less commercial guys out there and therefore, far more sharks than in years past. One shark in particular is overly plentiful and it's called "sandbar." This shark is among the top favorites to folks who enjoy eating shark steaks and their fins are widely sought in the Orient for shark fin soup.

According to environmentalists, this shark was considered "over-fished" as of 2012 and is "protected" until 2060, meaning that if rules don't change, the waters could get extremely over-filled with them!

Many fishermen say that there are already more sandbars than any other shark and in the Gulf of Mexico, and they are found very close to the beach. Commercial shark guys set gear overnight and pull it up the next day and have to release any sandbars they catch. This is in water as shallow as 15 feet. That's not very far from bathers and I know one thing: before I decide to take a midnight swim I'll keep that in mind. Remember, more sharks in the water means more bitten bathers.

Seals and Great White Sharks (Northern Waters)

Now let's talk about the also "protected" Great White Shark and what they love to eat — seals. One of the reasons that more great whites are around is because of the extreme overabundance of seals found up north. There are loads of seals found on the west coast of America and as a result, lots of great whites also. Worse though is the matter of the seals themselves up where I spend most of my time, Montauk Point, New York. We moved there in 1951 and hardly ever saw seals, especially in the winter. But now we have whole herds of seals out here the entire year round. This occurs too, to the north of us where I hear that some beaches have actually been closed to fishing because of the need to "protect" the seals in New England.

Simply, because seal-hunting was either stopped or drastically reduced in Canada, seals have reproduced in incredible numbers and have moved down the coast to ports as far south as Virginia. And as with porpoises, seals too have learned how to eat fish off of angler's hooks! Guys trolling for striped bass and bluefish discover that a hooked fish becomes seal food before the fish can be boated.

As winter arrives, much of the usual seal food such as stripers, and bluefish have moved south, and the inshore fish like porgies, sea bass and blackfish have moved out into deeper water. That leaves little for the seals to eat. But they satisfy their appetite by going into shallow water to feed on any flounder as well as eels that winter over in the inshore grounds. Some say that "over-fishing" may be blamed but I strongly feel that the main reason for the reduction in the flounder population is the fact that seals are eating them while in hibernation, preventing them from spawning early each spring. With no enemies, the seal population is growing rapidly and they are found the year round in Montauk and elsewhere.

Still More about Commercial Regulations in the Northeast

Commercial guys throw back way more fish then they are allowed to keep. "Draggers" use nets and they get a "catch-share" for the opening and closing of seasons. One problem though is while some fish may be legal, his nets don't know one fish from another and when he puts his net into the water and drags it back, the net cannot tell what is legal and what is not and as a result, the dragger has to put all kinds of otherwise good-tasting fish back in and many of these are dead. At times, thousands of pounds of fish have to be picked through to find what he can keep and what he must throw back in. The discards

The *Viking Freedom*, fishing in rough seas in the Gulf of Mexico, 10/12/2012.

are shoveled overboard to die and become shark and crab food. Untold millions of pounds of fish are being wasted this way each and every day!

The biomass of fish in the waters of the United States is way up, in fact, from what I understand, more than three-quarters of the fisheries are already at close to or even in excess of the desired biomass, even with these ridiculous, backwards and wasteful regulations. This waste of billions of good edible fish is considered good fisheries management by the National Marine Fisheries.

Over the last 30 years there have always been regulations to contend with. It's amazing that the fisheries have come back as well as they have along the coast around America. Some of these insane regulations are counterproductive in bringing fish back resulting needlessly in the loss of edible fish for the American public. It is unbelievable that the fishery could still survive and come back, especially after devastation wrought by foreign trawlers along our coastlines.

Man, you can look at my web page on this stuff. I'm not going to waste my time on issues. You can look it up and read about "Fight For Your Fishing Rights" on the web page. If you go back into the history, you will see some of the bad things that have gone on and what's happening to the fisheries and that's only part of it. Keep in mind that 85 percent of every piece of seafood consumed in America is imported, and it's not lack of fish in our ocean causing it. It's the lack of allowing the fishermen to go out and catch it, and that's what it's all about. There is a structure now so that big companies will take over the little people. The little fishermen will be gone. It will all be big business and the government will have control and have a piece of it. It's all about the money.

Chapter Twenty

The Coast Guard

More About The Coast Guard

Some Good, Some Bad

Back in Chapter 7, we discussed how I got my first license, with the help of a good but tough Coast Guard Inspector. Then in Chapter 11, I told you the story about the great friend we had, Commander Wolfe, of the U. S. Coast Guard. From time-to-time, I have complained about the Coast Guard, for sure, but more often than not, they do a very commendable job, trying to be certain that people are safe when on the water. However, every now and then I do feel that some go way overboard.

To the best of my knowledge, the passenger vessel industry is the only transportation industry that is supervised by a military force, which is the U. S. Coast Guard with inspections and regulations, etc. Some people feel that this is bad and others think it's good. I have mixed emotions about it. It is what it is and the safest vessel afloat in the world today is a small inspected vessel. However, sometimes we'll have a discrepancy in the interpretation of a regulation between the Inspector and the boat owner. When that happens, we are able to challenge the decision by use of an appeals process.

You can send in an appeal if you feel that the Inspector or Inspection Department is interpreting the regulation differently than you and the way that you have done things in the past. I've used the appeals system many times over the years and I've won most of my appeals. A lot of people are afraid to make appeals. I've talked to people in my business and some are afraid that the Inspector will be vindictive and retaliate against them if they appeal his decision and the next inspection will be even harder than ever. I've only had one Inspector through my career that held a grudge against me and retaliated and it was very obvious and he wound up sticking his foot in his mouth. I used the appeals process and the vendetta was over instantly and I did not allow him to inspect any of my vessels for a couple of years. However, just a short time ago he was allowed back on one of our vessels and he was a real gentleman and did a fine job and gave us a real good inspection. No matter what the problem, you always have the appeals process and that's what it's there for.

"Jack The Ripper"

On another occasion I had a problem with the guy I called "Jack The Ripper" at Montauk. I called him that because he liked to rip up lifejackets and I talked to others in my business and they told me that he had torn up a number of their lifejackets also. He didn't use proper procedures in inspecting the jackets; he used his own "method" and pulled on the straps that are used to strap the jackets together in opposite direction, as they were intended to be used and he wound up tearing the straps off and made them useless. They were in perfect condition before he ripped the straps off. Others in my business experienced this assault as well but figured that if they let him do his damage, that he would not bother them with other matters. But that simply meant that he could destroy countless good jackets.

We had 375 lifejackets on the *Viking Starliner* in Montauk and before Jack The Ripper got stopped by me he tore up 132 perfectly good lifejackets. Once again, I used the appeal process. (By the way, this took place right before the very busy Fourth Of July weekend that year!)

I went over his head and up the chain of command until a Commander came out and looked at the pile of otherwise perfect jackets in a pile in my parking lot. I left them there for just that purpose. It took a few months before the Commander came out and saw the mess his guy created and to make a long story a bit shorter, I was reimbursed for the replacement cost of all the jackets that "Jack The Ripper" had destroyed. I never saw him again, nor did any other boat owner I knew. He left the Coast Guard so the system really does work. The appeal process is a great system and many other skippers now use it successfully.

Chapter Twenty-One

Ports Of Call

Viking boats have sailed out of many a port, as you have already read. Depending on conditions, we've taken passengers out to sea from two ports in Massachusetts, two in Florida, one in Puerto Rico, and of course, Freeport and Montauk. One day, you may see a Viking near to where you live. If so, try to hop a ride, to see for yourself, just how hard we try to please our customers!

Chapter Twenty-Two

Remembering

Some Thoughts from
My Friend Harry Klauber

've known Paul quite well since I started fishing out of Montauk with Paul's dad Carl on the *Viking Star* and later with Paul on the *Viking Starlite* and some of his other boats. I fished with him on the *Andrea Doria* wreck which he discovered, as well as at many of the other sites he pioneered fishing. We became good friends and I loved fishing with him because he puts his all into every day and always had a huge smile on his face when big fish were coming over the rail.

I moved from Brooklyn to Florida in 1973 and while I returned to Montauk to fish with him several times, these were limited in number. I also fished on the *Starship* out of Key West when he had the big boat down there but I never did join him in Tarpon Springs until many years later.

However, our friendship came right back as if we had never grown apart. We agreed to meet and when we got together in his home and talked for hours it was as if those missing years had never passed. We went out to lunch and before I left he said that I was welcome to join him on the *Viking Freedom* any time I wanted. I took him up on his offer and since 2012 we have made numerous trips-just us two old men-in search of deep water fish.

Although we have both aged, when it comes to fishing Paul is exactly the same as he was when he was younger. His interests are in the places no one else has yet fished and he takes the time to explore, knowing that most often it will be a bust but on those occasions you hit it big it makes all the busts forgotten memories.

I speak with him 3-4 times a week and most of our conversations are about what government has done to the commercial fishermen and the industry. I live in Miami now and was one of the first anglers out of that port to recreationally day fish for swordfish and I do very well at it. But I still would prefer to fish on the *Viking Freedom* with Paul for ten days at a stretch in search for grouper and snapper.

Paul wants to take me to a spot that is 250 miles out at sea and when I asked him why, he said "Because no one else has done it!"

Harry Klauber

Endword

I would like to acknowledge the major assistance I obtained from two people who play a huge role in my life.

First, to Patricia, my far better-half and my dancing partner, for her love, of course, but also for the great part she played in making my scrambled words far better for you to understand. She spent countless hours improving the book greatly.

Second, to Eleanor, my wonderful office manager, for the significant part she has played in making the *Viking* fleet move smoothly when I'm not around, and for her huge changes that clearly made this a better book.

All the best. Good fishing.
Captain Paul G. Forsberg

P.S.: Before signing off, I wanted to tell you that I also answer to another name, "Cappy." Most of the local folks near me in Montauk and Tarpon Springs have called me that for many years.

How are these two photos for contrast?

This is the *Viking V* in 1953, backed into her slip.
She was our first boat in Montauk
and was the first head boat to ever fish Cox's Ledge.

This is my grandson Steven in the pilothouse of our newest boat,
the *Viking Fivestar,* wearing his Viking 77 T-Shirt,
celebrating our 77th Anniversary.

Ordering

utographed copies of this book can be purchased directly from Captain Forsberg by mailing your check in the amount of $21.95 (plus tax where applicable) to:

Captain Paul G. Forsberg
462 W. Lake Drive,Montauk, N. Y. 11954

He won't charge for shipping.

To order books in bulk, at discount, send him an e-mail to or contact the publisher, Gone Fishin' Enterprises, at mannyfishing@msn.com.

You can also obtain a special 75th Anniversary Shirt on the *Viking* web site as well as lots of other gifts for yourself or others. Go to www.Vikingfleet.com.